Changing
Children's
Behavior

Changing Children's Behavior

John D. Krumboltz
Stanford University

Helen Brandhorst Krumboltz
San Jose State College

Prentice-Hall, Inc., Englewood Cliffs, New Jersey

Library of Congress Catalog Card No.: 79–172945

ISBN: P 0–13–127944–0

       C 0–13–127951–3

Printed in the United States of America

20 19 18 17 16 15 14

Prentice-Hall International, Inc., London
Prentice-Hall of Australia, Pty. Ltd., Sydney
Prentice-Hall of Canada, Ltd., Toronto
Prentice-Hall of India Private Limited, New Delhi
Prentice-Hall of Japan, Inc., Tokyo

Acknowledgments

Dennis the Menace cartoons reproduced with permission from Publishers-Hall Syndicate ▪ Emmy Lou cartoon © 1969 United Feature Syndicate, Inc. ▪ Patrick cartoon reproduced with permission from Washington Star Syndicate ▪ Short Ribs, Carnival, Side Glances, and Born Loser cartoons reprinted by permission of Newspaper Enterprise Association ▪ Peanuts cartoons © United Feature Syndicate, Inc. ▪ Seventeen cartoon reproduced with permission from Chicago Tribune–New York News Syndicate, Inc. ▪ Cartoon on page 57 by Jan Van Wessum, reprinted from *Look*, December 1, 1970 ▪ Cartoon on page 109 by Robert Censoni. Copyright 1966 Saturday Review, Inc. ▪ Cartoon on page 159 by Al Ross. Copyright 1965 Saturday Review, Inc. ▪ Cartoon on page 176 by Leo Garel. Copyright 1966 Saturday Review, Inc. ▪ Cartoon on page 219 by Orlando Busino ▪ Letter to Ann Landers reprinted from San Francisco *Sunday Examiner and Chronicle*, December 5, 1965, by permission of Publishers-Hall Syndicate ▪ Letter from Dear Abby reprinted by permission of Abigail Van Buren from San Francisco *Examiner and Chronicle*, June 28, 1970 ▪ Charles McCabe column reprinted from San Francisco *Chronicle*, 1968 ▪ Poem on page 63 reprinted from Dorothy Law Nolte, *Children Learn What They Live*, with the permission of John Phillip Co., 1070 Florence Way, Campbell, Calif. 95008 ▪ Assistance in manuscript preparation provided by Eleanor Worden and Helen Leamey

To Ann and Jennifer

May your joy of life
remain undiminished
by our audacity

Contents

Behavior
Problems

A list of illustrations based on actual events

Changing Children's Behavior: What's in It for You?

If you feel any responsibility for the behavior of a child or a group of children, this book is designed for you. If you have ever been dissatisfied with the behavior of your children or with the progress of their learning, you will find in this book principles and examples on how to change the unsatisfactory behavior. If you are a teacher or parent, you will find many practical applications. But the same basic principles and same examples will also be valuable for psychologists, school counselors and administrators, psychiatrists, physicians, ministers, camp counselors, recreation workers, social workers, grandparents, parole officers, baby-sitters—in short, anyone who wants to help young people learn more effective ways of behaving.

Practical Research-Based Principles of Behavior

Psychologists have discovered much about human behavior that is true but not necessarily useful. We do not intend the behavioral principles presented in this book to represent all that psychology has to offer; rather we have chosen them for their usefulness to you. They summarize the most effective and practical ways known to help your children learn new behavior.

The principles are all based on recent psychological research findings. Although we have not described the research studies, we have included an annotated bibliography of pertinent references.

Real Life Illustrations

Each principle is liberally illustrated with concrete examples based on actual happenings. Some are from our own experiences, while others are derived from the experiences of teachers, parents, and others we have supervised. Over the years we have collected thousands of examples. We have included only those which best demonstrate the principles and which constitute frequent problems for adults concerned with children's welfare. Naturally we have changed names, locations, and identifying data.

Sometimes deliberately simplifying, we have chosen illustrations so that you might easily devise solutions under similar circumstances. Many of your problems will be more complicated than the cases we have presented since real life situations are usually more complicated than psychological generalities. But you will see how complicated problems can be analyzed into simpler behaviors which can then be treated one at a time.

˙ A Precise Way of Viewing the Behavior You Want

Behavior includes more than deportment. "Behave yourself!" a child is often told. Such advice commonly means "Be polite," or "Act properly." But a child is still behaving when he is impolite or acting improperly. Behavior is more than good manners. Behavior refers to any activity of human beings, whatever they do or say. Right now you are engaged in reading behavior.

We want to encourage you to think specifically about behavior you can see and hear. "Gail is lazy" is not an adequate description of a behavior problem. We do not know exactly what Gail does or says. However, "Gail was late to school three times last week" does describe something that she has done. It also specifies how often.

Let us try another example: "Clifford shows irresponsible behavior." This description is not useful since we do not know what Clifford did or said that led someone to describe his behavior as irresponsible. The word *behavior* does not make the description any clearer. A more adequate description is: "Clifford did not bring his homework back to school three times last week; twice he left his gym shoes on the floor in the locker room; and for the first time he failed to keep his promise to his mother that he would call her when he was going to be late for dinner." This more complete description of Clifford's activities tells us what he did or did not do, what he did or did not say, and how frequently.

Observing exactly what your children do or say and how often, you can then decide whether you want to increase or decrease the frequency. You can arrange conditions to change the frequency of specific behaviors. This book will tell you how.

A Common Sense Approach

Conscientious adults have been confused by the reams of contradictory advice on how to deal with children's behavior. We feel the systematic development of the principles in this book can help alleviate confusion.

Many persons have successfully applied a behavioral principle without at the time being able to state that principle. From their point of view they were using common sense. Only later were they able to recognize that they had applied a basic psychological principle. We like the idea of a "common sense" approach, especially at a time when common sense is not all that common.

We assume most behavior is learned. Both desirable and undesirable behaviors are learned. Children who have learned inappropriate ways of coping with their problems can also learn to substitute more desirable behaviors.

Of course some patterns of behavior may be attributed to factors other than learning, for example, hunger or fatigue, hormone or vitamin deficiency, illness or injury. We recommend that any child whose behavior does not respond to the types of environmental changes advocated in this book be given a complete physical examination by a qualified physician. Behavior is a complicated phenomenon, and all possible sources of help must be used. Many an underachieving child has been helped when it was discovered that he could not see the blackboard and needed glasses or that he suffered a correctable hearing loss.

Some familiar notions will not fit our common sense approach. We do not advocate that adults should be "permissive" with children any more than we think they should be "authoritarian." We do not tell you what kind of behavior to expect at each age with the idea that you will therefore try to put up with it until the behavior is outgrown. Although we do advocate that you learn how to listen to children and communicate with them about what they think and feel, we do not think understanding is enough; children need help in changing too. We do not speculate about unobservable, hypothetical entities such as ego, id, habit strength, and self-actualization since talking in these terms is too frequently a substitute for appropriate action.

No Guilt Feelings

Sometimes adults feel guilty about what they have done with their children. Certain theories have led people to believe that behavior is determined in the first few years of life and not much can be done about it later. We do not share that point of view. We recognize that past events shape present behavior. But present behavior can and does change for better or for worse. The question is: What shall we do *now*? What kind of environment can we arrange for the child now that will encourage desirable behavior and diminish undesirable behavior? We *can* take action that will make a difference.

A System for Reaching Your Goals, Not Ours

We will describe *how* you can change behavior, not *what* behavior you ought to change. You are the judge of what behavior is good. You must determine for yourself what kinds of behavior you wish to encourage among the young people for whom you bear responsibility.

For advice on what constitutes desirable behavior you may select from such sources as the Bible, the Koran, the Congressional Record, lists of educational goals, newspaper columns by Dear Abby or Ann Landers, Amy Vanderbilt's writings on etiquette, the behavior you learned from your parents and teachers, or the opinion of your next-door neighbor. You are certain to obtain contradictory advice when you consult many different authorities, but we feel that constructing your own standards of desirable behavior is important.

Suppose you were to ask: "Should I require my 16-year-old daughter to be in by midnight, or should I expect her to set reasonable hours for herself and keep her promise about the time she says when she will return?" We cannot decide for you what you should want your daughter to do. However, we can help you find an answer to either of these questions: "How can I teach my daughter to come in at midnight as I would like her to?" or "How can I teach my daughter to set reasonable hours for herself, tell us when she will return, and keep her promise?" When you have decided what behavior you feel is important, you will find this book helpful with its suggestions of possible methods for teaching that behavior.

At the same time our own values and opinions will become evident. We feel that children should learn the skills and values that will enable them to adapt creatively and successfully to new and unexpected demands when parents or teachers are no longer present. Most adults working with children will find no quarrel with this view. Unfortunately no one knows the precise sequence of behaviors that leads to this ideal. Well-intentioned adults will differ on the specific behaviors children need to learn in order to prepare for the future. You must be your own judge of what behavior you think best prepares your children for the years ahead.

A Challenge to Your Ideals

The principles of behavior described in this book are powerful. They could be used by unscrupulous persons for unworthy ends. Few adults deliberately try to teach their children improper behavior, but many adults unintentionally cause their children to engage in unethical or inappropriate behavior because they do not know what actions will create something better. Helping responsible adults devise better techniques seems more than worth the risk of possible misuse. Widespread dissemination of these ideas is the best defense against their misapplication.

If you test the principles in this book for yourself and find them successful, you may gradually come to adopt a more behavioral approach to dealing with problems. Then perhaps you will sense their relationship to larger issues in the world today—to problems of crime, welfare, truancy, vandalism, war, poverty, racism, and even overpopulation.

I

Strengthening Existing Behavior

1

Good
Behavior
Must Pay Off

LEARNING THE MORSE CODE

Dusty dashed into the house. "Hey, when's supper?" No answer. "Anybody home?" No answer.

Dusty went to his bedroom. He found a bright yellow sheet of paper on his pillow. "What's this?" He read:

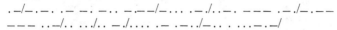

Dusty knew that his father wanted him to learn various Boy Scout skills, but with so many other things to do he just couldn't get around to tying knots and learning Morse Code.

Unable to read the code, Dusty threw it aside. He wandered aimlessly around the house, but as his curiosity grew he returned to the note, took it to his desk, and drew a scout handbook from a drawer. Gradually he deciphered the note: "A candy bar for you is in hall desk."

Several days later Dusty found another message which when decoded gave him advance information of a family outing. Finally his father left a series of longer messages, each in code, which led him eventually to a new scout knife.

Dusty soon learned Morse Code so that he could translate messages more quickly and find his rewards sooner. The scoutmaster mentioned Dusty's rapid progress, and with such encouragement Dusty began demonstrating his newly developed deciphering skill to his family and friends.

Having achieved one Boy Scout goal, he pitched in to other scout activities more enthusiastically.

Why didn't Dusty learn Morse Code earlier? He had no reason to do so. However, once he translated the strange coded message, he obtained immediate satisfaction. Later on, the satisfaction was only partly in the gift. It was also in the fun of playing a game with his father and demonstrating his newly developed skill to scoutmaster, family, and friends. Once Dusty had succeeded at one Boy Scout task, his interest in related scout activities increased.

Positive Reinforcement Principle: To improve or increase a child's performance of a certain activity, arrange for an immediate reward after each correct performance.

Translating Morse Code is certainly not the most important skill needed in this modern age. But many students fail to master the skills of their own written language or a foreign language because the benefits are too few or too far removed. A new skill will be learned quickly if its mastery brings direct and immediate benefits to the learner. It may not be learned at all if benefits are delayed

Arrange immediate reinforcement after each correct performance.

weeks, months, or years. One major problem for parents and teachers is to devise ways for children to receive immediate benefits from new learning.

Many problems in child behavior are solvable when we apply the Positive Reinforcement Principle.

- Mary pouts and sulks when things are not going her way.

- Ten-year-old Madeline does not enjoy reading books.
- Jack takes saxophone lessons but never practices unless someone nags at him first.
- Buck and Biggie fight constantly and invent ingenious ways to get the other blamed for starting their arguments.
- Libby has difficulty sticking to her diet to lose weight.

Reinforcement

REINFORCERS ARE REWARDS

Psychologists use the term *reinforcer* instead of pay-off or reward. When Dusty obtained the candy bar after successfully translating the Morse Code message, we say that he was reinforced for decoding the message. We could also have said that he was rewarded or paid off, but these more casual terms connote lost-and-found want ads and political skulduggery. Thus we shall use the more technical term *reinforcer* with increasing frequency. Reinforcement is the presentation of a reinforcer. Reinforcement occurred when Dusty received his candy bar.

GENERATING ENTHUSIASM FOR SCHOOL

Liz's sixth grade class was studying conservation. Mr. Williams had planned a library assignment, but as he began to present it, Liz raised her hand urgently.

"Mr. Williams, why can't we do more than talk and write about it? Why can't we *do* something for a change? You mentioned saving our trees. Maybe we should try to get people interested in the Gazette's newspaper recycling drive. Maybe our class could really help."

From the stirring in the class as Liz spoke, Mr. Williams knew he was reflecting their interest when he said, "Liz, that's a great idea. What would we need to know if we wanted to help?"

Students asked many questions: how and where paper could be collected, what would happen to the paper next, how paper was made originally, and the effect of recycling paper on workers' jobs. It soon became apparent that they needed more facts. Mr. Williams, sensing their continued interest, helped them organize committees to find answers and report back to the class.

The students learned on what days the papers would be collected, how they would have to be tied together, and how many pounds of paper would save one tree. Committees began work on reports about reforestation, paper milling, and economic effects of recycling.

Simultaneously each student was on an "action" committee to ask neighbors to save papers for the drive. One group wrote a supportive letter to the newspaper which was published. Mr. Williams helped students to find needed information and coordinate their energies, but he gave full credit to the class members for their efforts. On the date of the final pick-up he worked with some of the boys to load the bundled papers into the truck.

Liz appraised the project: "Most of us stopped being bored by school, really got with it, and learned a lot. I personally saved the lives of 5.3 trees."

Mr. Williams reinforced Liz by praising her suggestion. Students were also reinforced by parents and neighbors who cooperated, by the newspaper that printed their letter, by one another as they worked together, and by their growing knowledge that their actions preserved trees.

Boredom occurs when reinforcement is too infrequent. Mr. Williams capitalized on Liz's suggestion and arranged an environment that reinforced the children more frequently for beneficial learning activities.

Mr. Williams in turn was reinforced by seeing his students learning enthusiastically. He did not have to instruct each child personally. Instead he rewarded Liz's initiative and organized the group so that each child could reap some benefits from participating in the group activities.

A BEHAVIOR OCCURS MORE FREQUENTLY WHEN FOLLOWED BY A REINFORCER

We know that the candy bar was a reinforcer for Dusty because, after decoding the message and then receiving the candy, he subsequently increased the frequency with which he decoded Morse Code messages. If Dusty had found his old discarded baseball in the hall desk, he may well have stopped decoding messages, in which case the discarded ball would not have been a reinforcer for him, at least under these circumstances. Mr. Williams' praise for Liz's idea was a reinforcer for her since it increased related activities.

Experience with many children under varied circumstances has established certain kinds of events as frequently effective reinforcers:

- candy and other pleasant tasting food
- words of praise
- admiration or recognition
- money
- attention
- high grades in school
- opportunities to observe or participate in unusual events
- memberships in honorary organizations
- opportunities to associate with attractive members of the opposite sex
- opportunities to engage in mutual conversation with another human being

Whatever the child does just prior to reinforcing events is likely to increase in the future. Thus we can increase the probability that the child will engage in a particular behavior by arranging for him to receive one or more of such reinforcing events immediately thereafter.

Events Reinforcing One Person May Not Reinforce Another

A child who habitually receives D and F grades in school will probably be reinforced by a C grade. However, a child accustomed to A and B grades will probably perceive a C grade as punishing. An event is more likely to be reinforcing if it constitutes an improvement over what the child is accustomed to receiving.

A parent may reinforce some behavior by giving a child an allowance of ten cents a week if the allowance previously was five cents a week. However, if the allowance used to be twenty cents a week, a ten-cent allowance would constitute punishment. To understand whether any event is reinforcing one must know its relationship to preceding events for that person.

Events Reinforcing at One Time May Not Be Reinforcing at Another

To a child who has never been on an airplane an opportunity to fly might be a powerful reinforcer. If the child had just completed a long airplane trip, another extended ride immediately might have

EMMY LOU ® By Marty Links

"Wait till I get my hands on Amy — going around saying I'm a straight 'A' student!"

Events that reinforce one person may not reinforce another.

no reinforcement value at all. Other things being equal a reinforcer is more effective when the child has had little of it recently.

Similarly candy may be reinforcing if the child has had little of it for some time. However, it has less reinforcement value if the child has frequent access to it, and if too much is eaten at any one time it may be punishing. When satiated, a child is less likely to engage in a behavior which results in his receiving the reinforcer producing the satiation.

How to Make Reinforcement Effective

TIMING OF REINFORCEMENT IS CRUCIAL

How much time should elapse between a child's correct perfor-mance and the presentation of the reinforcer?

Reinforce Immediately During Initial Learning

Under most circumstances the sooner the reinforcer is presented after the correct behavior, the sooner the child learns to engage in the desired behavior.

> GETTING TO CLASS ON TIME
>
> Gary had developed a habit of rushing into American History class just after the bell stopped ringing every day, collapsing in his seat, and frequently missing the beginning instructions of the teacher. One day, for some unaccountable reason, he appeared early. The teacher, wishing to strengthen this chance change in Gary's time of arrival, immediately approached his desk, quietly thanked him for getting to class before the bell rang, and asked if he would take roll, a prestige job exchanged among the earlier arriving class members. Following this incident Gary began arriving at class on time more frequently.

Any new response is learned more quickly if the reinforcement appears immediately after the improved behavior. Undoubtedly Gary would need additional reinforcement, but because of the immediacy of the teacher's actions he could easily associate his improved behavior with the reinforcer.

Reinforcers are sometimes presented too soon, that is, before the child has actually begun to improve his behavior.

> UNINTENTIONALLY ENCOURAGING TEMPER TANTRUMS
>
> Three-and-a-half-year-old Melinda stayed with a baby-sitter five days a week while her mother worked. One evening when her mother came to pick her up, Melinda happened to be having an unusually good time playing with the dog. She refused to leave with her mother and threw a temper tantrum.

Her mother promised Melinda a surprise on the way home if she would leave the baby-sitter and stop crying. She stopped crying immediately and was eager to go. On the way home her mother shopped at a drugstore and bought Melinda a storybook.

The next evening when her mother came to pick her up again, Melinda threw another temper tantrum, this one even more violent than the one before.

Melinda's reinforcement was her mother's promise of a surprise. The reinforcement occurred immediately after Melinda had begun to cry and thus strengthened the child's future tendencies to engage in temper tantrums. Giving rewards to stop temper tantrums serves only to increase the frequency of temper tantrums.

If her mother wanted to reinforce her for leaving the baby-sitter's house cheerfully, she should have chosen a time when Melinda did in fact leave the baby-sitter more cheerfully and should then have given her the surprise. Melinda's mother was using reinforcement, but after the wrong behavior. Immediate reinforcement should follow the improved behavior.

Describe Past Good Behavior When Reinforcement Must Be Delayed

Sometimes a parent or a teacher does not learn about improved behavior until much later.

GOING TO BED PROMPTLY

Chip was typically uncooperative and slow about going to bed on time. At six years of age he would find all kinds of reasons for procrastinating, particularly when a baby-sitter was taking care of him. One evening when his parents returned home, the baby-sitter reported a slight improvement in Chip's going-to-bed behavior. His mother asked the sitter for a detailed description of what the boy had done.

The next morning she was able to say, "Chip, remember last night when the baby-sitter was here and you were watching television? Do you remember when the program ended and she asked you to get ready for bed? She told me that you got up and turned off the television set and scarcely complained at all. She also said that you got your pajamas on without dawdling as much as you did the last time she was here. Daddy and I are pleased to hear that. It sounds like you're really becoming more prompt."

The mother's words of praise were reinforcers for Chip. His mother was not there to praise him immediately after his improved behavior, so she did the next best thing. She reconstructed the behavior so that Chip could remember quite well what he had done. She then reinforced Chip with her praise immediately after the verbal description of his improved behavior. Although Chip's mother at first regretted she had missed the opportunity to reinforce him immediately, she found she was still able to capitalize on the situation.

Whenever immediate reward is not possible the child may be reminded of the circumstances and the details of his own improved behavior; the reminder may then be followed by either a verbal or a nonverbal reinforcer.

Delay Reinforcement When Teaching Patience and Dedication

In real life rewards are not always presented immediately after improved behavior. In some cases rewards are delayed weeks, months, or years after the behavior occurs. A business promotion, for example, is seldom awarded the first time an individual does well. Usually it takes years of constant effort and good work to earn a promotion. If a person expected to be promoted immediately the first time he did a good job, he would be disappointed and might cease working unless he had already learned the importance of continued good performance without immediate reward.

Immediate reinforcement is necessary to get the new or improved behavior firmly established. However, once the behavior is learned, it is usually desirable to help the child learn that immediate reinforcement does not always occur. Ways of tapering reinforcement to prepare children for the realistic conditions of life are described in Chapter 7.

Omit Reinforcement When Behavior Has Not Improved

If you wish a child to improve his behavior, you must reinforce him only when his behavior does begin to improve. Chapter 9 discusses further ways of omitting reinforcement to stop undesired behavior.

OVERCOMING SULKING

When eight-year-old Mary did not get her own way, she would go to her room, sit alone, pout and sulk. The sulking and pouting caused her mother and older sister to feel uncomfortable. In fact with despair her mother would frequently go to Mary's room and give in to some of her demands. If her mother did not give in, the older sister often offered sympathy or a piece of candy or agreed to play a game with Mary to make up for her unhappiness. Mary was usually able to get special favors and attention from her older sister even when her sulking did not sufficiently move her mother.

Mary also sulked and pouted in school. However, the teacher refused to give in when Mary sulked and instead talked with her parents about her behavior. When the family realized that Mary had been using this behavior to get her own way, they agreed to ignore it. When Mary did not get her own way and went to her room to sulk, her mother and sister would simply leave her alone. At first Mary sulked for increasingly long periods of time, but when she discovered that she was missing out on fun and activity and received no attention during these periods, she quickly reduced their frequency.

To help Mary overcome sulking no reinforcement should have occurred during the time it persisted. After she stopped sulking and joined the rest of the family or the class, she was being reinforced by renewed group acceptance and inclusion in ongoing activtities. Sulking was ignored but her voluntary return was reinforced.

REINFORCERS MUST BE SELECTED CAREFULLY

A Sufficiently Powerful Reinforcer Must Be Chosen

Reinforcers vary in their effectiveness. A reinforcer may be effective for one child but not for another, effective at one time and not at another time.

MOTIVATING A VOCAL MUSIC CLASS

The seventh grade vocal music students had had little music instruction in their grade school experience, and with a few exceptions they did not know how to read notes or sing part harmony. The teacher found difficulty in motivating the students, and the class progressed slowly.

When the music teacher was asked by a nearby junior college to bring her class to participate in a music festival, she presented the possibility to the students. She explained that acceptance meant learning five difficult songs with three-part harmony to be sung partly alone and partly together with a top-notch senior high choral group. The students would be bussed to the campus, have lunch in the cafeteria, and miss a half day of school.

The girls and boys voted overwhelmingly to participate even though they were aware that they would have to work hard to learn the songs well. There were extra practices at noon on four occasions but attendance was high.

The pride in preparing for this performance was in great contrast to the earlier apathy. Fellow students suddenly placed high value on being a member of the vocal music class.

What was the effective reward? Making a trip to a college campus? Missing a half day of school? Associating with an excellent older choral group? Being given a choice in the activity? Perhaps it was a combination of all these. These rewards might well be effective for seventh graders but ineffective for college students. We sometimes need to try a variety of reinforcers to find the right combination at the right time. By observing what children normally enjoy doing, we can pick reinforcers that will be effective for them.

Love Is a Dangerous Reinforcer

Parents and even teachers sometimes use love as a reinforcer. "How can I love you if you do this?" "I'll love you all the more if you do that!" Nonverbal evidences of love are often used as reinforcers. Hugs and kisses may be granted in exchange for good behavior. We would caution against the use of love for reinforcing purposes, not because love is ineffective but because there are side effects to the use of any reinforcer. Children learn to use the same reinforcers with others that we use with them. In fact they use the same reinforcers with us that we use with them.

If we use love as a reinforcer, we must be prepared to withhold it just as readily as we grant it. Most people are unable, fortunately, to turn their love on and off. Any attempt to use love as a reinforcer involves some falsifying of one's emotions.

A verbal or physical expression of love should be a spontaneous manifestation of feeling, not a way of reinforcing someone. A girl who has grown up in a family in which love is used as a reinforcer may well become the kind of girl who uses kisses to repay a boy-friend for spending money on her. A likely but untested hypothesis is that girls from families in which love is exchanged for favors more readily sell themselves for sex.

If we wish children to express love only when they feel it, we cannot use love as a reinforcer. A child should feel loved and cared for regardless of his behavior. So many other possibilities for reinforcers exist that there is no need to produce emotionally insecure children by giving and withdrawing love.

Value of the Reinforcer May Be Increased or Decreased

How large or valuable should a reinforcer be? Abraham Lincoln once said that a man's legs should be long enough to reach the ground. Similarly a reinforcer should be valuable enough to en-courage the child to engage in the behavior desired. Sometimes the size or value of the reinforcer needs to be varied in order to have it accomplish its results.

LEARNING TO ENJOY READING

Ten-year-old Madeline knew how to read but did not enjoy it. She spent much time playing and watching television but re-sisted persuasive efforts to get her to read. Her parents thought she should learn to enjoy the pleasures of good reading and at the same time improve her reading skill.

"Madeline," her father proposed, "if you can finish reading the book you checked out of the library by the end of the next week, I'll give you ten cents." Madeline agreed, but by the end of the next week she had not read more than five additional pages. The ten-cent reinforcer was insufficient.

Then her parents decided to find out what kinds of books interested Madeline. They consulted Madeline's teacher and the local librarian about books that children with Madeline's read-ing ability enjoyed. Madeline said that she liked mystery and ghost stories. Yet even when she was given the most attractive, well-written, and exciting stories, she showed little interest in reading.

"Madeline, you know that your mother and I want you to learn to enjoy reading, but you'll never learn how much fun it is unless you really give it a good try. We'd like you to pick one of the books you took out of the library and see if you can read it in your spare time before next Monday. If you can, we'll give you some money. How much do you think it's worth to you?''

"That's a hard job. A dollar and a half."

"That's a high price; but all right, it's a deal. If you finish reading the book by 8:00 P.M. on Monday, I'll give you a dollar and a half."

"You mean it? Really! A dollar and a half for reading that book? I'll start right now!"

The book, *Charlotte's Web* by E. B. White, was fortunately an ideal choice. Although intent on reading quickly merely to qualify for the financial reward, Madeline was soon engrossed in the book. In response to her parents' interest, she described the plot as it unfolded. Madeline was so touched by the story that she cried when she read that Charlotte, the spider, died. She finished the book ahead of schedule and was promptly reinforced with the dollar and a half. More important, however, was her reaction to the book. "That was the best book I've ever read. No other book could be that good."

Frequently a big incentive is necessary to get some activities started. In the case of Madeline ten cents proved to be insufficient but a dollar and a half did the job. Furthermore father and daughter held a rudimentary bargaining session to arrive at the price. The dollar and a half was Madeline's suggestion and somewhat exceeded her father's expectation as to what he wished to pay. However, he quickly decided to meet her price this one time because he considered it vital to Madeline's own future that she soon learn the joys of reading. If the girl had requested some exorbitant amount, say one hundred dollars, the father would have had to negotiate the amount to something within reason and possibly something other than money. The amount of the reinforcer must be such that both parties to the contract consider it in their own best interest to make the agreement. In this case both Madeline and her father thought a dollar and a half was a good bargain. For Madeline it seemed a fantastic sum for reading a book. For her father the chance that a dollar and a half would improve his daughter's reading skill and enjoyment seemed an inexpensive bargain.

The amount of the reinforcer at one time does not necessarily set a precedent for the amount at any subsequent time. Madeline later asked how much her father would give her to read a second book. If she had wanted more than he was willing to offer, they may have had to negotiate something attractive to them both a second time. As it was they agreed on a price of one dollar, and the careful selection of an appropriate book again led Madeline into the pages of an intriguing story. Her joy in discovering that the printed word could touch her emotions made future financial reinforcers unnecessary. Once over this initial hurdle Madeline ceased to ask for money in return for reading books and gradually began to read them on her own; the reading itself had become reinforcing. If at some future time it again appeared necessary to encourage Madeline's reading, a more tangible reward might again be used.

To some people it seems almost immoral to offer a child money as an incentive for reading a book, something the child should want to do by himself. A child should indeed want to read for the intrinsic enjoyment it brings, but if he has not yet found for himself that reading brings enjoyment and hence avoids all opportunities to engage in reading, some step is necessary to help him get over the initial hurdle.

Several Reinforcers May Be Combined

To encourage performance over a long period of time, one type of reinforcer alone often proves insufficient. Sometimes a series of reinforcers needs to be arranged.

IMPROVING SAXOPHONE SKILL

At eleven years of age Jack seldom practiced his saxophone. He was able to play moderately well but was not showing much improvement.

To encourage Jack members of the family began looking for things to praise when he practiced. First they pointed out certain tunes they enjoyed hearing him play. Later on, after a better-than-average practice period, his mother told him if he continued the good work he could practice during the time when he had previously helped wash the dinner dishes.

Jack continued to improve in his playing. Along the way, as further reinforcement, his family took him to a performance in which a professional saxophone player played. His father rewarded him for still further progress with the purchase of a new saxophone to replace the rented one he had been using. Finally, when he was taken in as a member of the school's concert band, his desire to improve his saxophone playing no longer needed family support. He became intrinsically interested in improving his own musical performance for the aesthetic enjoyment and social opportunities it brought to him.

Jack's family emphasized improvement in his playing, not the amount of time spent practicing. A frequent mistake of many parents and music teachers is to insist that a predetermined amount of time be devoted to practicing, for example, one hour per day. Obviously improvement cannot take place without practice, but the emphasis should be on improvement rather than on the amount of time to be spent. Assignments such as "See if by next Tuesday you can play these eight bars without a single mistake" focus attention on the job to be learned, not on the amount of time necessary to accomplish it. It is relatively easy to spend an hour a day going through the motions of practicing without really accomplishing anything.

A wise teacher chooses music the student will generally enjoy hearing as he learns it. If a child really wants to improve his musical performance, he will use his practice time efficiently to accomplish the job. A combination of reinforcers may sometimes be helpful in getting him to make sufficient progress so that the intrinsic joys of making beautiful music provide the subsequent reinforcers.

Use of the Same Reinforcer Can Reduce Its Effectiveness

When reinforcers are merely words or tokens, the constant use of the same reinforcer tends to reduce its value. The child simply tires of it. A better procedure is to combine praise with an exact description of the child's improved behavior.

PICKING UP TOYS

Kirk was learning to be responsible for putting away his toys. His mother always said "Good job" in response to Kirk's gradually improving behavior. But one day he said, "Good job, good job, that's all I ever hear. I get so tired of hearing you say 'good job'." Chagrined at her own rigidity, Kirk's mother devised alternative ways of letting him know how much she appreciated his increasing responsibility for maintaining and caring for his own toys and equipment. Instead of merely resorting to synonyms such as "fine" or "much better," Kirk's mother reduced her direct verbal remarks to him and began to describe the child's improved performance to his father. "Dad, you know what Kirk did today? He picked up all his toys in his room without my having to remind him. And he did it all by himself."

Sometimes the most effective verbal praise is directed not to the person who deserves it but to that person's immediate superior. The adage "Don't tell me, tell my boss" applies to children too. Suitable public praise is a powerful reinforcer.

Reinforcers Need Not Be Specified in Advance

The child does not need to know in advance exactly what kind of reinforcer he will receive. Surprise reinforcers are often very effective.

REDUCING SIBLING QUIBBLING

Buck and Biggie were constantly fighting with each other. In the past their parents had attempted to find out which child started the fight and had punished him. If Buck were punished, Biggie was delighted. If Biggie got caught, Buck was reinforced.

The two boys began to develop clever and subtle methods of provoking each other into some overt act which would bring parental punishment on the other. When either boy succeeded, the parents, without realizing it, were reinforcing him for provoking his brother.

"Look, boys, if the two of you play together this afternoon without either of you hitting, fighting, or calling each other a bad name, I am going to give you both a surprise. I can't tell you what the surprise is now, but it will be something you will like. It's two o'clock now, and if I hear absolutely no fighting of any kind between now and four o'clock, then you both get the surprise. But if either of you fights, then neither of you gets the surprise regardless of who is at fault and regardless of who starts the fight. If a fight starts, there's no surprise for anyone. If there is no fight for two hours, then you both get the surprise. Is that clear?"

The mother did not prescribe the precise method which the two boys were to use, but in effect she was willing to reinforce any alternative activities devised by the boys themselves which would enable them to get along together peacefully. If the boys were successful in avoiding a fight during the afternoon, the mother might give each of them a special snack or a small trinket. She might take them to the park or to the store or give them some other form of substantial reinforcement. It is essential, of course, that the mother keep her promise and present them with some reinforcer of value to them. A failure to keep her promise would reduce her effectiveness in the future.

If the children were unable to get along together peacefully, they should certainly receive no "surprise." No punishment is necessary or desirable. No attempt should be made to pinpoint which boy was responsible for the fight. Both children should be reinforced for cooperative behavior, and no reinforcement should be provided to either boy when fighting occurs. Under these conditions the boys will figure out their own method of getting along with each other because they will soon discover that it pays off. Fighting will diminish because the boys will find that nobody wins after a fight.

REINFORCING "AGENTS" VARY IN EFFECTIVENESS

The person who delivers the reinforcer to a child, the reinforcing agent, may be as important as the reinforcer. For example, from personal experience we know that praise from some people may mean more than the identical words from someone else.

Persons Prestigeful to the Child Are the Most Effective Reinforcing Agents

It is not always possible to predict in advance who will be able to administer a reinforcer to a child most effectively. In general, children, like adults, tend to respect persons who have demonstrated a mastery of various situations through their skill or knowledge, persons who are recognized by others as important and influential, and persons who have been attentive, kind, and loving to the child.

The following story is a mother's version of what took place with her children.

We were living in the greater Los Angeles area when Angie was eight and Dorey was fourteen. With an age difference of six years Angie looked up to her older sister and, perhaps too frequently, deferred to most of her wishes. She could usually count on her sister to organize neighborhood games and to stand up against their dad and me about watching the news on television.

The pollution crisis was just becoming apparent that year. Dorey's junior high social studies class decided to study the problem. At evening meals for several weeks she informed the family of the facts she had learned that day about air or water pollution. Each night she would search the papers for an article to add to her "Pollution Scrapbook" for school.

Angie began to get involved too. Not only did she want to demonstrate that she too could now read at least some of the evening paper, but Dorey thanked her genuinely for spotting any pollution article.

One smoggy day I was driving Angie and three of her third grade friends to a dance class.

"Eeooo!" from Angie. "Look at all that air pollution. We'd better stop breathing!" At this point she took a deep breath and held it until the others said, "Where? What do you mean?" And then the third grade version of our ninth grader's dinner lectures was given.

When we arrived home it was still on her mind. "I'm going to close all the doors so the pollution can't come in."

Angie's initial interest was in trying to please and to imitate her prestigeful older sister who was inadvertently the reinforcing agent. Along with the newly acquired knowledge, her friends further reinforced her interest—again quite unintentionally. Angie's awareness of ecological problems in our society had begun.

Adults Can Combine Efforts to Reinforce Improvement

Encouragement from two or more significant people in the child's life may often be more effective than the efforts of either person alone.

Rita seemed to have little desire to succeed in fifth grade arithmetic. She frequently put down anything on her paper just to have something there. At the blackboard she stood looking sullen, or if possible, copied from another student. She did poorly on tests. Her IQ was only slightly below average.

Her new teacher began by trying to eliminate all sources of pressure, punishment, and failure. This task was not completely possible, but she always tried to find something praiseworthy about Rita's work.

When she was certain Rita could succeed, the teacher would send her to the blackboard, praising her after the successful performance. She would also correct Rita's papers and tests as soon as possible, adding some comments of praise or encouragement in response to the best parts of Rita's work.

In this particular school district the policy was that only the accurate, neat papers could be displayed on the bulletin board. Since Rita's papers were seldom perfect, there was a danger that her parents would come to the open house and not find any of her work. The teacher devised an easy test on which Rita was able to make a perfect score, and this paper was displayed at the open house.

Along with individual encouragement the teacher also arranged for another pupil to assist her. As Rita's work began to improve, the teacher asked her to help another classmate who had been having difficulty.

Conferring with Rita's parents, the teacher told them what she was trying to do. They discussed ways they could all show an interest in Rita's work and praise her improvements. Prior to this time the parents had been pressuring their daughter to do well and had been extremely critical of failures. Now they began to take more interest in her homework papers and emphasized the problems that she had solved correctly. Even her classmates noticed and commented spontaneously on the change in Rita.

Successful performance combined with recognition from teacher, parents, and classmates changed Rita's previous attitude of inferiority. Motivated to succeed, she now viewed her mistakes as challenges to overcome instead of as glaring evidences of failure. Both her daily homework and her test scores improved.

The reinforcements from teacher, parents, and classmates undoubtedly combined to encourage Rita to succeed. Another element in her success was the realization that she could receive help from a classmate and also give it to another classmate. Not only was success emphasized, but failure was deemphasized. The classroom environment for Rita was restructured so that she would succeed as often as possible and fail as seldom as possible. Since the same emphasis on success and absence of criticism for failure occurred at home, Rita rather quickly overcame her resistance to arithmetic.

Everyone Is a Potential Reinforcing Agent

Reinforcing events occur constantly whether or not intended. Everyone with whom the child comes in contact may possibly serve to reinforce, or fail to reinforce, any given behavior. The unpredictable and often accidental reinforcements that each person receives, or does not receive, when accumulated over a lifetime contribute to the wide variety of behaviors that we observe among friends, acquaintances, and strangers. Both desirable and undesirable behaviors are learned through these chance encounters.

CRYING IN A RESTAURANT

Even though Jay was only 18 months old his parents enjoyed taking him on weekend excursions. One Saturday they stopped in a restaurant for a cup of coffee. Although it was not mealtime Jay, for no obvious reason, began crying and fussing. The waiter immediately came to the child and presented him with a cookie. Jay stopped crying, ate the cookie, and soon began crying again. The waiter came running with another cookie, but a third one was confiscated by the parents who then picked up their howling baby and left. When Jay and his parents entered other eating places after that incident, he would begin fussing as soon as he was seated unless someone quickly presented him with food.

In this case the waiter unwittingly served as a reinforcing agent by presenting Jay with cookies soon after he had begun to cry. Babies announce their discomfort chiefly by crying, and to a certain extent parents can only reinforce crying behavior if they are to meet the baby's needs. As the child grows older, however, he can learn to express desires in more acceptable forms. In this instance Jay was probably not hungry, but his crying behavior had been reinforced by the presentation of cookies. In the future the parents could remedy this problem by giving food to Jay before he started to cry in the restaurant. If he did begin to cry first, they could ignore him (most unfair to the restaurant management, employees, and patrons) or take him back to the car.

However, if the child is hungry and announces his hunger by crying, then it is far better to give him some food when he first begins crying than to wait five, ten, or fifteen minutes and then give him some food. If some crying behavior must inevitably be reinforced, it is better to reinforce ten seconds of it than twenty minutes of it.

BEING LATE FOR SCHOOL

Sixteen-year-old Patty had always been prompt at getting to the school bus stop in the morning. One morning she overslept. Since she had recently obtained her driver's license, her mother allowed her to take the family car to school.

After that morning, Patty began to oversleep more often. Or she would eat her breakfast slowly so that she often missed the school bus. Her mother always allowed her to take the family car on such occasions.

Obviously the use of the family car was a reinforcing event for Patty. Without realizing it, her mother was reinforcing oversleeping and dawdling.

CREATING DISORDER IN THE CLASSROOM

Van was noisy and inattentive in class. Although his teacher spoke to him several times, he continued making a disturbance. She then asked him to come up and sit by her. She spoke angrily to him and interrupted the entire class when she verbally chastised him. Then she asked him to sit beside her at the front of the class while she kept her hand on his shoulder. Shortly after the teacher allowed him to return to his regular seat, Van again began making disturbances.

Contrary to her intentions the teacher was actually reinforcing Van with the attention from her and from his classmates. Every member of the class was able to observe how Van behaved. The teacher's hand on his shoulder may even have seemed affectionate to him rather than the controlling gesture she intended.

A Child Can Learn to Reinforce Himself

Ultimately each child should learn to reinforce himself. A truly mature and self-directed individual has learned what goals he wants to accomplish for himself and is inwardly pleased with his own activities. An independent person can reinforce himself for his own actions even in the face of pressure to engage in other behavior by influential people.

Children should be encouraged to learn standards for judging their own behavior and should be helped to develop methods for reinforcing themselves when they feel they deserve it.

> LOSING WEIGHT
>
> Libby was seventeen years old and overweight. She wanted to lose weight, and her physician had recommended an appropriate diet. Unfortunately she had difficulty sticking to the diet partly because any progress she made was not immediately apparent.
>
> Her father suggested that she make a graph, weigh herself twice each day, and plot her weight on the graph. Libby weighed herself just before breakfast and just before her evening meal. She mounted the graph in the hallway so that every member of the family could observe her progress although family reinforcement was probably not as important to Libby as the observation that her weight was decreasing.

Perhaps as important as the weight loss itself was Libby's finding that she could in fact control her behavior. Keeping a record of one's progress is an aid in developing control.

Correcting Common Misconceptions About Reinforcement

REINFORCEMENT IS NOT COAXING

> GETTING DRESSED WITHOUT HELP
>
> Binky was three-and-a-half years old but refused to dress himself. For several months his mother had been urging him to do

so, but all her attempts had proved futile. "Binky, please try to put on your shirt. I know you can do it. You are such a big boy. You can do so many other things. I know you can do this, too." Binky refused to participate, and his mother eventually dressed him herself. The mother's coaxing did not convince Binky that he should dress himself.

Eventually his mother stopped coaxing. She also stopped doing such a conscientious job of getting him dressed. One morning Binky came into the kitchen with his shirt on. Even though it was inside out his mother was delighted with his effort and let him know. The next morning he put his shoes on the wrong feet and without socks, but again his mother showed pleasure at his effort. From that point Binky made rapid progress in learning to dress himself.

Coaxing involves an attempt to persuade, inveigle, or flatter someone to engage in some behavior before he actually does so. It really constitutes reinforcement for *not* trying since it is attention directed to a person immediately following his resistance to participate. We frequently find that prolonged coaxing serves to strengthen a person's resolution not to participate. Coaxing is reinforcement for behavior opposite to that desired: it is flattering attention following refusal, not praise following performance. When Binky's mother stopped coaxing and waited for him to begin even small efforts to dress himself, she was sincerely pleased and reinforced his improvements by letting him know her pleasure.

REINFORCEMENT IS NOT BRIBERY

Webster's Collegiate Dictionary defines bribery as a prize, reward, gift, or favor bestowed or promised to pervert the judgment or corrupt the conduct of a person (in a position of trust).

Our language contains many words to represent the exchange of services, products, or money. Wage, salary, commission, honorarium, fee, prize, reward, reparation, bribe, ransom, tip, blackmail, pay, and compensation all refer to the exchange of one valuable for another. However, each different word connotes different circumstances. Only if you wish to pervert the judgment of a child or corrupt the conduct of a child could it be said that you are bribing him by offering him some reinforcer.

Reinforcement, as we have already seen, can be used to promote desirable or undesirable behavior. It is a powerful tool and can be abused as well as used wisely. Bribery is a misuse of reinforcement.

Since people in our society have different ideas of what constitutes desirable behavior, a behavior considered desirable by one parent or teacher may well be considered corrupt or perverted to another. Reinforcing a child for saying his prayers may be considered highly desirable to a devout Christian but corrupt to an agnostic or atheist. However, the distinction rests on the type of behavior that is thought of as desirable, not on the use of reinforcement itself. Just as a physician's scalpel may be used either to save lives or to murder, so can reinforcement be used to promote worthy or unworthy behavior.

REINFORCEMENT HAS LIMITATIONS

No amount of reinforcement will ever enable a snake to fly or a cat to read. In the same way each person has limitations as to what he can accomplish. A young child has more limitations than an older child. Skills which can be taught quickly to an older child may require an inordinate amount of effort to teach a younger child.

Children vary widely in their rates of development, and it is impossible to prescribe that any given child should learn any given skill at a definite age. If a child is making no progress, perhaps he is not yet ready (has not yet matured sufficiently) to learn what you wish him to learn. Perhaps in a few weeks, months, or years he will be better able to benefit from instruction, or perhaps the skills or behaviors you wish to teach him need to be broken down into some prerequisite skills or behaviors which must be learned first (see Chapter 2).

Some adults are more concerned about their children and more eager for them to do well than are other adults. A parent with musical ability may wish his child to display similar proficiency and be extremely disappointed if the child does not make rapid progress. An English teacher may want every student in his class to experience pleasure from reading Shakespeare. For unknown hereditary or environmental reasons, however, the child may simply get his kicks from other pursuits. Adults should make available opportunities for children to engage in a wide variety of activities that will permit children to test their own skills and reactions. Youngsters will probably choose to engage most in those activities in which they make the greatest progress and gain some satisfaction quickly. These activities may not necessarily be the ones that the adults would prefer, but if the activities are worthwhile, the adults should not discourage progress.

CHILDREN REINFORCE ADULTS TOO

Parents, teachers, and other adults are not the only people who can administer reinforcers. Any human being may reinforce or be reinforced by any other human being with whom he comes in contact. A child reinforces his parents or teachers, for example, when he plays happily, stops crying, learns new skills efficiently, or expresses joy.

Reinforcement is a mutual affair. In any harmonious relationship each party to the interchange reinforces the other. This mutual reinforcement is so automatic that most people are not aware that it is happening. Adults who use reinforcement techniques will soon become aware that children also use these techniques to modify adult behavior. By reinforcing or by withholding reinforcement, the child informs the adult of the activities he wishes just as the adult similarly informs the child. Harmonious human relationships exist when each person reinforces the other.

II

Developing New Behavior

2

Gradual
Improvements
Become
New
Behaviors

DEVELOPING INDEPENDENT STUDY SKILLS

To Mr. Healy the assignment was perfectly clear: "I want each of you to choose one foreign country, read all you can about it from many different sources, independently decide what the most important features of the country are, and then write a report summarizing your findings." But when the reports came in, he was chagrined to find that his students had merely copied paragraphs from the encyclopedia. The better students had occasionally copied paragraphs from two different encyclopedias, sometimes containing contradictory information.

Instead of chastising the pupils for their uncritical and unimaginative performance, Mr. Healy reexamined his assignment and the skills that he had expected the students to perform. He discovered that many of the students did not know how to use an index. None of them had ever before been asked to compare two independent sources on the same question. Many did not remember how to use the card catalog in the library. Most of the students did not know what kind of questions were important to ask. Their skills in outlining were markedly deficient. Furthermore he found that most of the boys and girls were unconcerned about the foreign country they had selected, having engaged in the exercise as a sterile academic requirement without any intellectual curiosity.

Mr. Healy listed the skills he had found missing and organized a series of instructional experiences designed to improve each skill. Finally, to integrate the skills he capitalized on a classroom argument concerning the most important business activity in their own state. He asked the students to list the most plausible alternatives, to formulate the key questions, to find answers from a variety of sources, to compare and evaluate the answers they received from different sources, and finally to write a report summarizing the evidence and their own conclusions.

Mr. Healy had at first expected his pupils to engage in a complicated type of activity before they had mastered the prerequisite skills. When he found they were unable to master the complex task, he decided to break it down into smaller, easier skills which could be tackled one at a time. By reinforcing the children for accomplishing each small skill (or approximation of the more complex skill), he gradually helped them master the total behavior.

Successive Approximations Principle: To teach a child to act in a manner in which he has seldom or never before behaved, reward successive steps to the final behavior.

The difficulties some children have both in school and at home

PATRICK - - - By MAL HANCOCK

Reward successive steps to the final behavior.

frequently result because they have not mastered the skills necessary for performing the more complicated behaviors expected of them. The wise adult attempts to help a child identify precisely what prerequisite skills he needs to master in order to learn the more complex task.

The Successive Approximations Principle implies that adults must not wait for a behavior to be perfect before using reinforcement. Any tendency to improve must be reinforced. A series of small improvements gradually becomes the desired behavior. Applying this principle is sometimes difficult for adults who desire perfection. Sometimes reinforcement is necessary for an improved behavior which is still "wrong." A child who improves his spelling of the word *receive* from *reesief* to *resief* deserves some reinforcement for his improvement even though he is still far from perfect. A child needs to know he is making progress as well as to know how to remedy his deficiencies. Catch him doing better.

Many types of behavior problems can be remedied by an application of the Successive Approximations Principle:

"That's where my Mom pastes a gold star on the days I'm good."

Reward successive improvements instead of waiting for perfect behavior.

- Art is discouraged and hates math because he receives failing grades even though he claims he knows what he is doing.
- Three-year-old Hugh will eat no vegetables and deliberately drops his food on the floor at mealtime.
- Kay, confident and able to work with plastics in art class, refuses to try any other medium.
- Dale feels humiliated in his physical education class because he cannot hit the volleyball properly.

- Since Buddy's grandfather has come to town, Buddy cannot go into a store without demanding toys and candy.

How to Identify Intermediate Steps

Identifying each step or each part of any performance is not always easy. There are four ways of breaking down a complex skill to reinforce behavior approximating the desired performance.

LEARNING EACH PART OF A COMPLEX SKILL MAY BE REINFORCED

HITTING CURVE BALLS WITHOUT FLINCHING

Smitty lunged off balance and rarely hit a curve ball that came at the plate and broke away. Because he was off balance, he swung at many bad pitches. He also flinched, went back on his heels, and failed to swing at curve balls that broke over the plate. Although he could hit other kinds of pitches well, he struck out two or three times a game on curves. He complained "I just can't hit a curve. How can you hit a ball that looks as if it's going to hit you and then breaks over for a strike? I guess I am just afraid of the ball."

Despite this weakness the coach felt certain that Smitty was a baseball player of exceptional ability. He had speed, strength, and remarkable reflexes. He could hit the fastest pitcher in the league, but he could not hit a curve ball. After a fast start in his sophomore year, Smitty found that opposing pitchers and coaches had discovered his weakness and had started to take advantage of it. Soon he became so worried about the curves that he couldn't hit anything else either.

The coach reported the story as it developed: I discussed Smitty's problem with him, and we agreed to get together with a few boys informally on several consecutive Saturdays to see if we could help him. I outlined briefly what we would do, emphasizing that he could *learn* to hit a curve. I began the first session by telling Smitty that he wouldn't be hit if he watched the ball carefully and remained balanced. "Remember, you get hit when you flinch and lose your balance so that you can't react to the ball," I told him. Then as he simply stood at the plate, I pitched curve after curve to him. I praised him each time he watched the ball and remained properly balanced. When he involuntarily flinched, I said nothing. In a short while he didn't flinch at even the closest pitches. After praising him for doing well in this phase, I then described the next step to him.

In the second session I mixed up the pitches I threw. Since he didn't know what to look for each time, he flinched at a few curve balls, but I praised him whenever he stayed balanced. Soon he gained confidence in this phase also and began facing both types of pitches equally well.

Then I asked him to call out the kind of pitch I was throwing as soon as he could detect it after it had left my hand. I praised him for the correctness of his call and for the speed with which he could detect what it was when he was correct.

In the last session I let him swing the bat for the first time. "Now when you call the pitch, Smitty, if it's a fast ball, swing immediately. If it's a curve, coil slightly around toward the catcher first and then swing when you see the ball in the hitting area. The coil will delay your swing to allow for the slower speed of the curve and will insure that you stay in position to hit the ball if it's over the plate."

I threw him a few curves so that he could practice the coiling. Then I began mixing the pitches up. Smitty demonstrated that he had learned the steps we had practiced previously by reacting properly to several curve balls and hitting them hard. At this point my praise was unnecessary; the successful application of what he had learned was enough. He wore me out as he insisted on curve after curve to see how far he could hit each one.

The coach broke the complex skill of hitting a curve ball into several subskills: remaining balanced and unflinching as the curve ball approached the batter, remaining balanced and unflinching when curve balls were mixed with fast balls, predicting the type of pitch, swinging the bat differently for different types of pitches, and hitting both curve balls and fast balls as they were pitched in a mixed order. Each subskill was complex in itself, but Smitty had progressed far enough in his baseball skill that he could master each part successfully. If he had had difficulty with any part, the coach could have helped him further by breaking down one of the subskills into even finer parts.

The coach praised Smitty for successfully mastering each part of the task. He even praised him for simply being able to stand balanced at the plate without flinching when a curve ball came toward him. Since this ability constituted a considerable improvement over what Smitty could do before, he clearly deserved praise for it.

Thirteen-year-old Art was developing a strong aversion to mathematics. He received zeros on many of his test papers, not because he knew nothing of the subject but because he made foolish arithmetical mistakes. His teacher gave this account:

My policy had always been to give full credit if the answer were correct and no credit if the answer were wrong. I noticed that Art would frequently work all the way through a rather complicated problem using the proper method throughout but making some simple addition error which would cause an incorrect answer. I discussed with Art's parents his growing hostility and discouragement; as a result I experimented with a different grading procedure for the class.

I began to give partial credit for those parts of a problem that were handled correctly. As a result everyone's grades became higher since the parts that were correct got credit. Furthermore, by keeping a record of the most frequent mistakes I was able to identify the kind each pupil made most often so that he could work to improve that particular skill. Art's particular difficulty was in adding numbers to nine, especially nine plus six, nine plus seven, and nine plus eight.

His parents now report that Art is happier and more enthusiastic about math than he ever was before. Certainly his class interest and performance have improved remarkably.

Art's teacher made a twofold attack on the problem: She began giving credit to those parts of his work that were done correctly, and she identified the particular performance (addition with nine's) that seemed to cause most of his difficulties. Not only Art but the entire class began to benefit from this more analytic approach. Clearly this approach made more work for the teacher but the reward for this additional effort came from Art's improved attitude and performance, the satisfaction of his parents, and the improved motivation and skill of all the other class members.

INCREASING ACCURACY MAY BE REINFORCED

Breaking a complex skill into its component parts is not always easy or even necessary. For some types of performance merely rewarding the child for improvements in accuracy is sufficient. For example, a child developing his archery skills might first be rewarded for being able to launch an arrow, then for being able to shoot as far as the target, then for being able to hit any part of the target, and then gradually for hitting closer to the bullseye. Although it would be possible and sometimes highly desirable to analyze the task by describing the proper stance and the proper position for hands, arms, and shoulders, such a detailed analysis may not be necessary as long as the child can see that his performance is improving.

MAKING ONE'S OWN BED

Six-year-old Polly had never before attempted to make her own bed. One day she pulled up the blanket on the bed. Her mother told her that her bed looked nice. The next day Polly pulled up the blanket and also straightened her pillow. Again her mother noticed the improvement. On successive days Polly began pulling up the sheet along with the blanket and finally the bedspread. Although the bed would not pass military inspection, it represented a substantial improvement for Polly, and her mother expressed her appreciation.

Polly's mother did not wait for her to do a perfect job of making the bed. As the bed began to look neater with each attempt, her mother merely commented on the improvements. If Polly had ceased improving her bed making, her mother would have made no comment. The pleasure Polly got from the increased ability to make her own bed would likely generalize to future responsibilities. If she finds satisfaction in making her bed well, she might also begin to find satisfaction in picking up her toys, keeping her room neat, and taking care of her clothes.

IMPROVING EATING HABITS

Three-year-old Hugh scattered large portions of his food all over himself, his high chair, and the floor. His mother explained what she did about it:

Hugh had a great fondness for peaches. I told him that he could have peaches for dessert if he did not mess his food up so much. I showed him the peaches he could expect and pointed out that he should put the food in his mouth, not on the floor. He did better, although liberal amounts of food still fell on the floor. I gave him the peaches. The next day Hugh was in an exuberant mood and scattered his vegetables far and wide. Hugh received no peaches. Subsequently each day that Hugh did a better job of putting the food in his mouth instead of elsewhere I rewarded him with peaches. He improved rapidly and was eventually willing to substitute other fruits for his reward.

Hugh's mother did not provide detailed instruction on how to hold his spoon or where to place the food. As Hugh's accuracy increased, his mother continued to reward him. When he regressed to his previous level of sloppy eating, she simply omitted the reward. Since he found that increasing accuracy paid off, Hugh gradually improved his eating habits.

LONGER INTERVALS OF GOOD BEHAVIOR MAY BE REINFORCED

Some types of behaviors cannot be easily broken down into subskills and increasing accuracy cannot be identified. Whether or not a behavior is performed, the length of time that "good behavior" lasts can be counted. For example, in the case of Buck and Biggie (p. 18) the absence of fighting for a period of two hours was reinforced. The time interval could gradually be increased as Buck and Biggie were able to go for longer periods of time without fighting.

Habits such as squabbling, thumb sucking, and family bickering are not necessarily different from such habits as smoking, drinking, overeating, or taking dope. If the individual is to control or give up a habit, reinforcement for longer intervals between indulgence is one way to assist in bringing it under control.

When working with juvenile delinquents authorities would do well to pay more attention to constructive behavior during probation. A child showing an increasingly longer time interval with good behavior between offenses is giving evidence of progress along the road to rehabilitation. A youngster should be rewarded when increasing lengths of time go by without a repeated offense so that he comes to realize that good behavior is more profitable than bad behavior.

INCREASING EFFORT FOR PARTICIPATION MAY BE REINFORCED

Sometimes simply encouraging a child to try is desirable. Particularly in learning new skills, children may resist making an effort because they fear failure or because they are content with the previous way of doing things. Teachers and parents who would like their children to be exposed to new experiences and gain new skills may need to reward even the slightest beginnings of approaches to the new activities.

LEARNING A NEW CRAFT SKILL

Kay was a thirteen-year-old girl enrolled in a seventh and eighth grade craft class that had been set up to work with nine different media. The group had completed several projects with plastics, the first medium. Making designs of differing colors and shapes for necklaces and charms was the favored project.

The second goal in the craft class was to learn how to make small copper pictures from plain copper sheets. Immediately problems began to develop. Everyone wanted to make more plastic jewelry. Kay was a special problem. Her teacher described what took place:

Although she was not strong academically, Kay was artistic and dexterous. Her plastic designs were imaginative, and she had received high praise from her classmates, her mother, and me. But when she was presented with the copper picture project, she was not interested and said she did not want to do it. As resistance gave way to downright obstinacy it became very evident that she only wanted to work with more plastics.

Finally I said, "Look, Kay, if you will just try, really try, to learn how to work with copper, you can then return to making more plastic designs."

Kay's fingers and hands began to fly and the copper picture soon took shape. It was a fine job for the first try. Kay and I evaluated it together, and we found some spots where improvements could be made. I gave her the plastic materials so that she could return to making plastic designs.

The next day Kay finished her copper picture and toned it for color. All the class members including Kay herself admired it, for it was really good. She was too excited to start making plastics until the last few minutes of class, but I assured her she could work on them the next day. However, when she came to class the next day, she asked for another sheet of copper so that she could make a pair of copper pictures for her mother. She wanted to know if she could come in after school or on the weekend to work. I reminded her of her initial reluctance, and she replied that she did not realize how much fun it was to work with copper sheeting. After this experience she went from one medium to the next with less reluctance.

The teacher used as a reward the opportunity to engage in a previous activity which had been highly satisfying to Kay. However, when the time came for Kay to receive this reward, she preferred the new activity.

There was the risk that Kay might have become so enthusiastic about working with copper that she would then reject the next new experience when it was presented, or that she would not have found copper work as satisfying as plastics. Luckily in this instance the teacher helped Kay to see that she could not really judge how satisfying an artistic medium would be until she had first given it a try.

SPEAKING COMFORTABLY IN A FOREIGN LANGUAGE

Miss Ziller was teaching French, using the Aural–Oral method which requires class members to speak in French in response to her speaking in French. Sam would never speak. No matter what she said he remained silent. Miss Ziller described what happened:

I did not penalize Sam for his silence. I continued the drills, passing on to the next student without interrupting the work or embarrassing Sam. One day Sam muttered some words while covering his mouth with his hand. I acknowledged Sam's response with a smile and a nod and continued the drill as if Sam had given the correct answer. Actually at that point I had not understood what he had said. I acknowledged each effort that Sam made to respond even though his pronunciation was not flawless. Gradually he began to speak more distinctly, no longer covering his mouth with his hand. He seemed much less embarrassed by the inevitable errors one makes in the process of learning to speak a foreign language.

The teacher helped Sam by gently reinforcing his beginning efforts to speak. Her reinforcements were inconspicuous to the class since any fuss over Sam would have embarrassed him. Sam began to discover that no matter what he did, no matter how poorly he spoke, the teacher did not humiliate or embarrass him. When a child is reticent to participate at all, the most important task for a teacher or a parent is to encourage his effort, not to correct his mistakes.

Improved Competency Is Its Own Reinforcer

Almost everyone wants to be able to control his life, to be master of his environment, and to be free and independent from the aversive consequences of nature and other individuals. One way of achieving increased autonomy is by learning to master problems independently. Most children are eager to master new skills as long as the learning process is not too painful. A parent or teacher needs to provide little in the way of reinforcers if the learning task is relatively pleasant and if the child can observe his own increasing mastery of the skill.

REWARDS MAY BE BUILT INTO THE PERFORMANCE ITSELF

SERVING A VOLLEYBALL SUCCESSFULLY

Fourteen-year-old Dale was unable to serve a volleyball in the direction he wanted. The other boys in his gym class teased him about his poor aim, and the coach, seeing that the boy needed help, described what he did about the situation:

I took Dale aside and asked him if he would like to learn a better way to hit the ball. He was eager to learn. I demonstrated an improved stance and suggested he try hitting the ball with his hand instead of with his forearm.

I then arranged a spot in the gym so that he could practice by himself and know immediately when he hit a good serve. I had him serve to a blank wall. If the ball hit higher than a certain spot on the wall and if it returned straight back over a certain line on the floor, he would know he had hit correctly. He was eager to practice by himself, and before the hour was over, he had mastered serving well enough to reenter the volleyball game.

The coach had only to arrange a suitable way for Dale to practice and observe his improving skill. Dale's increasing competence was all the reinforcement he needed.

KNOWING PERFORMANCE STANDARDS HELPS A CHILD
BECOME INDEPENDENT

Merely reinforcing a child for improvements is not always sufficient. If we wish to help a child judge his progress and reinforce
himself, we usually need to give him a good idea of the goal to
which his improvements will lead—that is, the ultimate standard
of performance toward which he may strive. He also needs to
understand the reasons why the standard of performance has
been established. In this way he can make judgments and become increasingly independent. Standards of performance can
be taught for simple physical and academic skills as well as for
complicated moral decisions.

IMPROVING CURSIVE HANDWRITING

Doug was a ten year old whose handwriting was fast but
illegible. His primary fault was that he did not close the letters
d or *a* so the *d* looked like *cl* and the *a* resembled *u*. His teacher
felt he needed help and told how she gave it to him:
   One day when I returned an assignment to Doug, I circled the
best *a* he had written. It was not good, but I said to him, "Doug,
here is the best *a* you have written on this paper. Your *a* still
looks a little bit like a *u*, but I'm sure you know that it ought to
look more like this (demonstrating a closed *a*). Here's how the *d*
should look. See how both are completely closed." Whenever
I saw on Doug's papers an *a* or a *d* that was closer to the standard, I circled it and wrote "better" beside it. One time I asked
Doug to look over one of his own papers and tell me which *a*
he thought was best and which *d* best. I did not comment on the
poorly written letters.
   After three weeks his handwriting had improved markedly.
I retrieved one of the papers he had written a month earlier, and
we compared it with his current handwriting. He was impressed
with the difference and could see how much he had improved.

His teacher did several valuable things for Doug. She set a standard of performance for him. She reinforced him for each successive improvement even when his writing was far from the
standard. She helped him evaluate his own performance so that
he could see for himself when he was improving.
   Helping a child set appropriate standards of performance is

important so that he can become his own judge and reinforcing agent.

Tendencies Toward Poor Behavior May Be Mistakenly Reinforced

We have seen in Chapter 1 that poor behavior as well as good behavior may be reinforced. The Principle of Successive Approximations applies equally to good and to poor behavior. The reinforcement of gradually worsening behavior is usually not a deliberate act on the part of the involved adult. Sometimes it is beyond the control of anyone. Sometimes it is accidental, resulting from carelessness or expediency. The process begins usually in one of two ways: by ignoring the child when he should be reinforced or by reinforcing the child when he should be ignored.

IGNORING A CHILD WHEN HE SHOULD BE REINFORCED

LEARNING TO SCREAM FOR ATTENTION

Two-year-old Pia, her mother, and her mother's friend were having lunch in a restaurant. Her mother explained that she and her friend were deeply engrossed in a conversation. This is her report:

When Pia asked, "Mommy, may I have piece of bread?" I must admit I ignored her and continued to converse with my friend. Pia repeated the request more loudly. This time I heard her clearly but was still reluctant to interrupt the conversation. Finally, Pia screamed, "Mommy, gimme, gimme!" No longer able to ignore her, I gave Pia a piece of bread and returned to my conversation.

The beginning of a vicious circle is evident here. Pia has discovered that polite, quiet requests are ignored while noisy, obnoxious behavior in public is rewarded. Inadvertently the mother began to teach Pia to act in an unruly way in public by reinforcing the screaming, but ignoring the polite request.

In the future the mother will be less able to converse with her friends undisturbed because Pia is learning that noisy interruptions are reinforced. Both parent and child will be less happy with each other as time goes on unless this vicious circle is stopped. Parents are people with their own needs. But when Pia's mother became engrossed with her own needs, she neglected to pay attention to Pia's. In the long run her mother would be better able to carry on her conversations if she rewarded Pia for quiet requests rather than for noisy interruptions.

REINFORCING A CHILD WHEN HE SHOULD BE IGNORED

Sometimes adults give attention to children when it would be far wiser to give no attention at all.

FORGETTING POSSESSIONS

Twelve-year-old David went to school Monday morning without his physical education clothes which his mother had placed on the table after reminding him to take them. She told the events that followed:

David phoned from school, two miles away, and asked me to bring his clothes before gym so that he would not receive any demerits. I did, leaving them in the school office. The office secretary then called his name over the loudspeaker system and asked him to pick up his clothes. On successive days the next week he forgot his lunch money, his English workbook, and a textbook containing an assignment he needed to turn in.

I discovered my mistake in this situation when David told me with pride and satisfaction, "This is the fourth time I have had my name called over the loudspeaker." I then realized that my effort to keep him from getting demerit marks for not having his equipment was the first step in reinforcing his forgetfulness and thoughtlessness.

If David's mother had really wanted him to remember to take things he needed to school, she might better have let him accept the demerits in his physical education class.* Her attempt to protect him from the consequences of his mistake actually encouraged him to continue making the same kind of mistake. The reward

---

*We do not advocate a demerit mark system in schools. The existence of such systems, however, is an unfortunate fact of life which must be considered in making decisions about appropriate behavior. See Chapters 8, 9, 10, 11 for alternative ways of stopping undesired behavior.

turned out to be the attention he received by having his name announced over the loudspeaker system. To David such a public announcement was reinforcing although to other children it might have been embarrassing.

Giving Rewards When Requested

Acquiescing to a request for a reward frequently serves only to reinforce "gimmie" behavior.

BEGGING FOR TREATS

When Buddy's grandfather came to visit, he would occasionally go shopping and bring candy home to him. Since Buddy's mother seldom allowed him to eat much candy, he was delighted and thanked his grandfather.

As time went on he began accompanying his grandfather on shopping expeditions to get an extra treat. His grandfather tended to buy many of the things that Buddy requested, but he was particularly likely to buy something if Buddy make a strong protest about passing it by.

Eventually he made so many outrageous demands that his grandfather refused to take him to the store any more.

The indulgent grandfather, well able to afford the requests Buddy made, undoubtedly wanted Buddy to like him. However, as the requests mounted, the grandfather gradually became unwilling to grant them and eventually damaged the previously good relationship with his grandson.

No one can quarrel with a parent's or grandparent's wanting to give gifts to a child, but a gift given in response to a request rewards requesting behavior. If the grandfather does decide to grant a request for an ice cream cone during a shopping trip, he should agree to it when it is first requested and not after much pleading and protesting, unless he wants to encourage prolonged begging.

The type of behavior occurring just prior to granting the request will be the type of behavior most likely to occur in the future. It is better to reinforce one specific request than ten minutes of begging. For the same reason Jay, the small boy who cried and was given cookies by the restaurant waiter (page 22), should if hungry be fed immediately rather than only after the crying persists. (Of course if a parent wants to teach his child to cry persistently, he should reward increasingly longer intervals of crying.) The adult's actions, not his intentions, influence the child's behavior.

Taking Over the Child's Responsibility

Frequently it is easier to do a child's job yourself than it is to help him do it right. If getting the job done quickly takes precedence over teaching the child to do his part, the child may be reinforced for neglecting his duty.

> NEGLECTING TO SET THE TABLE
>
> Everyone in the Brown family had some job. Lori had the job of setting the kitchen table. She was proud of her responsibility and worked well. Her mother described the events that changed Lori's performance:
>
> One day Lori forgot to place a fork beside my plate. I said, "Never mind, Lori, I'll get it myself." Several days later Lori forgot to put the napkins at all the places. I again did the job for her. Sometimes when Lori would come in late, I would set the whole table for her. She seemed to lose pride in her job and had to be prodded and reminded to do it. Even when she did attempt the job, it was frequently sloppy and incomplete.

Parents who pick up toys or clothes for their children may be rewarded by having a neater house sooner, but they are not teaching their children to assume responsibilities. In effect the child is often getting credit for work he has not performed.

Teachers face a similar temptation. Whenever there is to be a public display of children's work, the teacher, desiring to make a favorable impression, may be tempted to display a little too much of her own efforts and not enough of the representative work of her children. This display seldom fools the children's parents, although it may make for an extremely neat and attractive bulletin board. The unfortunate aspect is that the children know the work is not their own and therefore are not reinforced for their own attempts. If children are going to learn new competencies, then they should recognize their own gradual improvements, even though they lack perfection. Adults can help most not by catching children doing poorly, but by catching them doing better.

3

The
Good
Example

LEARNING SPEECH PATTERNS

The kindergarten teacher sent Larry to the school speech specialist because of his inability to speak so others could understand him. When he would try to say "My name is Larry Mc-Monihan," it would come out, "M'nim 'Ar' M'Mahun."

Larry's mother was called in for a conference to explain to her why he should be referred for help. The school also needed a medical clearance from her because of the possibility that he might have some birth defect or other physical problem. Larry's mother appeared at the appointed time and announced herself: "M' nims Mizz M'Mahun. Ahm 'Ar's munr."

A child learns to speak correctly best by hearing others speak correctly. Larry was an only child when his father died. With few children to talk to in the neighborhood he had simply copied his mother's slurred speech pattern. Patterns of speech are learned through imitation. Both good and poor habits of speech can be accounted for in large part by the examples provided through parents, brothers, sisters, friends, and teachers.

Children imitate many other kinds of behavior in addition to speech patterns. The people whose behavior is imitated are called "models."

Modeling is frequently unintentional. Larry's mother certainly did not plan deliberately for him to imitate her speech, but the modeling behavior occurred anyway. If she had modeled clear enunciation, Larry might just as readily have acquired more understandable speech.

Modeling Principle: To teach a child a new way of behaving, allow him to observe a prestigeful person performing the desired behavior.

Adequate or inadequate models can influence a variety of behaviors:

- Paul, a child with cystic fibrosis, hates to do the exercises that are a part of his treatment.
- A tall girl for her age, Jean slouches and slumps to appear shorter.
- Jeff is a poor sport when he strikes out in baseball.
- Robbie is a bright tenth grade boy who has not learned the rigors of scientific investigation.
- Sandy enters college having never examined what she believes.

CARNIVAL   By Dick Turner

8-9

© 1965 by NEA, Inc. T.M. Reg. U.S. Pat. Off.

**"I almost wish Mom would catch us! She's always
holding you up as an example!"**

Modeling can promote either desirable or undesirable behavior.

Who Can Become a Prestigeful Model?

ANYONE WHO DISPENSES REINFORCERS

The President of the United States, whoever he may be at the
time, is always a prestigeful model because of his power to control
reinforcers for many people. His power to spend or withhold
money for certain persons and projects, his power to appoint or
not appoint persons to high office, and his power to increase or

decrease aid to innumerable projects, persons, and countries establish him as a powerful model. People who respect him are likely to imitate him, his manner of speaking, his attitudes, his dress, his qualities of personal courage and integrity.

But one does not need to be President of the United States to be a prestigeful model. Parents, teachers, relatives, friends, and even total strangers can be prestigeful models since under certain circumstances they control the dispensing of many reinforcers.

Parents

Mothers and fathers give their children a great number of reinforcers and are usually the first natural models for their children. They provide the child with daily meals, a place to sleep, help in understanding problems, money, transportation, birthday presents, and hopefully a generous dose of love and affection. With such powerful reinforcers, parents generally cannot help being prestigeful models especially for young children.

PERFORMING PHYSICAL EXERCISES REGULARLY

Paul, a cystic fibrosis child, had to do upside-down tilting exercises as part of his treatment. The tilted block of wood and the upside-down position were frightening to him, and he resisted doing these exercises.

To help him overcome his fear Paul's father did exercises with him, attempting to make the exercises seem like a game. His dad would say, "Time for my exercises," and then do sit-ups which were similar to Paul's. Paul simply watched at first. For a while he was reluctant, but gradually his dad's interest and enthusiasm took hold. He decided to attempt one exercise with his father helping him. After that point Paul performed his exercises, which they called his "upside downies," more frequently until they became a regular routine with his father's assistance.

From seeing the example set by his father, Paul soon began to act as if his "upside downies" were a game as well as an exercise.

Teachers

A teacher also controls the administration of many reinforcers important to most children. The teacher grades the child's progress, gives encouragement when the work is hard, provides novel experiences, and gives approval when the child's work is improving or meets the teacher's standards. A warm, supportive, friendly teacher provides a strong model for many children.

Such a teacher will find that the students begin to imitate some of her behaviors. Hence by modifying an aspect of her behavior, the teacher can help a child try a new response.

PARTICIPATING IN PLAYGROUND ACTIVITIES

Seven-year-old Kit would not play kickball with the class. She said that kickball was for boys and would even try to talk some of her girl friends into staying out of the game. Her teacher had noticed that Kit considered her a model. The teacher gave this report:

Kit would bring me things from home and come to my room before school to talk. She tried to emulate me in small ways, such as using some of my expressions and tying her hair back as I did. Her mother had told me that Kit liked to be the teacher and frequently used my name when she played school at home.

From this information I had a fairly good idea that if I played kickball myself, her behavior might change. One day I put myself on a team that was short one player. The whole class got so excited that they were simply screaming. I kicked a good ball and almost scored a run.

Kit was as excited as the rest of the class. Never again did she ask to be left out of the game or claim that kickball was only for boys. She even practiced her kicking skills when she was not playing in a formal game.

Good Friends and Siblings

Good friends and brothers or sisters are often powerful models. The reinforcers which they provide are less material and less formal than those from parents and teachers. Good friends share special possessions and secrets. They listen to each other's stories. They stick up for each other when either one is in trouble. They provide companionship. What one can do, the other usually wants to do.

LEARNING TO RIDE A BICYCLE

Tammy had been given a bicycle at age five, but for months she took no interest in it and would not learn to ride. She invented excuses for not trying to learn whenever her parents offered to help her.

One day Tammy's best friend, Linda, was given a bicycle for her sixth birthday. Linda learned to ride almost immediately and was able to travel more places faster than Tammy. Tammy began to feel left out.

Although she was still fearful of falling from the bicycle, she began practicing by herself. She was cautious while learning, but she would not give up. Within three days she had mastered the bicycle and reestablished her relationship with Linda.

Adults sometimes mistakenly ridicule a child for performing less well than a model. Children need encouragement for gradually approximating a model's behavior, not punishment or ridicule for failing to achieve an ideal performance.

Special Persons

The best model for a child with a special problem is a person who has faced and solved that identical problem. If such a person can be brought in contact with the child and is the kind of person who provides some attention and warmth toward the child, it is highly likely that such a special person can be a most beneficial model. Alcoholics are often helped best by former alcoholics. The same basic idea also applies to less severe problems in the average child.

OVERCOMING SENSITIVITY ABOUT BEING TALL

At the age of twelve Jean had a spurt of growth which brought her to the height of five feet ten and one-half inches. She was extremely self-conscious about her height since all her friends were much shorter. In trying to remain the height of her friends, she would slump and slouch and was becoming increasingly roundshouldered. Her poor posture made her look much less attractive. Her parents were distraught because nothing they could say or do seemed to make Jean feel any better about her problem. Here is the story as told by Jean's mother:

Last December a young couple bought the house next to us and proved to be ideal neighbors. Mrs. Smith is young, pretty, vivacious, has a keen interest in young people, and is six feet tall. She has excellent posture, looks lovely in everything she wears, and seems proud of her height. I confided to Mrs. Smith my concern about Jean. One day she asked Jean to come over and help her with a job, and soon the two of them became good friends. Mrs. Smith showed Jean some advantages of being tall. Jean is now trying hard to stand erect and improve her posture. She plans soon to enroll in a charm course (which Mrs. Smith also did at one time). She studies fashion magazines to determine the best clothes for tall girls. She seems determined to make her height an asset rather than a liability.

New Acquaintances

A total stranger can quickly become a powerful model if he provides the kind of reinforcement needed by another person. A model is not necessarily a person everyone would hold in high respect, but if he provides needed reinforcement to a young person, it is quite likely for him to become prestigeful.

CREATING AN ADOLESCENT DELINQUENT

Connie had run away from home at the age of 15. Although ordinarily this "first offense" would not have been punished, her obvious fear of returning home was so great that the judge felt it would be in her best interest to remain in the "girl's school" for a while to stabilize her situation.

Connie was frightened and self-conscious the day she first entered the school. However on the second day she was singled out by Wanda, a sixteen-year-old habitual offender who had a long record of home difficulties and sex offenses. When Wanda's friends deliberately excluded Connie from a game, Wanda called to Connie in front of the others and said, "I won't play unless you do too. Anyone who runs away from home is a friend of mine." Connie, feeling lonely and misunderstood by everyone, was so grateful for Wanda's attention and support that Wanda soon became the object of her hero worship.

Connie spent all her free periods with Wanda and adopted

her arrogance and several of her descriptive expressions, the mildest of which were, "I'm hot to go" and "Shuck'er baby." The environment that was supposed to stabilize Connie's situation actually put her in contact with a model who led her in the opposite direction.

Young people getting no support, encouragement, attention, or positive reinforcers from parents, teachers, or siblings will most likely turn to someone who will provide these reinforcers. If he is able to provide the needed reinforcement, that person will become a powerful model regardless of his moral standards.

Parents are sometimes worried about their children falling under the influence of bad companions. However bad companions are a serious danger only if the good companions fail to provide the reinforcement needed by a child.

ANYONE POSSESSING DESIRED SKILLS OR ATTRIBUTES

A model need not necessarily be a person who distributes reinforcers. Powerful models frequently are persons who demonstrate competencies which the child would like to attain himself or has been taught to admire. The model may also possess personality characteristics, physical attributes, or even material possessions which the youngster admires.

A parent or teacher can frequently help a child learn new behaviors by arranging for him to become acquainted with a potential model. The model should possess some skill or characteristic the child admires and should also practice the type of behavior the adult is trying to teach. Such models may be found in a variety of situations.

In the Child's Everyday Environment

Sometimes it is possible to bring into a school or classroom a former graduate whose skills or possessions are respected by the students.

APPRECIATING THE VALUE OF A FOREIGN LANGUAGE

Tom was apathetic toward his beginning course in German. His homework was frequently incomplete or carelessly done, he mumbled halfheartedly through oral work, he was satisfied with barely passing grades, and he appeared to be indifferent, inattentive, or bored with class activities, assignments, and exercises. Although his performance in other courses was satisfactory he considered learning German to be a useless activity and not worth his time or effort. His German teacher reported the following sequence of events:

I invited Clay, a former student of mine who had just returned from military duty in Europe, to visit my German class and tell of his experiences. Clay was well known to most of the members of the class. He had graduated from our school two years previously and had been known as a cool guy. Clay had been a better than average student; he participated in athletics, had quite a few friends, drove his own car, and was a prestige figure among the teen-age set.

When he entered the classroom, Clay greeted me in German and we had a short lively conversation. I introduced him to the class, first in German and then in English. Clay spoke in English but with a few expressions and comments in German. He told how useful his knowledge of German had been while traveling in Europe. He related his excitement of making new friends in a foreign country, the special dividends of being able to talk to people in their own language, being able to read newspapers, go to movies, date, ask for directions and information, and interpret for other Americans who couldn't speak German.

I noticed that Tom listened attentively to Clay's account.

Probably it is too much to assume that this single incident produced Tom's change in attitude and behavior, but I do believe it provided the catalyst which made the change possible. Tom's former apathy virtually disappeared. He did his homework assignments more conscientiously, and showed definite improvement in pronunciation. Within six weeks he raised his average from D to C and was "shooting for a B." He now showed signs of being annoyed with other students who acted as he previously had. He even tried to sell some younger students on the value of studying German.

I think the significant factor was that Tom could not believe me when I spoke of the advantages of learning a foreign language. Clay was a far more credible source for Tom than I could ever have been. Clay represented the kind of person that Tom would have liked to be.

It is not always necessary to bring in a model from the outside. Sometimes desirable models exist in one's classroom or family. Older siblings frequently become models since the age difference makes them more skilled and knowledgeable, and if they are also liked as a good friend, the effect is increased.

LEARNING GOOD SPORTSMANSHIP

It was Jeff's first year playing Little League baseball. Whenever he struck out he would throw his bat into the screen, shout insults at the opposing players, and argue with the umpire, particularly on a called third strike.

His parents often took him to baseball games in which his older brother, Tony, was one of the star players. Once when Jeff and his parents sat just behind the dugout Tony, usually a strong hitter, struck out stranding men on first and third in the fourth inning. Tony walked back to the dugout, laid his bat down with the others, said "Sorry about that," and ran out to assume his fielding position.

Jeff's reaction was one of letdown. He had been anticipating something spectacular from his brother, and figured both Tony and his teammates should at least have been upset if not downright mad. Later when Tony arrived home Jeff said as much.

Tony's reply: "After you pull a goof like that the only way you can save face is to show you're a good sport about it."

Although Jeff said no more, his parents noticed something had clicked. From then on when he struck out in Little League he returned to the bench trying hard to control his temper. Once they observed him showing some compassion for his teammates' foibles.

The power of a model is usually enhanced if the child has already attained some partial competence in the same area as the model or if he has expressed some desire to achieve that competence.

Among Prominent Entertainers, Sports Stars, or Political Figures

Young people often admire prominent figures from television, movies, athletics, music, art, and politics. Even though such prominent figures are already well exploited for testimonials to advertise breakfast cereals and cosmetics, they may also serve as models for other kinds of behavior, both desirable and undesirable.

The local visit of a prominent personality is often an ideal opportunity to exploit his potential for being a desirable model.

Behaviors of prestigeful persons are modeled.

LEARNING TO DEVELOP MORE TENNIS SKILL

The thirteen- and fourteen-year-old girls in the tennis class were just learning the correct way to stroke the ball. They frequently became impatient with learning the correct form and preferred the easier badminton-type stroke. Their tennis instructor reported an event which changed their minds.

Billy Talbert, at that time coach for the United States Tennis Team, was visiting our city due to a state tennis tournament. During this time he gave a tennis demonstration and clinic. An attractive and charming man, he interested many females in the clinic including all the girls from my tennis class. Mr. Talbert observed their tennis strokes, giving each one some individual suggestions for improvement. Then he demonstrated playing techniques, first with a boy and then with a pretty, vivacious girl who was a state champion. He commented on her strong tennis strokes. As soon as they finished playing, a number of the boys wanted a chance to play tennis with her.

After that I noticed a pronounced difference among my tennis pupils in the way they wanted to learn to hit the ball. They practiced longer and asked for more help and advice.

In this case it is difficult to know who was the more powerful model—Mr. Talbert or the attractive state champion. Undoubtedly the combination of Mr. Talbert's comments and the champion's popularity with the boys combined to make the entire situation a motivating one for aspiring female tennis players.

Among Fictional Heroes

Characters in books, movies, and television may make powerful models, with the potential to exert either a negative or a positive influence over a youngster. For this reason there is a general concern to develop the best possible television programs for children. The following episode illustrates that even cartoon characters can have an influence on a child.

EATING SPINACH WITHOUT URGING

Some years back Josh, then six years old, refused to eat any vegetables. He wouldn't even let his mother put them on his plate.

Josh watched cartoons on television every afternoon. His favorite program was *Popeye the Sailor.* Popeye's amazing strength after eating spinach made an obvious impact on Josh. He began to ask for spinach and said it tasted good. Although he would not eat any other vegetable, Josh was willing to eat spinach whenever it was served, even though his mother was not convinced he really liked it.

Among Historical Figures

It is possible to learn a great deal and gain much inspiration from studying the lives and actions of famous people in history. John F. Kennedy, while immobilized with a painful back injury, wrote his best-selling book *Profiles in Courage,* an account of courageous actions taken by famous men in history. John Kennedy's courage may have been derived in part from his study of these other lives.

The following report of a music teacher shows how the life story of a famous musician affected recruitment for the school band.

GENERATING INTEREST IN MUSICAL INSTRUMENTS

One of my jobs as band leader was to encourage junior high youngsters to start working on some musical instrument. Since getting into the band was considered an honor, the job was not too difficult.

However the year that I began the job, I checked the future prospects for various sections and found that there was not a single child in junior high working on the trombone to replace our graduating trombonists. My inquiry among the younger set revealed that they did not like the trombone. Knowing better than to try to pressure anyone into taking it, I hit upon the idea of letting them observe a skilled trombonist.

At that time a movie was available on the life of the late Glen Miller, the famous trombonist. With the approval of the rest of the faculty, I showed the movie at the next assembly and made no further comment. Within a week five junior high boys asked me if they could begin taking trombone lessons.

ANYONE ADMIRED BY PRESTIGEFUL PERSONS

The power to be an effective model can be transferred from one person to another. Any person who has become a prestigeful model through his achievements, competencies, attributes, or his power to dispense reinforcers can transfer at least some of that power to a third party by expressing admiration for him. Political candidates frequently try to secure a favorable endorsement from a highly respected political figure. For example, a former president, even if he no longer wields any power, can influence some admiring voters to support another candidate.

Young children have traditionally tended to adopt the political party and the religious preferences of their parents; in such a case the parents obviously serve as models for the child. Political or religious figures or beliefs are automatically accepted by the child because they are respected by the parent. As children become older, of course, their parents are no longer their only models; in fact, the parents sometimes lose their power as positive models completely.

Teachers frequently establish reputations which affect the behavior of pupils year after year. The reputation of a teacher as being good, tough, or easy is passed by word of mouth from one generation of students to the next and influences how the new students behave when they come in contact with that teacher.

A teacher may influence the students' attitude toward a textbook, for example. If the instructor speaks disparagingly of the textbook, students will complain about being required to read it. If instead the instructor points out desirable features of the identical book, the students will tend to report finding it of value. The instructor's prestige as a model can be transferred so as to affect the reputation of an author.

The opinions of alleged experts affect our appreciation of many musical and artistic productions. We admire art objects that experts have declared to be masterpieces even though objectively we may not be able to pick them out of a lineup of ten mediocre art productions. Usually the less we know about a subject, the more influential prestige models can be in influencing our judgments.

DEVELOPING AESTHETIC TASTES

Thirteen-year-old Joy listened to modern rock-and-roll music like other girls her age. A senior high school combo called "The Lions Roar" became quite popular with the older high school boys and girls. Joy's older sister and her friends said that "The Lions Roar" was even better than some of the nationally known rock bands.

Joy had never heard "The Lions Roar" play. Nevertheless, she would frequently say that they were far better than the records she and her friends listened to.

Copycats or Independent Thinkers?

Some people worry that the deliberate use of modeling in teaching children will produce youngsters incapable of thinking for themselves. They warn that children taught to mimic in a "monkey see, monkey do" fashion will be citizens incapable of making wise and rational decisions in a free and open society. Actually it is a good sign that people are worried; the very awareness of the possibility tends to minimize the chance that it will occur.

However, we must recognize that the process of modeling can be used for either moral or immoral purposes. A child can learn blind obedience to authority by modeling the example of his elders, as we saw on a mass scale in Hitler's Germany. Knowing the potential power of the modeling process should awaken us to the importance of making available models well calculated to produce thoughtful, rational, and independent citizens.

MODELING IS INEVITABLE

The process of learning by modeling is inevitable. If teachers and parents could deliberately avoid being models themselves and refrain from providing examples of desirable behavior for youngsters, the youngsters would simply turn elsewhere for their models. It is impossible for a parent or teacher not to be a model to some extent. Even if a parent or teacher stopped dispensing positive reinforcement and demonstrated no admired skills or attributes, his very presence might serve as a negative model. The children might well decide to do the opposite of whatever this negative model did.

Our actions and characteristics determine whether we will be strong models, weak models, or even negative models for the young people with whom we come in contact. However, as adults there is nothing we can do to avoid being models of one kind or another. Our best recourse is to serve as desirable models and make sure that, insofar as possible, other people likely to be perceived as models by our children represent the creative and self-reliant characteristics we want our own children to develop.

INDEPENDENT THINKING CAN BE MODELED

If we want our children to become creative and independent thinkers, then one of the most powerful methods for achieving this end is to provide them with models who are creative and independent thinkers.

DEVELOPING SCIENTIFIC CURIOSITY

Robbie enrolled in tenth grade biology with the same perfunctory spirit with which he enrolled in any course. It was merely to fulfill a requirement.

The biology teacher, Mr. Barnett, was a favorite among many of the students in Robbie's class, especially the boys. He would occasionally plan short field trips during laboratory periods. At the request of some of the students he also devoted some of his Saturday mornings to taking longer field trips with students who volunteered. They would look for specimens of plants and insects, observe their characteristics carefully, write down their observations, and classify their findings. Mr. Barnett asked many questions and encouraged his students to ask questions also. He was never satisfied with mere opinions. He insisted that the students answer questions from their own direct observations or the observations of the scientists who wrote biological reference books.

Robbie became an avid information seeker. He spent much of his free time on hikes looking for insects for his new collection. He kept a notebook on his "research work" and shared his findings enthusiastically with his classmates and his family.

Appropriate models can develop not only habits of careful scientific observation but the ability to weigh evidence on more than one side of an issue.

SEEING BOTH SIDES OF ISSUES

When she entered college, Sandy tended to accept the ideas of her parents and other authority figures pretty much without question. Her opinions were the opinions of those she respected. She had not carefully examined any of them in the light of her own experience.

Sandy's first encounter with the intellectual world at college included a professor whose course in sociology she took as a freshman. At her particular college the instructors and students ate lunch in the same dining hall, each instructor eating at a table with a group of students. At Dr. Young's table sociological issues were frequently the topic of conversation. Sandy was so stimulated by what he had to say that she would get to the dining hall early to be sure of a seat at his table. In discussing important issues, Dr. Young would argue one side, presenting evidence and reasons to support that side until most of the students at the table were convinced of the merits of that argument. He would then take the opposite side of the issue, bringing forth counterevidence and counterarguments which made the ultimate decision as to the wisest course of action much more difficult. Sandy began to see that many of the complicated issues in society were not as easy to resolve as she had first thought. She began to see the merits of arguments on both sides.

After two quarters at college her old friends were surprised to find her deliberately changing sides in a discussion. She said that she was much better able to make up her own mind about issues after she had argued both sides with her friends.

Virtually any kind of behavior can be modeled. Even the behavior of being a good model can be modeled. Everyone has been influenced by models. Children will inevitably find persons whose lives will influence them. An adult's job is to model as best he can and to help children find other models that represent the best the world has to offer.

CHILDREN LEARN WHAT THEY LIVE

If a child lives with criticism,
   He learns to condemn.
If a child lives with hostility,
   He learns to fight.
If a child lives with ridicule,
   He learns to be shy.
If a child lives with shame,
   He learns to feel guilty.
If a child lives with tolerance,
   He learns to be patient.
If a child lives with encouragement,
   He learns confidence.

If a child lives with praise,
He learns to appreciate.
If a child lives with fairness,
He learns justice.
If a child lives with security,
He learns to have faith.
If a child lives with approval,
He learns to like himself.
If a child lives with acceptance and friendship,
He learns to find love in the world.

Dorothy Law Nolte

4

Signals
for Appropriate
Behavior

WIPING SHOES ON THE DOORMAT

Matt's play yard contained a large dirt area that was dusty when dry and muddy when wet. A typically exuberant seven year old, Matt would usually forget to wipe his feet on the doormat before entering the house and would thus track sand, dirt, or mud over his mother's previously spotless floor. Despite daily reminders and scoldings Matt continued to aggravate his mother with his unintentional carelessness. His usual reply was, "I forgot."

Some method of reminding Matt was necessary to save his mother's sanity. The solution came in the form of a twenty-five cent hollow rubber duck which would squawk when squeezed. His mother put the rubber duck underneath the doormat and told him the duck's quack was to remind him to wipe his shoes. Any time he heard the duck quack he was to wipe his shoes thoroughly on the mat to make the duck quack at least five more times.

Whenever Matt approached the door, he could not avoid stepping on the doormat. The duck would quack and Matt would be reminded to wipe his feet. The five additional quacks would notify Matt's mother that he had indeed remembered. The first time the system worked she was so pleased that she gave him a cookie for himself and one for his friend in the back yard.

Many people have similar problems. Matt wanted to do the right thing, but at the exact moment the action was required, he was thinking of something else. The rubber duck's quack was the signal that reminded Matt to wipe his shoes. The toy under the doormat would not have to be a permanent addition to the household. Once he had developed the habit of wiping his feet before entering the house, his mother could remove the rubber duck. His own approach to the door would become a sufficient cue.

Matt's mother's previous scoldings and reminders didn't work because they always came after he had made the mistake. But the rubber duck served as a reminder just before he was expected to wipe his feet. If it had squawked after he had already finished tracking dirt on the floor, the duck would have been no more a successful reminder than his mother's scoldings.

Matt's mother made perfectly clear that the quack was to help him remember. When he finally did remember, she reinforced him with a cookie.

The experience of Matt and his mother illustrates the **Cueing Principle: To teach a child to remember to act at a specific time, arrange for him to receive a cue for the correct performance just**

before the action is expected rather than after he has performed incorrectly.

Certain types of behavior difficulties are especially adaptable to this principle:

- The children at Marble Elementary School are so boisterous and rowdy in the hallways that one child had a tooth knocked out.
- So as not to hurt the other girls' feelings, Lois often acquiesces too easily to their demands.
- Alan has difficulty remembering to feed his pets each day.
- Mrs. Morse dislikes reminding each of her four children about their daily chores.
- Claude can't seem to break his thumbsucking habit.

Who Benefits from Cueing?

Cueing seems to work better under some circumstances than under others. When cues are verbal, they are sometimes confused with nagging but there is an important distinction. Nagging is persistent unpleasant urging or scolding by finding fault. Cueing is a simple nonhostile direction when the child needs a reminder or when he needs help in learning.

CHILDREN NEEDING HELP IN LEARNING

Children who want to learn a new skill can benefit by receiving cues from a skilled performer. A skillful teacher can diagnose exactly what the learner is doing wrong and can give a timely cue. An ineffective teacher may be just as skillful in diagnosing the difficulty but gives the cue after the mistake instead of just prior to the time the action is needed.

HITTING A GOLF BALL

Joe was one of the slowest learners in a beginning golf class. In attempting to hit the ball he usually jerked his head up at the last second to see where the ball would go. However, as a result of moving his head, his body would also move, and his club would miss the ball completely. The golf instructor reported these remedial measures:

I first taught Joe how to swing the golf club without a ball. Then I told him, "When I give you the ball to hit, Joe, I'm going to remind you to keep your head down just before you swing."

Joe addressed the ball. Right at the top of his backswing I said, "Head down." His head did stay down and he hit the ball. I continued the same cue three more times and then shortened it to "down." After that I asked him to say "down" himself at the top of his own backswing. He learned to give himself the cue and no longer jerked his head up as he hit the ball.

People who want to learn are eager to obtain cues as to what they must do to perform correctly. Joe was eager to play golf. The cue "Head down," given just before the desired performance, helped him to master the complex movement. The skilled golf instructor then taught Joe to cue himself and become self-sufficient on the golf course.

CHILDREN NEEDING REMINDERS

Frequently people need help in remembering to do things that they really want to do. Tying a string around one's finger has been advocated, but the string may not be an efficient cue because the string bears no relationship to the action to be remembered.

Efficient cues are those whose very nature reminds the person what he needs to do just before he should do it.

IMPROVING CHORAL SINGING

Members of the ninth and tenth grade chorus would frequently forget to take a deep breath just before two long musical phrases. Without that deep breath they would be unable to complete the phrases properly. The director first told them to put an X on their sheet music at the spot where they should take a deep breath. Still half of them forgot.

The director then asked the chorus to watch him carefully. He told them he would give them a cue when they were supposed to breathe. Just before they were to take a deep breath, he opened his mouth wide and simulated, in an exaggerated fashion, taking a deep breath.

The singers without exception remembered to breathe at the proper time and also tended to watch the director more carefully for other cues. With continued practice the group remembered to breathe properly without the exaggerated cue.

The director's cue was a good one. His exaggerated intake clearly conveyed what action was needed.

The Time to Cue

METHODS OF PRESENTING THE CUE BEFORE THE ACT

The cue is best presented just before the desired behavior, not after an error has been made. When a child makes a mistake, the natural response of many parents and teachers is to tell him immediately he was wrong and then perhaps give further instructions. The child's mistake unfortunately becomes the parent's cue to give instructions. However, if they are going to be reinforced by seeing their children learn better ways of behaving, knowledgeable adults will learn to give their cues at more appropriate times.

Advance Planning

An adult with the habit of correcting mistakes as soon as they occur will have to devote some effort to overcoming the habit. At first it will require a good deal of thought to anticipate just when a cue can most advantageously be given. Waiting for the best moment requires some vigilance. Advance planning pays off.

WALKING, NOT RUNNING, IN SCHOOL

Last year the children at Marble Elementary School had become increasingly loud and boisterous when they were dismissed for recess to go to the playground. The children were lectured for their pushing, shouting, and horseplay but with little effect. One little girl had a tooth knocked out when she was pushed into the drinking fountain.

In planning for the new school year the teachers vowed to start out differently. Just before classes were dismissed for the first recess each teacher reminded her students that they were to move through the halls in a quiet, orderly manner without running, pushing, or yelling. The teachers then moved into the hall. Any child who ran, pushed, or shouted was not scolded; he was merely asked to return to his classroom and walk through the hall again on his way to the playground. No punishment was involved, but obviously the children who walked slowly, quietly, and orderly got to the playground equipment sooner than their more boisterous companions.

As a result of consistently enforcing this new procedure, movement in the halls was more orderly from the first day on. No serious incidents occurred that school year.

Some children in this school probably did not want to learn to move in an orderly fashion through the halls. For them a simple cue was not sufficient; some additional reinforcement was required. The children who did follow the rules were reinforced by being first to the playground equipment. In effect they became models of how to get outdoors fast. Those who failed to follow the rules received no punishment, ridicule, or humiliation; they were merely asked to try again. As soon as they walked through the halls properly, they too reached the playground but not until some of the choicest equipment was already in use.

On the basis of their experience from the previous year the teachers anticipated what they would have to do the next year to change the situation. They planned just when they could give the cues most effectively and exercised vigilance to be sure that the students were following the rules.

Verbal Instructions

Children are sometimes chastised for not living up to adult expectations when they do not know exactly what those expectations are. They have not been "cued-in" as to what is required of them. But adults have a problem too. They cannot always give a cue at the moment it is required.

LEARNING TO SPEAK TO GUESTS

When his parents were entertaining company in the living room, fifteen-year-old Eric walked through the room without speaking to any of the guests. Later his father asked him why he had not spoken to anyone, including several people he had met previously. Eric replied, "I thought it was your party, not mine."

Eric's parents realized that he did not know that ignoring the guests would be considered rude. They wanted him to act according to their own expectations without really communicating to him what those expectations were.

On the afternoon before the evening they next entertained Eric's mother spoke to him: "Eric, when the people come tonight, we'd appreciate your presence just briefly to say hello to those you know. We will introduce you to those you don't. You don't have to stick around. We know this is your night for television. Would you come in for just a few minutes right after your program is over? You could see everyone then all at once."

When he was approached in this manner, Eric was quite

willing to oblige his parents. At the second party he spoke to several people he knew and responded appropriately when introduced to the other guests.

Although Eric had no particular desire to learn the social amenities, his parents made it as easy as possible for him to do so. They did not scold or punish him for ignoring guests the previous time. Such punishment or scolding tends to arouse hostility and defensiveness which cause even more difficulty for learning to take place. At the same time his parents realized that giving Eric a cue when the company was present would be inappropriate. Both Eric and the guests would be embarrassed by an "Eric, don't you want to say hello to the Parks?" The instruction was given close enough to the time of the required action so that Eric would remember but far enough in advance so that neither he nor the guests would be embarrassed.

Role-Playing

Verbal instructions may not be sufficient in some situations. When a new skill is somewhat complicated, role-playing of the problem situation may be more effective and more fun. The adult and child can alternate in playing each part. They can pretend to be each other or the person who may be the source of a problem. Young children especially seem to enjoy this role-playing; however it adapts well to any age.

SAYING "NO" POLITELY BUT FIRMLY

Lois had been taught to be polite to her friends and acquaint-ances. At the age of twelve she was already well aware that she should at times acquiesce to the wishes of others. Unfortunately she seemed to have learned this too well. She was unable to complete her own plans whenever they conflicted with plans of her friends or acquaintances. Her difficulty was that she did not know how to decline without offending her friends. She talked the problem over with her mother:

"Whenever Nancy calls and wants to come over to our house to play, I never know what to say if I don't want her to come," complained Lois.

"Why can't you simply tell her that this is not a good time?"

"She'll just ask me what I'm doing, and if I say I'm working on my stamp collection or anything else, she'll just say that she'll come over and help me. And I never know what to say then, so I just say OK, and then I have to play with her even though I don't really feel like it."

"Well, that is a hard problem. I think everyone has trouble knowing just how to say 'no' to someone else's request. Why don't you pretend to be Nancy? And I'll pretend to be you. You call me up," suggested her mother.

Lois, having previously played this game, immediately pretended to dial a number on an imaginary telephone.

"Hello, Lois, this is Nancy," said Lois, throwing herself into the new role. "Can I come over to your house and play?"

"I'm afraid this isn't a very good time, Nancy."

"Why not?"

"I'm busy with some other things, so I don't have time to play now."

"What things are you busy with?"

"Oh, quite a few. Hey, Nancy, did you understand those new math problems we had in school this afternoon?"

"Not very well. They were awfully hard."

"I thought they were too. I certainly hope the teacher explains how to do them tomorrow. Thanks for calling, Nancy. I'll see you in school tomorrow. Good-bye."

Lois and her mother rehearsed a number of different variations depending upon alternative things that Nancy might say. Lois would play herself while her mother would be Nancy. Her mother stressed that it was not desirable to give in to others just because you were under pressure. She wanted to teach Lois how to withstand pressure without offending, without telling lies, and without having to reveal information she did not wish to reveal. She and Lois figured out ways to handle some problems that neither had known how to handle previously. They also discussed some solutions they did not like. When Lois did want to play with Nancy, they decided that she would call Nancy and invite her, rather than leave the impression that she would only play when Nancy was the instigator.

Whenever a new problem situation would arise, Lois and her mother would role-play some possible ways to handle it. Lois would try these techniques to find which ones seemed to work best for her. She became able to control what she would do with her spare time without succumbing to undue pressure from her friends.

THE CUE FOR THE CUE

At the beginning of a race the starter will say, "On your mark, get set, go." The word "go" is the cue for the runner to begin running.

The words "on your mark" and "get set" are anticipatory cues to prepare the runners for the signal to go. At times it is important for children to react promptly when a cue is given. Anticipatory cues serve to alert them that when the final cue is given, they must move quickly.

TERMINATING PLAY CHEERFULLY

Ricky was a good swimmer and enjoyed playing with the other children in the community pool. However, when his mother asked him to get out of the pool to go home, he protested the interruption of his play and delayed as long as possible getting out of the water.

The next time they drove to the swimming pool Ricky's mother said, "I know you never like to leave the swimming pool, but it is not much fun for either you or me when you complain and dawdle after it is time to leave. How would it be if I gave you a little advance notice about five minutes before it's time to go?" Ricky was willing to give it a try. Five minutes before it was time to get out, his mother said, "Ricky, you have five minutes left to play." He continued playing with his friends. When his mother said, "Let's go," Ricky jumped out of the pool and got into the car without protest.

Both he and his mother liked the new system. Eventually she did not need to speak the anticipatory cue but merely got his attention and held up five fingers. One tension spot in the family had been removed.

Many people appreciate anticipatory cues. Even some alarm clocks are built with an anticipatory cue called a "snooze alarm." A person can be awakened gently ten minutes before the final alarm signals him that he must arise. During those ten minutes his body can relax while his mind gradually prepares to accept the inevitable.

The success in Ricky's case was due not merely to the use of an anticipatory cue but to the fact that he and his mother discussed the problem and agreed together on a solution that they could try. Agreement upon the use of an anticipatory cue seemed to work for Ricky and his mother. When two people face a problem and agree that something ought to be done about it, they have taken the first step toward resolving many difficulties. In other situations more complicated solutions might well be necessary.

A SERIES OF CUES FOR MORE COMPLEX LEARNING

The more complicated the behavior that is to be learned, the more cues become necessary during the initial period.

LEARNING TO ENJOY DRAWING

Beth was a seventeen-year-old girl hospitalized with arthritis. The job of the nurse's aide was to teach Beth some enjoyable skill which would require her to begin moving her fingers and arms. The nurse's aide describes how she taught Beth to draw:

When I first asked Beth to draw a picture of a person, specifically the girl in the bed across from hers, Beth drew a vague round circle with two circles in the middle. She put down her pencil immediately and covered her picture, saying she wanted to throw it away and do something else. She had not even looked up to observe the other girl.

I had hoped that, despite her arthritic pain, Beth would be able to gain pleasure and satisfaction from drawing by becoming a more accurate observer of visual detail. It seemed I had expected too much when I asked that she draw a complete human figure.

I then suggested that she look carefully at just my face and draw what she saw. Again she drew a big circle with two circles inside for eyes. I asked Beth to look at my eyes carefully and to notice the corners. She erased her two small circles and began to draw shapes that appeared more like eyes, looking at mine frequently for a reference. I praised her for observing my face so carefully. I then pointed out the shape of my face, asking her to look at my chin, cheekbones, and forehead. Beth erased the circle outline and carefully drew a new one representing the shape of my head. With each new detail—eyebrows, eyelashes, hair, lips, nose—I commented on what she had accurately observed. For the first time she smiled as she viewed the picture she was drawing. I knew the main job had been accomplished when she showed her picture to the girl in the next bed.

In the following weeks I noticed that Beth continued to draw on her own. I took notice and gave encouragement. The activity did not cure her arthritis but did seem to provide an enjoyable activity during her confinement.

The nurse's aide was successful not only because she called a series of cues to Beth's attention but because she gave warmth and recognition to Beth for her progress. Beth saw for herself that she was learning to draw. She took pride in her own accomplishment and also had something to share with her visitors. Asking Beth to draw an entire human figure at first was simply too difficult for a person with Beth's handicaps and inexperience. By taking one step at a time, starting with the shape of the eyes, the aide presented a more manageable task and Beth responded to each new cue to produce a satisfying picture.

CUEING OVER LONG INTERVALS OF TIME

Over the years a child gradually accumulates information on complex topics. The accompanying attitudes may depend on the manner in which his questions are answered and discussed over a long period of time.

LEARNING ABOUT SEX

Carol's parents believed in giving frank answers to her questions about sex, and in so doing they presented her with basic terminology without being evasive.
Age 3: "Why don't I have a penis?"
"A little girl has a clitoris and vagina."
Age 4: "Where do babies come from?"
"Babies come from inside a mother's body."
Age 5: "How do babies get inside a mommy's body?"
"The daddy puts his penis in the mommy's vagina and plants a seed that starts the baby growing."
Once Carol had learned the initial vocabulary, her parents could easily refine their answers, amplifying on these terms and related topics.

The cues in sex education, as in education about any topic, are given simply in answer to each question. The answers are not made complicated. The adult can tell from further questions how well the child understands the answers. Some questions might need answering several times.

If the child does not ask particular questions about sex, the parent can introduce the subject. Just as Beth could not draw a reproduction of a human figure in its entirety the first time she tried, so a child cannot be expected to understand the entire process of human reproduction and its ramifications the first time it is explained. Each stage is built upon the last over a long period of time.

A sequence of cues provided by adults over the years is a useful supplement to the kind of information learned from playmates. Full knowledge of the facts is a child's best defense against misunderstandings, irrational fears, and unhealthy attitudes.

How to Cue

CUEING SHOULD BE AS PLEASANT AS POSSIBLE

Even under the best circumstances most people do not like to depend on others to give them cues. They want to be independent and will readily interpret someone else's deliberate cue as an effort to control. Adolescents in their strenuous efforts to achieve an independent identity are particularly sensitive to cues which they may perceive as a challenge to their own good judgment.

Cues should be used as seldom as possible. A child who knows what to do, knows when to do it, and has every intention of so doing will resent having someone give him an additional cue.

A child already upset about some other problem might be particularly sensitive about unnecessary cues. As in the case of Eric, a cue given in the presence of other people may be potentially embarrassing and should be avoided whenever it could be perceived as inappropriate. Considerable human sensitivity is necessary in deciding when and how to cue.

A Matter-of-Fact Approach

Adults can easily become aggravated when youngsters fail to remember their duties. It is all too easy to shout and become emotional when reminding youngsters what to do. Insofar as possible an adult should give verbal cues in a matter-of-fact tone of voice. A calm, objective tone keeps open the lines of communication between adult and child and facilitates future working relationships.

ACCEPTING RESPONSIBILITY FOR LOST POSSESSION

Amy was in the final stages of having her teeth straightened and was required to wear a dental retainer to hold her teeth in position. The process had been an expensive one for the family.

Since she had to remove her retainer whenever she ate, Amy had been instructed to put it away carefully so that it would not be lost or damaged during mealtimes.

One day the school secretary called Amy's father who worked nearby to report that during lunchtime Amy had placed her retainer in her lunch bag while eating, had forgotten where it was, and had thrown the lunch bag away. She asked Amy's father whether he would like to come down to the school and go through all the waste material in search of the retainer.

Amy's father replied, "No, thank you, I wouldn't, but I wonder if you would be willing to pass a message along to Amy?"

"Certainly," replied the secretary.

"Would you please tell Amy that it is her responsibility to find the retainer? Please ask her to search through every discarded lunch bag after school until she finds it."

The secretary passed the word to Amy who recruited several of her sixth-grade girl friends. They sorted through 200 discarded paper sacks, removing waxed paper, banana peels, and apple cores, but were unable to locate the missing retainer.

Amy was extremely disappointed as she reported her failure at home. "Honey, you searched that trash pile as well as anyone could. It's too bad you were not able to find your retainer. What should we do now?"

"I'm never going to put my retainer in my lunch bag again. I'll always put it in my pocket or purse."

"Good idea. But where are you going to get your next retainer?"

"I guess we'll have to ask the dentist to make another one."

"And who's going to pay for it?"

"I guess I should pay since I lost it."

Amy and her father then worked out an arrangement so that she would pay part of the cost of replacing the retainer, the last one the dentist ever had to replace for her.

It would have been easy for Amy's father to become angry at her losing the retainer. He had spent a great deal of money having her teeth straightened and was justifiably disturbed about further expense. However, he knew that Amy was already upset at having lost it. Further displays of anger would not help and would only confound the difficulty. Nevertheless he politely refused to participate in the search himself but made Amy solely responsible. When she was unsuccessful, he still did not become angry but kept the responsibility centered on his daughter. The cues which informed Amy of her responsibility were given matter-of-factly and even sympathetically, but Amy never forgot whose responsibility it was to take care of her possessions.

Cues That Minimize Potential Friction

Tactful wording is helpful. A parent or teacher is a model for his children. If he wants them to be polite and tactful, he may best teach them by his own example. The cues may be either direct or indirect.

EXAMPLES OF DIRECT CUES

1. A mother says to her child as he comes in from playing in the snow: "Let's pull those boots off on the back porch. Then we won't get the kitchen dirty."

2. A journalism teacher says to her class: "Since this is a news article, let's remember to write up the story just as objectively as possible even though we may feel it's a one-sided issue."

3. A second grade teacher says, "Lunch pail!" to a boy who is learning to tuck his lunch pail under his arm instead of swinging it around and injuring others.

4. A father suggests: "How about turning the television off if you are going out to play now, Ken?"

5. A student council advisor asks: "Is there any way we can get more facts before we reach a decision?"

EXAMPLES OF INDIRECT CUES

1. A father whispers to his son who looks as if he is about to talk during the family's favorite program: "Perry, you certainly are good for not interrupting while we're watching television."

2. A mother asks, "How about talking about the mother–daughter picnic as soon as you finish your homework?"

3. A teacher says to her students who tend to forget to put on their wraps at recess: "Let's look out the window to see whether it appears cold outside today."

4. For Christmas Betty receives "stocking stuffers" of gelatin capsules and "Hard-As-Nails" since she had expressed a desire to stop biting her fingernails.

5. A father asks, "Anybody want to use the bathroom before

we get in the car? It'll be at least two hours before we stop for gas."

6. A civics teacher says to his class: "Now you have the facts of the case. Pretend you are the jury. How would you argue?"

Indirect cues have advantages in that they not only are more tactful but are closer to not being a cue at all. Ideally an adult should be able to see what action is needed without anyone deliberately giving him a cue. Sensitive, self-sufficient people can detect when to respond from minimal cues. Gradually moving from direct to indirect cues is a first step toward helping a child develop this sensitivity to minimal cues.

CUES MUST BE CLEAR TO THE CHILD

A cue that is clear to an adult may not be clear to a child. Adults frequently forget that a child has a limited vocabulary. For example, a mother may tell her four-year-old son who is going to a birthday party, "Now, be polite." The mother knows what she means by "polite," but the son may not be sure what he is expected to do. A more specific "When you leave the party, remember to say thank you to Mrs. Cutler" may be far more understandable to a four-year-old child.

CUES MAY BE AUTOMATED

Frequently the task of giving cues to children is not particularly pleasant for an adult. Whenever possible the adult should structure the situation to administer the cues "automatically." Matt's mother (p. 66) arranged an automatic cue by placing a squeaky rubber duck under the doormat. Other ways of arranging automatic reminders are evident in the following examples.

REMEMBERING TO FEED PETS

Eleven-year-old Alan was unreliable in taking care of his turtle and his dog. He was responsible for keeping them fed and clean. His parents' reminders that it was "time to take care of the animals" every morning and evening caused mutual aggravation.

His parents devised a reversible cardboard sign. On one side

SHORT RIBS   By FRANK O'NEAL

Cues must be clear to the learner.

the sign said, "Alan, we're hungry. Woofer and Humpback." The other side read, "Now we're full. Thanks. Woofer and Humpback." The sign was hung by a string at Alan's eye level by the back door. When he completed his care of the animals, he turned the sign over himself.

The sign was objective; it never irritated Alan, and his mother was able to stop nagging.

REMEMBERING HOMEWORK ASSIGNMENTS

Dina was constantly forgetting or losing her homework assignments. The teacher aide reports what was done about the problem:

I asked Dina if she would like to be able to remember her homework assignments better. She said she wanted to remember but always forgot. I thought if she had something valuable to put the homework assignments in she would not lose them. So I made her a folder with her name on it in big letters. She helped decorate the outside of the folder. We agreed that she would put her homework assignments in this special folder so she wouldn't lose them.

The next day she completed her homework for the first time in weeks. Perhaps I was congratulating myself as I praised her for remembering. It has been three weeks now and so far she has not once forgotten those assignments.

WATERING THE LAWN

John's yard had a sprinkler system, and his responsibility was to turn on four different spigots, one at a time, for ten- or fifteen-minute intervals several times a week. However, he often left the water on too long, flooding the grass, because he would forget when it was time to turn one spigot off and turn the next one on.

Then he came upon a solution. He began planning his job of watering during the evening when he watched television. Each time a commercial appeared it was his cue to run outside to change the sprinkler. He would finish the watering about the time an hour program ended without having missed anything except the commercials.

CUEING MAY BE COMBINED WITH OTHER LEARNING PRINCIPLES

Cueing and Reinforcement

When a child performs the desired act after being cued, reinforcement should certainly follow whenever possible. The following example is an intriguing method of combining "automated cues" with a cooperative type of reinforcement for the entire family.

COOPERATING ON FAMILY CHORES

The four children in the Morse family each had a number of home responsibilities. Their mother and father both worked full time, and the children were expected to carry their fair share of the chores at home. Each child had some duties he was expected to perform daily and weekly.

Reminding the children to do their chores every day was an additional burden that neither Mr. Morse nor his wife wished to assume.

Mrs. Morse constructed a chart which she posted in a conspicuous place in the front hall. Each child's name and his duties were listed across the top of the chart. Down the side of the chart were listed the thirty days of the month. Each child was expected to put a check mark on the chart under his name for every chore he performed that day. For jobs that were to be performed only once a week Mrs. Morse blackened out the squares for the days the job need not be performed. At the end of each day she could quickly scan across the chart to see whether every square had been marked.

As an additional incentive the family agreed that whenever all the children compiled a perfect record seven days in a row, the entire family would be entitled to go out for dinner at one of their favorite restaurants. The incentive encouraged the children to work together and remind one another of their duties. No single person had to provide the daily cues. The entire family cooperated so they might enjoy a restaurant dinner together.

Cueing and Modeling

Cueing given by a prestigeful person outside the family may sometimes help more than reminders from a mother or father. In this illustration the prestigeful person provided a cue that then became a built-in reminder.

OVERCOMING THUMBSUCKING

Claude's parents were concerned because at age eight he was still sucking his thumb. Their orthodontist told them that the boy's dental problems would be increased if he did not stop. Claude claimed he wanted to stop the habit but couldn't.

Dr. Brant, the orthodontist, taught Claude how to break a popsicle stick in half without splintering it. Then Claude practiced taping it to his thumb with one hand. In this way whenever he started to put his thumb in his mouth, the stick would remind him that he wanted to stop. Next, Dr. Brant recommended to his parents that they help him make a chart for the hours of each day. Claude was to plot each day for a week how long he could go without thumb sucking. Dr. Brant advised the parents to be sure to let the boy know they were interested in how he was doing and to praise all efforts. After the first week Claude decided he didn't need the popsicle stick; nevertheless his parents extended the chart so that he could continue to map his progress. After thirty days he felt he had broken the habit and no longer needed the system at all.

Dr. Brant's popsicle stick served as an automatic cue and relieved Claude's parents of constantly having to remind him themselves. The chart was an additional cue. The fact that a prestigeful person outside his family instigated the system gave Claude confidence that he would succeed.

CUES SHOULD GRADUALLY BE DIMINISHED

As the child learns a new pattern of behavior, the cues given to him should gradually be diminished. The child should learn to cue himself. Each stage of a task provides its own cue for the next stage. A mature and sensitive adult should have few occasions when he would need deliberate cues from others. An elementary example of how cues are gradually diminished is provided in this account by a kindergarten teacher.

REMEMBERING TO WASH HANDS

Pogo could not seem to remember to wash his hands after going to the bathroom. The kindergarten children in our school have their own lavatory facilities adjacent to the room. The teacher is expected to teach the youngsters the cleanliness habit of washing their hands after using the bathroom.

At the beginning of the school year I discussed with all the children why we wash our hands. Pogo was always so eager to return to his activities that he could never seem to remember. When he rushed into the lavatory, I would remind him, "Pogo, do you remember what you are to do when you come out?" His answer was, "Yup, wash my hands." As I continued cueing him, my words became fewer. I would say, "Pogo, don't forget," and then, "Pogo?" After only a few weeks he usually remembered to wash his hands without further cues from me.

Cueing should proceed so that the learner gradually becomes independent of the cues from others. Cues should diminish both in number and in intensity while at the same time the learner develops the skill of administering cues to himself.

The adult who writes down his appointments in a datebook has developed a self-cueing system. The housewife who makes out a shopping list before going to the grocery store has a self-administered cueing system. The airline pilot who goes through every item in a checklist before taking off self-administers cues which insure his safety and that of his passengers.

5

A Time
and a Place
for
Which
Things

TATTLING ONLY WHEN NECESSARY

Buffy had developed the habit of tattling to her mother every time the neighborhood children had a dispute. Here is her mother's story:

As a result of Buffy's constant tattling I had become the local arbitrator of all children's problems. (I realize now that I probably brought this behavior on myself. When Buffy's older brother teased her, she tattled and I usually intervened in her behalf.) The neighborhood children were beginning to call Buffy a "tattletale." I didn't want her to come to me about every little dispute. Yet I did not want to tell her *never* to tattle because there were times when I thought I should know what was going on. My first problem was to decide when I wanted her to tattle and when I didn't want her to tattle. Then we had a talk.

I explained to Buffy that when someone got hurt or when someone might get hurt or when something valuable might get broken and she could not prevent it herself, I wanted her to come and tell me. However she should learn to settle her other disputes by herself as best she could. I told her that I would be glad to talk the problem over with her later, but that I would not intervene at the time.

To make sure she understood I asked her about several hypothetical situations:

"Would you come tell me if you and Patty couldn't agree on a game to play?"

"No."

"Would you come tell me if another child called you a bad name?"

"No."

"Would you come tell me if another child was throwing a knife?"

"Yes."

Things didn't always go perfectly because both of us found it difficult to stick to what we had agreed. But the situation improved as I realized what I was trying to teach Buffy. When she came running in tearfully because another girl wouldn't take turns "being mother," I told her she would have to settle it herself. However later that evening we talked about what she might have done. On another occasion the boys across the alley were throwing mud-covered rocks at a group of girls, and this time I stepped in immediately, telling Buffy I was glad she remembered to tell me when someone might get hurt.

Buffy is gradually learning when to tattle and when not to tattle. Recently I overheard her say in a group of her playmates who were strenuously arguing, "It won't help to tell Mommy. She'll just say we'll have to settle it ourselves."

In most of the problems of life no one is around to give us a cue as to what an appropriate response might be. Buffy's mother could not be present at all times to cue her—"Now is the time to tattle" or "Now is not the time to tattle." Buffy had to learn to decide for herself whether the circumstances warranted a report to her mother. Her mother first had to decide what she wanted Buffy to learn: She wanted Buffy to tattle only when someone was hurt, when someone might get hurt, or when something valuable might get broken. Other parents might have had different conditions under which they would want their children to tattle. Buffy's mother explained to her when to tattle and then tested her to see if she had the idea.

But the hard part for the mother was sticking to the agreement herself. Actions, not words, teach a child when an adult is serious. Her mother had to refrain from intervening whenever the conditions were not met. She had to intervene quickly when the conditions were met. In this way Buffy learned that it was a waste of time to tattle when nothing would come of it but that she would receive fast support in more serious situations.

A child may sometimes attempt to control his playmates by threatening to tattle when he doesn't get his own way. Other children, however, are usually quick to expose the bluff as long as a parent seldom intervenes.

There are circumstances under which a wide variety of behaviors are appropriate. The problem is in teaching a child to distinguish the cues which indicate the appropriate circumstances. Buffy's experience leads us to the **Discrimination Principle: To teach a child to act in a particular way under one set of circumstances but not another, help him to identify the cues that differentiate the circumstances and reward him only when his action is appropriate to the cue.**

Many situations involve discriminating between closely related sets of circumstances:

- Dinner time gives Wally the forum he enjoys to talk about his insect hobby, much to the discomfort of his mother, who feels he should choose another time when people are not eating.
- Three-year-old Kelly, having just received her first crayons, uses them to color her coloring book and the walls and the floor of her room.
- Bill faces the prospect of seeing his good friend blackballed

when he knows that by breaking a fraternity rule he could probably make it possible for his friend to join.

- Andy feels he must fight with anyone who teases him.
- Harriet is brutally honest with her friends about everything and apparently unconcerned about how much she occasionally hurts their feelings as a result.

What Are Some Identifying Cues?

Four kinds of cues signal appropriate behavior: time, place, person, and anticipated consequences.

TIME

The notion that a behavior might be appropriate at one time but not at another is certainly not a new idea. The Old Testament is eloquent on this point:

> To everything there is a season, and a time to every
> purpose under the heaven;
> A time to be born, and a time to die; a time to plant,
> and a time to pluck up that which is planted;
> A time to kill, and a time to heal; a time to break
> down, and a time to build up;
> A time to weep, and a time to laugh; a time to mourn,
> and a time to dance.

Ecclesiastes 3:1–4

Few people would dispute that an appropriate time can be found for almost any kind of behavior. The difficulty comes in specifying which time is appropriate for what behavior; and even more difficult: Is *now* the right time? It is not sufficient to teach a child the generality that sometimes a behavior is appropriate and other times it is not. He needs help in distinguishing which time is which.

CHOOSING AGREEABLE CONVERSATION TOPICS FOR MEALS

Wally at age thirteen was fascinated by spiders and beetles. He was an intelligent boy and spent much time studying and learning about insects. Because of his strong interest in insects he wanted to talk about them much of the time—including dinner time. His parents had no wish to discourage his interest, but some family members found his detailed discussion of bugs at dinner time to be unappetizing. His father reported the sequence of events:

I explained to Wally as gently as I could that, although we were glad he was interested in insects, his mother and I found that the discussion of them over the dinner table spoiled our appetite. Wally found this difficult to understand and insisted that there was nothing unappetizing about bugs. While I had to agree there was no necessary connection, nevertheless, to his mother and me, his mother especially, dinner and bugs simply did not go together.

I am afraid our talk did not have much effect on his behavior. The next night he launched into a detailed analysis of the anatomy of a beetle. However this time we were prepared. No one asked any questions or acted at all interested. Whenever Wally stopped to catch his breath, someone simply started to discuss another topic. This action might have hurt Wally's feelings a bit.

But then immediately after dinner I took Wally into the living room and asked him, "Now what was this you were telling me you found out about beetles?" He had learned a surprising amount, and I found myself fascinated by the elaborate structure of a beetle body.

A somewhat similar sequence of events happened the second night. On the third night he did not mention anything about insects during dinner time. But again after dinner I asked him, "What's new in the bug world?"

On the fourth night he again said nothing about insects at dinner time. I felt he had learned the appropriate time to discuss bugs and so did not bother to ask him any questions after dinner. But he came up to me and said, "Aren't you going to ask me any questions about insects? It's after dinner, isn't it?"

Wally's father helped him identify the appropriate time to talk about bugs. He reinforced Wally with attention and interest after dinner time but not during dinner time. Youngsters learn to identify many cues associated with time. Here are a few additional examples.

EXAMPLES OF TIME CUES

1. When the 8:30 tardy bell rings, it is the cue for Mr. Burgoyne's government students to find their seats in the classroom and get ready for work.

2. When four-year-old Jamie is told it is a "daddy day" (Saturday or Sunday), it is his cue that his father might play with him at home. On other days Jamie has learned his father will not be around until supper time.

3. Craig knows the key day when he may apply for his first driver's license is his sixteenth birthday.

4. Mrs. Scott looks forward to the time each morning when the children go off to school, for she knows then she can leisurely have her second cup of coffee.

5. The first grader learns to cross the street when the light is green but to wait when it is red.

6. Charlie learns not to ask for help on art work during his math lesson.

PLACE

The advice "When in Rome, do as the Romans do" acknowledges that a location is also an important cue. Behavior appropriate to some places is often inappropriate elsewhere. But children need help in learning exactly which places are appropriate for what behavior.

COLORING ON PAPER, NOT WALLS

Three-year-old Kelly used her crayons not only for coloring pictures in her coloring book but for scribbling on the walls and floor. Her mother reported how she taught her to distinguish the appropriate place for coloring:

I found a discarded doll and took a crayon and scribbled all over it in front of Kelly. I showed Kelly that the marks had disfigured the doll's face and body. In simple language I told her that marking on the walls and floors destroyed them for us just as marking on the doll ruined it for her. I then gave her a coloring book and a pad of blank paper and told her to use her crayons only on them. I asked her to color a picture for me. When she finished, I told her it was a fine picture, so good in fact that we ought to put it up on the wall. "See, we color on the paper and then put the paper on the wall."

Kelly seemed pleased with her aesthetic contribution to our home. She produced many more artistic creations, and I selected with her help the ones she wanted to put up on the wall.

Kelly's mother did not punish her, much as she may have been aggravated by the disfiguring marks on the wall and floor. Kelly was not engaging in malicious mischief. She simply had not learned the appropriate place to use her crayons. Her mother's rather dramatic disfiguring of an old doll was probably not essential, but in any event she got across the idea that paper, not a wall, was the appropriate surface for crayons. Equally important, she taught Kelly this discrimination without inhibiting Kelly's artistic creativity. On the contrary she encouraged Kelly's creative expression by giving recognition to her productions.

Many other behaviors are appropriate in one place but not in another.

EXAMPLES OF PLACE CUES

1. When she goes to the beach, Judy wears a bathing suit or play clothes rather than her school dress.

2. Marv has found that although his parents make certain he is in bed by nine o'clock at home, he can stay up until ten at his grandparents' house.

3. Betsy has been taught to squeeze the juice out of a grapefruit at home but not to do it when she eats out.

4. One of the cues Rosie has learned for spelling is that in e–i combinations i usually comes before e except after c.

5. Whereas nineteen-year-old Pepe in Mexico would freely embrace a boy friend whom he has not seen recently, he has learned that in the United States he is less conspicuous showing his affection by warmly shaking hands instead.

6. Penny has learned she may eat cookies in the playroom but not in the living room on the new gold carpet.

PERSON

Our associates provide cues as to what is appropriate. In any group of people their sex, their past experiences, and even the number of people present influence what might be appropriate to say or do.

LEARNING WHEN TO SPEAK LOUDER

Marie had a soft, quiet voice which could seldom be heard when she was speaking to her thirty second grade classmates. Her voice was adequate for small groups and committees, but she did not seem to realize that in larger groups she could not be heard. The teacher told of taking the following steps to help Marie:

At first I thought there might be something physically wrong with Marie's voice. But when I observed her on the playground, it was obvious that she could shout as loudly as any child when she was excited. The school nurse checked her hearing and found it normal. I asked Marie if she could talk louder. She could when asked but quickly slipped back into her whispering tone.

I asked her if she would be willing to let members of the class help her speak louder. She agreed. I told the class that whenever they could not hear Marie speak when she was before the class, they were to cup both hands behind their ears. When they could just barely hear, they were to cup one hand. The cues helped Marie remember to speak louder. She was reinforced for her improvements during our critique session by remarks from other class members who praised her report.

After a few weeks it was no longer necessary for the children to give the cupped-ear cue. She had learned to project her voice when she spoke to the whole class but continued her soft voice in a small group.

Many situations exist in which the particular people present influence behavior.

EXAMPLES OF PERSON CUES

1. Sibyl and Madge have long been best friends in junior high school. When they are alone together, they tell each other things they wouldn't consider saying to anyone else.

2. By age six Milly has learned to ask for presents from the Santa Claus in the department store but not from her parents' friends.

3. Fred finds he can speak out almost any time in Mr. Wright's class but will be in trouble with Miss Lewis if he does the same thing in her room.

4. Hank has learned not to criticize people in public even though he expresses his feelings fully within his own family.

5. Howard tips a waitress but not a filling station attendant.

6. Viv has freely discussed smoking pot with certain friends but says absolutely nothing about it to her parents.

ANTICIPATED CONSEQUENCES

The cues of time, place, and person are merely signals that the consequences of an action will vary. But a single identifying cue does not easily resolve many real-life dilemmas. Sometimes a combination of persons, places, and times is necessary. Sometimes a particular combination of circumstances or some anticipated consequences make an action desirable that would be undesirable under other circumstances.

OBEYING OR DISOBEYING THE RULES

Karl was an ordinary college sophomore who was eager to join the ABC fraternity. Bill, a senior in college and one of the leaders of ABC, gave this report:

Karl went through rush during his freshman year, but quite a few of the fellows thought he wasn't good enough and voted him down. During the year, however, he became good friends with several in the fraternity who encouraged him to go through rush again. Karl was eager to get into any fraternity but definitely preferred ABC.

The procedure for matching students and fraternities was something like this. At midnight after the last rush party on Friday night each fraternity met and prepared a list of the rushees they were willing to have in the fraternity. Independently each rushee was to list in the order of his preference the fraternities he was willing to join. A fraternity could reject any rushee who listed it as a second, third, or fourth choice, however, even if that rushee were otherwise acceptable. This policy was rationalized, "If he doesn't have enough sense to know that we're the best, then we don't want him."

One ironclad rule was that no member of any fraternity could communicate with any rushee about anything between midnight and noon after the last rush party. The policy was designed to ensure independent judgments, to prevent unfair rush practices, and to prevent rushees from learning the results of the voting. The choices of the fraternities and all rushees had to be turned in to the office of the Interfraternity Council between 9:00 and 10:00 A.M. Saturday morning.

At midnight Friday our fraternity members met as scheduled and found general agreement on most names. When Karl's name came up, however, I was surprised by the amount of discussion. Although some of the brothers really liked him, a few still objected to the idea of his membership and two members blackballed him. Since unanimous agreement was required, Karl was denied admission for the second time.

I was troubled. I knew that Karl had been greatly upset the first time he was turned down. I knew he was going to list ABC as his first choice and XYZ fraternity as his second choice. XYZ had the same policy as ours, denying admission to anyone who listed them as second choice. I knew the rules. It was absolutely forbidden to communicate with any rushee, let alone tell him the result of the fraternity's vote.

But what were the consequences of that rule for Karl? I remembered a discussion in our philosophy class. The professor considered it important to act lawfully and to work for changes in the law when any regulation appeared unjust. He said ultimately any law must be judged by its consequences. I slept fitfully that night. Should I call Karl and tell him, breaking my pledge to the fraternity? Were the consequences of obeying the law more desirable than the consequences of disobeying it?

At 7:00 A.M. Saturday I arrived at my answer. I called Karl and, without mentioning names, explained what had happened. I extended him my personal best wishes, went back to bed, and slept a dreamless sleep. Karl became a member of XYZ fraternity. I never regretted breaking that rule.

An orderly society depends upon its members obeying its rules. Yet occasionally special circumstances arise in which members of that society must consider whether a particular rule fits a particular situation. In this instance Bill evaluated the rule barring communication with rushees by considering the consequences of obeying or disobeying this rule. There was not time to legislate a change in the rule itself. If Karl were to be saved from a cruel rejection for a second time, Bill had to break the rule and break it quickly. He elected to do so. Others might well have elected another course. Bill's philosophy professor probably had no idea that his discussion on obedience would have the effect it did. His statement that any law must be justified by its consequences caused Bill to stop and think. Bill took action which in his judgment produced far happier consequences than following the rule would have produced.

But did Bill consider *all* the possible consequences? Would he have been willing to accept penalties from his fraternity if others had discovered his action? What might have happened if Karl told members of XYZ about Bill's action? What precedent was Bill setting by violating the regulation? Would a more responsible course of action have been to revise the entire system in which blackballing potential members was possible?

Responsible adults should not teach children always to obey blindly. The millions of "good Germans" who merely followed Hitler's orders produced a record of cruelty, barbarism, and inhumanity without equal in history. Children need to learn to evaluate laws and engage in orderly processes to change laws when change is needed. In rare instances they may need to break regulations and accept the consequences.

To teach children to evaluate rules, adults must permit their own rules to be discussed openly with the exceptions to these rules considered. The benefits of rule obedience must be shown to outweigh the benefits of rule disobedience. If they don't, maybe the rule *should* be changed.

How Do You Help a Child Distinguish the Cues?

BY DESCRIBING EXAMPLES

When a child is old enough to understand, simple verbal descriptions of concrete identifying cues are often helpful.

LEARNING WHEN TO CALL FOR HELP

Five-year-old Sharon was immobilized in bed following an operation. She was lonesome upstairs in her room. She would call her mother almost every five minutes for some attention. Usually she did not want anything in particular, just someone to be with her and talk with her. Her mother had a number of other household duties since Sharon had four brothers and sisters. It was often inconvenient and sometimes even impossible for her mother to run and answer Sharon everytime she called. Providing her with books, toys, a radio, and even a television set did not prove to be sufficient. Her mother wanted to give Sharon the attention she needed but did not want to be called so often. The problem was to help Sharon distinguish between circumstances in which she needed to call her mother and circumstances in which she did not.

Her mother found a large piece of cardboard. On one side she labeled "BIG THINGS" in large red letters. On the other side she labeled "little things" in blue letters. Picture diagrams illustrated the difference between big and little problems. Red and blue pencils were attached on a string to the chart. Sharon's mother explained to Sharon that sometimes she was busy and couldn't come every time Sharon called. "So let's try this. Before you call me next time, you decide whether it is about a big thing or a little thing. Big things include when something hurts, when you're thirsty, or when you need the bedpan. Little things include asking me to look at your book, asking me to pick up a toy you dropped, telling me something funny. If it's a big thing, put a red check on this side of the chart where the drinking glass is pictured. If it's a little thing, put a blue check on this side of the chart with the doll picture. I want you to call me only about big things."

Her mother realized that Sharon's need for love and attention was also a "big thing" and made a point of talking with Sharon or reading her a story at times when she had not called. She thanked Sharon for not calling her for "little things."

Sharon was pleased with her chart. She called her mother much less often about trivia.

Sharon's mother did not merely say, "Call me only when it is important. Don't call me when it is not important." Sharon did not know the difference. To Sharon, a toy on the floor was probably just as important as a drink of water. She needed help in distinguishing the specific situations that would justify a call to her mother. The chart was a method of dramatizing the two sets of circumstances. If Sharon had been a little older, the situations illustrating "big things" and "little things" could have been listed on the chart itself. Since she couldn't read, they had to be pictured and described for her. By asking Sharon to make a checkmark on the chart before she called, her mother required her to think of the distinction between "big things" and "little things" before calling.

Sharon's mother not only helped her to distinguish the circumstances but also reinforced her for not calling: Her mother gave her some additional time when she had not called for it. In this way Sharon learned that sometimes she would get attention even when she had not requested it. Then when she really needed her mother, she could count on prompt attention.

BY MODELING

Members of a family provide models for one another. Fathers are often models for their sons, mothers for daughters, and older children for younger children. Younger children can observe the cues that a model uses to distinguish appropriate action, particularly if the model points out what the cues are.

FIGHTING IF OR WHEN

Andy was the youngest in a family of four boys. At age seven he would box and wrestle with his older brothers, also taking turns with them to hit the punching bag in the garage. But he had not yet learned when it was appropriate to fight with people outside the family. His brother describes the situation:

As the youngest, Andy took the most guff, but he took it well. One day, however, he came home from school with skinned knuckles. I asked him what happened. Andy said that a boy had teased him, so he had beaten up the boy. Actually, we found out later that the other boy was just joking, had no intention of insulting Andy, in fact didn't even know that Andy was getting angry at his taunts.

Our dad was pretty upset because he thought Andy may have been a poor sport. In Andy's presence we older boys talked over how such a situation might have been handled and agreed on several things: We should never hit a person because of words. If someone else starts pushing us around, we should give him fair warning before hitting back. Dad concurred.

Andy got the idea. I remember he came home one time after that situation and told us how he had "told a guy I was warning him for the last time to lay off or he'd really get it—and he layed off!"

The problem of when to fight and when not to fight is frequently a difficult one to resolve. Most parents do not want their children to be aggressors. Yet at the same time they want them to be able to defend themselves against unwarranted aggression. In Andy's family the older brothers and father provided models of a middle ground between the "hawk" and "dove" positions. Other families might have different standards as to what might justify a fight. In any event the model provided by the parents and older children influences the cues that a younger child will use.

BY REINFORCING ACTIONS CONSISTENT WITH THE CUES

When a child does act appropriately in a situation, some prompt reinforcement helps him to learn and remember the appropriate cues. Sometimes additional practice and reinforcement can be provided through role-playing.

At age fourteen Harriet was still quite a tomboy, preferring to play baseball with her two brothers and their friends than participate in girls' activities. She was brutally frank in her talk with other girls to the point that she either intimidated them or made them hostile. Her camp counselor recalled some significant events:

Harriet, or Hat as we called her, reminded me of the way I had been at her age—honest to the nth degree, let the chips fall where they may. A few instances may serve to illustrate.

"Hat, would you like more of these cookies that my mother sent?"

"No, I don't like the way they taste."

"Hat, how come I didn't get into the advanced swimming class?"

"You aren't well coordinated."

Some people may think that the whole truth should be spoken always but there are times when part of the truth might best go unspoken. One day Harriet and I were alone together and we got on the subject of being honest. It was a long bull session, but the essential points I made were these:

1. Before giving a frank opinion, consider whether it might hurt someone's feelings.
2. If it would hurt someone's feelings, something important needs to be at stake to justify the frank expression.
3. There may be times when it is better to say nothing at all or to give a noncommittal answer.
4. There may be times when a frank opinion makes an issue out of something that is unimportant.

We discussed situations that we both agreed warranted complete and open honesty—so important that failure to tell the whole truth is really unfair. I said, for example, that it's unfair to let a boy think you love him if you really don't. We made a distinction between telling lies, even white lies, and the withholding of an opinion. We agreed that it is unwise to tell even white lies, but we would not actually consider it dishonest to withhold an opinion.

For about a week I had no idea whether our discussion had meant anything to Hat. Then one evening I overheard a camper who had just put on a rather poorly prepared skit ask Harriet how she had liked it. "I stayed awake all the way through," Hat replied. Then she and I exchanged a shared-secret glance.

Not everyone will agree with the behavior Harriet learned. Some people believe that children should be taught to tell little white lies under certain circumstances. Other people believe children should be taught to be completely honest at all times regardless of the consequences. Some people may openly advocate one course of action while actually behaving in the opposite.

The camp counselor used principles of modeling, cueing, and reinforcement in helping Harriet modify some of her frank responses. The older girl was a model for Harriet; her description of her own responses suggested possible behavior that Harriet could try in similar situations. They might also have taken the additional step of role-playing various situations to explore the pros and cons of different responses. The only reinforcement that Harriet needed was a significant glance. In the counselor's judgment Harriet had correctly identified a situation that did not call for another brutal truth.

Reasons for Learning "Poor" Discriminations

In the same way that they learn cues for appropriate actions, children also identify times when "poor" behavior seems to pay off. Regardless of an adult's intentions, children will learn to distinguish cues for appropriate or inappropriate actions. The basic principles apply equally to the learning of either desired or undesired behavior.

Why do children learn undesirable behavior in some situations in spite of their parents' and teachers' best intentions? There are several reasons.

IGNORANCE OF THE LEARNING PROCESS

NEEDING PARENTS NEARBY TO FALL ASLEEP

At two months of age Lisa would go to sleep only when her parents held her. If they put her in the crib, she would cry until either her mother or her father came to pick her up. Then she would go to sleep. Lisa had learned this discrimination naturally. At first she would go to sleep after nursing as she was being held in her mother's arms. Her parents never allowed her to go to sleep in any other situation. Extended crying always brought them to her.

Anxious to be good parents and not wanting her to feel rejected, Lisa's mother and father spent hours every night getting her to sleep. They could put her in the crib only after she had gone fast asleep in their arms. If she awoke during the middle of the night, the entire process had to be repeated. They were getting progressively more tired, irritable, and fearful about the future.

Lisa's parents did not realize that they were cueing her to sleep in the wrong place by letting her fall asleep in their arms. Unwittingly they consistently provided the wrong cue.

Parents who want to avoid such a dilemma may take some precautions. When it is nap time and their new infant shows signs of being sleepy, they should not allow him to go to sleep in their arms because they would be cueing him to do so in the future. Instead they should take him to his crib and put him in it, thereby helping him to learn to associate sleepiness with his crib. If the child cries for a period of time even though his parents have fulfilled his bodily needs, they should let him cry himself to sleep. Since the child always goes to sleep in his crib and never in their arms, the parents are free of unreasonable demands such as those Lisa was unknowingly making on her parents. No child will feel rejected simply because he is not held when he goes to sleep.

INCONSISTENT REINFORCEMENT PRACTICES

GAINING EXTRA PRIVILEGES IN FRONT OF COMPANY

Michele has learned to ask for cookies when her mother is entertaining company. Her mother is afraid that the company will think her a poor mother if Michele fusses and cries. As a result the girl has learned that when company is present she can get away with many things that she can't get away with when no guests are in the house. Taking full advantage of this knowledge Michele demands not only cookies but many other privileges whenever guests are present. Her mother gives in to her requests at the time even though she scolds her afterward for "asking for things that you know you shouldn't have." The scoldings after-the-fact make no impression. Michele gets what she wants when she wants it, and the scoldings afterward are a small price to pay.

Michele's mother certainly did not intend to teach her to make demands in the presence of company but not in their absence. Nevertheless by her actions she did teach Michele this discrimination. She reinforced Michele by granting requests only when company was present.

A parent not wishing to teach a child this discrimination would enforce the same rules in the presence of company as are enforced otherwise. Michele's mother was caught in a vicious circle: Afraid that her guests might think she could not cope with her own daughter, she temporarily prevented fussing and crying by giving in to the child, thereby reinforcing her. This reinforcement led to more demands which caused the guests to conclude that Michele was a spoiled child. The solution to the problem is in not yielding to fussing, whining, crying, or pouting even in the presence of company. If poor behavior is reinforced under certain circumstances but not others, the child will quickly learn under which circumstances he can get away with his inappropriate behavior. Guests might even respect a parent more for resisting a child's pressure than for keeping the child quiet.

VALUE CONFLICTS—REAL OR IMAGINED

Sometimes an adult is uncertain about what the most desirable behavior ought to be. As a result he may sometimes reinforce one behavior and at other times reinforce something quite different. A child may take understandable advantage of this uncertainty.

CHOOSING BETWEEN CLEANLINESS AND CREATIVITY

Jeanine would reluctantly, slowly, and haphazardly clean her room but only with a great deal of prodding and nagging from her mother. Following is the mother's account:

When I told Jeanine to clean up her room (the repository of the neighborhood's junk and refuse), she would pretend to work at it for a few moments, then noises from her room would subside, and I would forget about her. Later she would come out smiling with some ingeniously constructed junk sculpture, some witty little poem or drawing. I would simply have to admire and exclaim over her creative production.

Too late I would realize that she had been spending room-cleaning time this way. It seemed narrow-minded for me to complain that she hadn't gotten her room cleaned; after all she had produced a new marvel in the world! Now room-cleaning time is so thoroughly connected in her thoughts with creativity time that she is horrified at me when I crack down and say, "All right, that's nice, but it is not what you are supposed to be doing, and I don't want you to make anything else until you have a clean room to make it in."

She never really succeeds in getting very far in her room cleaning because she always thinks of something impressively creative to do instead. I end up cleaning the room myself while puzzling over the quandary of whether to squelch a free artistic spirit or let a member of the household get away with murder.

Jeanine was indeed creative. She had developed a creative method of avoiding her household responsibility by producing art work instead. Her mother, valuing artistic creativity more than routine middle-class cleanliness, reinforced her daughter in two ways: She praised Jeanine's artistic productions created during the time when she was supposed to be cleaning her room. She eventually cleaned Jeanine's room herself thus relieving her daughter of the responsibility entirely.

Creativity and conformity are not antithetical. A person can be both creative and clean. There is no reason to assume that creative powers belong only to those who are dirty and disorderly. Jeanine's mother was laboring under the mistaken notion that if she insisted her daughter conform by maintaining a clean and orderly room, she would inhibit her creative spirit. Jeanine took full advantage of this misconception and used clean-up time for her creative artistry.

Jeanine's mother could have reinforced both creativity and cleanliness. She could have reinforced her daughter for efforts to beautify her room in original ways, one of which might be cleaning it. An attractive room is a creative production in itself. In addition, she could have insisted on a distinction between work time and art time. During work time she would reinforce Jeanine only for activities resulting in a cleaner and more attractive room. During art time she would reinforce Jeanine for her creative productions. Thus Jeanine would develop both her creative spirit and her sense of responsibility.

AUDIENCES WITH DIFFERENT VIEWS

Sometimes a person is reinforced by one group of people but not by another. The person therefore learns two different patterns of behavior. A boss may tell jokes to his employees but not at his country club because only his employees laugh at his stories. Sometimes children learn to tell whopping lies because of the reinforcement they get from particular people.

LYING FOR ATTENTION

Eight-year-old Bobby was developing a reputation for telling enormous lies. He would visit other families in the neighborhood and regale them with imaginary incidents which seemed to build his prestige.

"I have a horse all of my own."

"How exciting! Where did you get it?"

"I have a rich uncle in Wyoming who is sending it to me. It's a championship race horse and has won many races."

"Wonderful, you're lucky to have such a fine horse."

A discreet inquiry to his parents revealed a different picture. Not only was Bobby not about to receive a championship race horse, no horse of any type had ever been discussed and he did not have an uncle of any description in Wyoming.

Bobby never discovered, however, that his enormous stories revealed him as a liar. So far as he knew, he received a great deal of attention and admiration from the neighbors in response to the stories he told them. The more fantastic the story, the more attention he seemed to receive. As he grew older, Bobby developed increasing skill at telling whoppers that were difficult to check for accuracy. He only told these stories to people who he thought would not check on his veracity.

It is difficult to teach a child to tell the truth if he is reinforced for telling lies and receives little or no attention when he tells the truth. Parents must be willing to listen attentively to their child as he describes accurately the events of the day. They must not allow him to exaggerate or tell stories contrary to the facts. The problem may be difficult to control because the parent does not always know what the actual facts are. Others who encourage storytelling provide an additional complication.

A child starved for attention will use extreme measures to obtain it.

A child who admits a transgression should be praised for his honesty if his parents want him to continue telling them the truth. Children learn quickly to whom they can speak the truth and to whom they must lie. The benefits of morality must outweigh the benefits of immorality if we wish children to choose a more moral life.

Maintaining
New
Behavior

6

New
and Better
Rewards

MAKING PROMPTNESS WORTHWHILE

In spite of threats and punishments, Mike was often tardy to his eighth grade classes. He averaged between five and ten tardies per week. Here is his teacher's report of the circumstances that altered Mike's behavior:

Our first attempt to help Mike get to class on time involved a new idea in our school, the Positive Progress Report. Instead of reporting to parents the bad things their children did, we began emphasizing the positive aspects. We would send home Positive Progress Reports whenever a student showed improvement. The idea proved successful with many students, but in Mike's case it did not work. After the first weeks he continued to be tardy at about the same rate as before.

Mike was a good athlete and enjoyed attending high school football and basketball games. A few of us teachers made a regular practice of taking some of the junior high boys to these games on Friday nights. Capitalizing on Mike's interest in sports I told him that each week that he received a Positive Progress Report for being prompt to class, he would be included among the boys we took to the game that Friday night.

A remarkable change overcame Mike. Eager to earn a Positive Progress Report each week, he suddenly began arriving at his classes on time. It was a rare occasion when he was late.

Why did the Positive Progress Report work so well for some students but not at all for Mike? Mike's parents probably did not give him much reinforcement for the reports he brought home. For Mike these Positive Progress Reports were simply slips of paper that had no significance.

The event which gave significance to the Positive Progress Reports was granting an important privilege to Mike if he earned one of the reports. The privilege was an activity that Mike desired, an activity that would be considered a reward in itself. When the privilege became contingent on his obtaining a Positive Progress Report, the slip of paper suddenly came to have value to Mike: That which previously had no value became something he worked hard to obtain.

Sometimes it is desirable or necessary to substitute one type of reward for another. The basic principle by which rewards are learned is illustrated in Mike's situation and may be called the **Substitution Principle: To reinforce a child with a previously ineffective reward, present it just before (or as soon as possible to) the time you present the more effective reward.**

Positive Progress Reports were previously ineffective for Mike. But by arranging for him to receive one before including him in the Friday activities, his teacher turned them into effective re-inforcers.

Will Mike continue to be prompt after the basketball season is over? The answer might depend on whether Mike finds any other advantages to being on time to class. He probably would not want to be late to any class which started promptly with interesting and valuable activities.

Changing rewards has advantages in many situations.

- Cleaning Miss Gibson's blackboard is a far different ex-perience from cleaning Miss Robb's blackboard.
- The Bristol School safety patrol suffers from general lack of interest and low morale.
- Anne's demanding of her ten cent reward for each A paper distresses her mother.
- Todd is learning that being "selfish" can make life better for others as well as for himself.
- Getting a gold star for each perfect spelling paper leaves Miss Schroeder's sixth graders cold.

How Are New Rewards Learned?

A newborn baby cannot be rewarded with many reinforcers that are effective with older children. Giving the baby a special privi-lege, a dollar bill, or a word of praise would not strengthen any of his current behaviors. However, providing him with a bottle of warm milk would be an effective reinforcer. How then does the baby learn to value these other reinforcers as he grows older?

THROUGH EVENTS OCCURRING AT ABOUT THE SAME TIME

At first the baby will stop crying only when a nipple is put in his mouth. Later he stops crying when he sees his mother. How does it happen that the mere presence of his mother becomes reinforc-ing? His mother has always appeared just prior to the time that he receives his nourishment. Occurrence of these two events— the appearance of his mother and the receipt of nourishment— close together in time means that the child will learn to value the appearance of the mother as a reinforcer. Learning is most rapid when the new event (mother's presence) is presented just before the older and more effective reinforcer (nourishment). Learning

"Yes, dammit! I was a good boy today. Now give me my vodka Martini!"

The previously ineffective reward must be presented just prior to the more effective reward.

seems to occur most rapidly when the interval between the new and old reinforcers is just a split second. With older children and adults, learning may also occur when the interval is considerably longer and sometimes even when the old reinforcer precedes the new one.

Once the mother's presence is established as a reinforcer, the child learns that specific actions of the mother are reinforcers too. His mother's smile precedes other good things happening to him. Then he learns that certain words, "That's good," "That's nice," "Good boy," tend to precede other favorable things happening to him. In this same way certain words and a variety of other events become established as reinforcers.

THROUGH WORDS

Mastery of a language enables people to establish connections between events that are separated in time. The high risk of contracting lung cancer from cigarette smoking appears to be well established. But since many years may intervene between the time one starts smoking and the time one may suffer from the consequences, many people find it difficult to give up smoking, the reward for giving it up being too distant in time. Other people, however, are able to give it up because the connection between smoking and cancer has been communicated to them in clear, striking, highly believable language, making the possible consequences seem much less remote.

Language may also be used to establish whether any given event is a reinforcer. Simply labeling a certain activity as a reward may often make it serve as a reward.

LABELING ACTIVITIES AS REWARDS

As a reward for her second grade class, Miss Robb granted a special privilege. "Whoever finishes both pages in his workbook without any mistakes today may come in after school and help me wash the blackboard." Each day Miss Robb would have a different activity which would qualify children to be chosen for the special privilege of helping her wash the blackboards. The second graders vied with each other to qualify for the reward. Miss Robb managed to arrange things so that over the course of the year every child in the class received this reward several times.

The next fall a new teacher arrived to teach the third grade class. Miss Gibson made it clear that she would tolerate no nonsense. "If any of you causes any trouble, you will have to come in after school to help me wash the blackboards."

The same children who valued the honor of washing blackboards after school for Miss Robb now felt shamed when they were required to perform the same activity for Miss Gibson.

Why Change Rewards?

If a child learns to act appropriately with one reward, why should it ever be changed? Let us look at some of the circumstances which may call for supplementing or replacing the first reward with another.

THE OLD REWARD MAY LOSE ITS EFFECTIVENESS

Overreliance on a single reinforcer usually results in a loss of effectiveness for that reinforcer. Even though it may have been highly effective at first, the children may well outgrow it as their interests change, or they may simply tire of it.

GIVING THE PATROL A NEW IMAGE

The boys and girls on safety patrol at Bristol Elementary School started out with great enthusiasm. But as the months went by morale suffered. Many dropped out of what seemed a tedious and unrewarding chore. Those who remained did so mainly for their early release from class.

The teacher in charge recognized that the old rewards were no longer effective. He arranged a special bimonthly noon meeting at which refreshments were served to those children serving on the safety patrol. He led them in a discussion of the value of their work. He pointed out that no child had been injured while crossing a street where the safety patrol was on duty. Common problem situations were discussed, and the children devised their own solutions.

The series of noon meetings with the recognition of their good work seemed to give the safety patrol a new sense of responsibility. They began to see themselves as making a valuable contribution to the safety of the other children. Morale grew as more children volunteered to serve.

Initially, being selected as a member of the safety patrol was in itself a rewarding event. Continued membership in the patrol, however, ceased to have reward value until it was strengthened by additional reinforcement. On other occasions, however, an adult may want a child to get tired of certain reinforcers (see Chapter 8).

YOU MAY WANT THE CHILD TO APPRECIATE
LESS TANGIBLE REWARDS

Madeline's father (page 14) rewarded her with money for reading a book. Some external reward was necessary to get her started in reading. However, it would certainly be unrealistic if throughout her life Madeline expected to be paid whenever she read a book. She also needed to learn that she would benefit in other ways as a result of reading.

For many types of behavior which ultimately bring their own reward the initial reinforcer is merely a temporary expedient to get the behavior started. Sometimes a shift from a concrete reward to a less tangible one is a step toward gradually helping the child become independent of external rewards.

CHANGING REWARDS FOR ACADEMIC SUCCESS

At the time that Anne was in the fourth grade her parents instigated the practice of giving her a dime for every A she earned in school. Anne was an intelligent girl and had no trouble getting the As. She frequently came home from school saying, "Here's an A paper, where's my dime?"

Her mother became concerned. Anne seemed to be getting careless in her work. Even though she still made As, she seemed to be working only for the money and did not seem particularly proud of her work or interested in the material she was learning.

One day Anne came home with an A on her math paper and took it to her mother. Before she could say a word, her mother praised the paper and posted it on a family bulletin board. When the rest of the family came home, her mother pointed the paper out to them, but she did not give Anne any money. (The transition might have been smoother if her mother had also given the dime a few more times.) On subsequent days her mother examined the A papers that Anne brought home. She posted only those papers that looked as if Anne had put her best effort into them. She commented favorably on those that looked neat and had required some thought and effort.

Anne soon stopped asking for money. She began to take pride in the work she was doing for other reasons. She knew that every A paper would not necessarily go up on the bulletin board.

Several years later when Anne was sixteen, she was still making A grades. She seemed proud of her work, but she received no money and her mother no longer posted her papers on the family bulletin board.

In Anne's case putting carefully done papers on the bulletin board gradually became more valued than the money. She outgrew the reward of having her work displayed because the habit of doing careful work produced many other satisfactions for her.

THE CHILD MAY LEARN NEW SKILLS FROM THE NEW REWARDS

A wide variety of materials, words, and privileges can be used as rewards. Favorite activities can also be used as rewards for engaging in less preferred activities. For example, even a mundane chore like helping a teacher wash blackboards after class can be considered a reward.

How can we discover what activities are likely to be considered as rewards by a child? One way is to observe the kinds of activities in which a child normally engages during his free time. We can also determine a child's favorite activities by asking him what he likes or what he wants. Most children freely express their preferences.

ENJOYING INCREASED RESPONSIBILITY

Thirteen-year-old Leo had a weekly task of mowing the lawn. At his request he was rewarded by being allowed to attend the Saturday afternoon movie matinee.

While Leo mowed the lawn, his father performed other chores about the yard, trimming the hedge, pruning trees, or building a rock garden. Leo had asked his father whether he could help with these other jobs because he was tired of just mowing the lawn. His father told him he was not old enough yet.

But one Saturday his father observed how well he had mowed the lawn: "You did such a good job on the lawn today I'm going to let you help me trim the hedge."

For several weeks after mowing the lawn, Leo's father helped him learn a new skill or allowed him to help on some job. On the fourth week after these new responsibilities started, Leo was designing an area in the rock garden. "Aren't you going to the movie this afternoon, Leo?" asked his father. Leo replied, "Not this week. I'm having more fun here."

Assuming responsibilities like those of his father proved to be more rewarding to Leo than the old reward of attending a movie. At the same time Leo was learning some new skills, was building a friendly relationship with his father, and was assuming the responsibilities of manhood.

YOU MAY WANT THE CHILD TO BECOME LESS SELFISH

Some people worry that the use of rewards in child training may tend to make children more selfish. We do not share that worry. Selfishness cannot be eliminated; it can only be disguised. So far we have never discovered an unselfish child, nor for that matter have we ever discovered an unselfish adult. Every human being is very much concerned with his own survival and welfare.

Attempts have been made to teach children that other people are more important than they are. Attempts at teaching a sense of unworthiness have unfortunate consequences. If a child really accepts the notion that he is unworthy, he suffers a lifetime of humiliation from others. Even a successful self-degrader produces the obvious paradox: He becomes proud of being humble.

A more workable solution to the problem of "selfishness" is to help the child learn that his welfare is intimately bound up in the welfare of the entire human race. He can learn to serve others, not because he is altruistic and unselfish, but because he understands that he is selfish and gains for himself by being of assistance to others.

Aesop's fable of the lion who preserved the mouse's life and was in turn rescued by the mouse gnawing a net of ropes closes with this moral: No act of kindness is ever wasted. Those who give the most to others gain the most from others in the long run. It is hard for a child to appreciate this fact because he has not lived long enough to value "the long run." This important lesson can be learned in many little ways as a child grows.

PROFITING FROM A CLEAN PUBLIC PARK

When five-year-old Todd goes with his family to the public park for a picnic, he hears his mother say, "Let's spread our blanket and food here. Whoever was here before us certainly left this place looking neat and clean for us. We'll have to do the same for those who come later."

Todd can observe his family's helping to clean up the area after their picnic. And if he were to help carry waste material to the trash basket, his parents might respond, "Thank you for helping, Todd. Our picnic area looks beautiful now."

The attempt to instill unselfishness as a virtue tends to produce either self-deception or feelings of guilt and unworthiness. It is far better to tie the natural self-centeredness of the human being into the welfare of all humanity. "I work for this political candidate because I believe I will live in a happier world if he gets elected." "I give generously to the United Fund because the services provided make this a better community in which to live and work." "l do volunteer work in the hospital and old peoples' home because they appreciate my services so much and because I know that someday I too will appreciate help like this."

DEVELOPING TEAMWORK IN LEARNING

Miss Schroeder, the sixth grade teacher, had the policy of giving a gold star to every child who got 100 percent on the spelling test. The star had little significance for most of the children. Scarcely a third of the class was ever able to get 100 percent on the spelling test. Here is Miss Schroeder's story of how she solved the problem:

I decided to change my approach and make the star more worthwhile as an incentive. I also wanted the children to work together instead of competing with one another. So I announced my new plan. "If 90 percent of the class members get gold stars on any one test, the entire class can have an additional 15 minutes of physical education on Friday." An extra 15 minutes of physical education delighted them. Two things began to happen. They not only worked harder to earn the gold star for themselves, but they worked together to help fellow classmates who were having trouble. They studied together, gave informal tests to one another, and offered extra help to those class members who seemed to be having the most difficulty.

The star became an important symbol. Grades on the spelling tests improved significantly. Each child strived to get his gold star because he did not want to let down the rest of the class. I was mainly pleased, however, because the children seemed genuinely concerned with the welfare of one another. I guess they realized that by helping one another they helped themselves.

Rewarding cooperation worked out well in a class where every student had the ability to perform adequately and was not pressured into trying to perform at a level that was too difficult for him. Learning to cooperate to achieve a common goal is certainly more valuable than simply acquiring stars and may well have been a more important outcome to these students than the words they learned to spell. In the words of John Donne,

No man is an island, entire of itself; every man is a piece of the continent, a part of the main.

7

Scheduling
Rewards
to
Develop
Persistence

DEVELOPING PERSISTENCE

Mr. Tracy wanted his son, Chris, to develop into a good competitor, one who would try to win, who would not be easily discouraged by defeat, and who would be eager to accept new challenges. How he set about helping Chris learn these behaviors is illustrated by the way in which he taught him to play chess when the boy was six years old.

After Mr. Tracy judged that Chris was old enough to learn and eager to try, his first step was to make sure his son understood the object of the game. "Chris, you have the white pieces; I have the black pieces. You win the game if you can capture my black king, this piece right here. I win if I capture your white king."

"How do you capture the king?" asked Chris.

"All you have to do is move any one of your white pieces into the square occupied by my king. Of course at the same time you must be careful that first I do not move any one of my black pieces into the square occupied by your white king."

The second step was to explain the basic rules to Chris. Mr. Tracy explained how each chess piece could move. He asked Chris to practice moving his pieces to make sure that he knew exactly the allowable moves for each piece.

The third step was to play a game together.

The fourth step was to insure that Chris won that first game. Mr. Tracy deliberately made errors which exposed his king to capture.

Delighted with his victory Chris wanted to play chess with his father again. On subsequent days new games were played. Chris won the second game, but his father won the third. Chris was disappointed that he lost and wondered why. His father pointed out a new strategy that would help him win. Chris then won the fourth game, employing the new strategy.

Over the months they played many games. Mr. Tracy accepted a handicap by giving Chris the privilege of removing in advance as many of his father's chess pieces as he desired. In that way Mr. Tracy could try to win instead of deliberately making errors. At first Chris would only allow his father to retain eight pawns, the king, and one knight. When he could win easily against inferior forces, Chris began to allow his father more men on the board. Eventually he said, "Dad, I want to see if I can beat you when we both start out with the same number of pieces." He came close to winning despite Mr. Tracy's best efforts.

Chris enjoyed playing games with his brothers and sister and friends as well as his father and mother. One day he asked his mother to play a game with him. "What's your favorite game?"

> asked his mother. Mulling the question over for a moment, Chris replied, "My favorite game is daddy-teach-me-a-new-game."

Chris' enthusiasm for competitive events, his desire to keep playing even when he lost, and his eagerness to learn new games was clearly a result of the carefully sequenced experiences provided by his father. Mr. Tracy made sure that his son was successful on the first attempt. However he did not allow Chris to be successful on every attempt. He carefully intermingled successes and losses in a way to keep him challenged by new difficulties which he could eventually overcome.

If Mr. Tracy had provided him with 100 percent success, Chris may have tended to give up the first time he encountered real difficulties. If Mr. Tracy had provided him with constant failure experiences by causing him to lose every time, the boy would probably have become discouraged and would have refused to play.

Chris was reinforced intermittently in his chess playing. Sometimes he was successful and sometimes he lost. He discovered that he could learn something useful from his losses as well as from his successes.

One clever gimmick in this learning experience is the way in which Mr. Tracy allowed his son to set the handicap. Before the game started the boy could remove as many of his father's chess pieces as he desired. In essense this allowed Chris to arrange his own schedule of reinforcement. When he felt that he needed to win, he could remove more of his father's pieces. When he felt he wanted more of a challenge, he could allow his father to keep additional pieces.

Chris' willingness to continue playing chess and to persist in learning new games can be attributed in large part to this irregular schedule of successes and failures, this intermittent schedule of reinforcement. The experience of Chris and his father illustrates the **Intermittent Reinforcement Principle: To encourage a child to continue performing an established behavior with few or no rewards, gradually and intermittently decrease the frequency with which the correct behavior is rewarded.**

Intermittent reinforcement may be useful in a variety of situations.

- Miss Wright's fifth grade class becomes noisy and unruly the minute she leaves the room.
- Ten-year-old Ellen wants to learn to make her favorite dessert, a complicated and time-consuming recipe.

■   The mother of two-year-old Danny is determined not to have the same unpleasant problems toilet training him that she had with his older sister.

■   Miss Corpus, the Latin teacher, finds that her students have "beat her system" and get away with not studying for class.

■   Holly is afraid to take the initiative and relies needlessly on her teacher.

Intermittent Rewards Have Special Advantages

When a child is learning a new behavior, continuous reinforcement is best. At first the learner needs to be reinforced every time he improves or performs correctly. Once the new behavior is well established, a change to an intermittent schedule of reinforcement is advantageous. Chris won twice, then lost the third game. Some youngsters might need more, or fewer, victories to establish the same level of interest. There is no precise method for predicting how long continuous reinforcement should be retained for any given child. The child's reactions can tell us if we have moved to an intermittent schedule too quickly.

WHEN A BEHAVIOR CANNOT CONSTANTLY BE OBSERVED

The true test of a person's character is his actions when he is not observed. The skills, competencies, habits, and ethical standards we hope children will learn involve behaviors that they will frequently demonstrate when no one is there to observe and reinforce them.

Behavior learned under continuous reinforcement usually ceases quickly when reinforcement is no longer forthcoming. However if intermittent reinforcement is provided after the initial learning has been established, the behavior will usually persist.

WORKING WITHOUT THE TEACHER PRESENT

Miss Wright's fifth grade class was noisy, unruly, and unproductive whenever she left the room. She describes how she helped the children learn to remain productive even in her absence:

I told the children that they needed to develop good work habits even when I was not in the room: "I will be so happy if I come back into the room and find it as quiet as when I am here."

I then left the room and returned again after about two minutes. There was a considerable amount of noise and talking as I entered the room, but I did notice that four or five of the pupils were still at work. I complimented those students who were working, telling them how pleased I was that they were old enough to continue work without supervision. I said nothing to those who had been causing the disruption.

During the next two weeks I found many opportunities to step out of the classroom. Each time I returned I commented favorably to those children who were continuing with their work. Each time more children were working.

I would vary the interval of time that I would be gone. Sometimes it was for only thirty seconds; other times it might be as long as ten or fifteen minutes. The class improved remarkably. I told them, "I guess you don't even need a teacher. You work so beautifully without one."

One morning I became sick. I had to leave the classroom four different times at about ten-minute intervals. Each time I returned I was astonished to find that the group was continuing their work. Once I complimented them on it, but the other three times I said nothing. When a substitute teacher arrived to relieve me, I told the substitute in front of the class that they were a wonderful group of children and that she should have no problem with them. She didn't.

Miss Wright provided intermittent reinforcement in three ways: (1) She varied the interval that she was gone from the classroom. Sometimes she was gone for only a few seconds, at other times for up to a quarter of an hour. The children never knew exactly at what moment she would return. (2) Miss Wright reinforced the children who were working, paying no attention to those who were idle. But she could not spot quickly every child who had continued to work. She missed some. Therefore even some of the children who had continued to work did not get reinforced every time. (3) Once the class had learned to continue working in her absence, Miss Wright gradually reduced the number of times she complimented them.

With this irregular, intermittent schedule of reinforcement the children gradually learned to work for longer intervals of time without supervision. The ability to work without constant supervision is an important skill, one that is the mark of every mature individual.

WHEN PERSISTENCE, PATIENCE, AND DEDICATION
ARE DESIRED

A dedicated person is one who works for long periods of time
without receiving rewards. Why do some people work for days,
months, or even years without much reward whereas others give
up quickly when things are not going their way? In all probability
the different schedules of reinforcement to which they were accidentally exposed influence the extent to which these people
persist.

If you want a child to learn to wait patiently, you would reward
him at first for waiting only a few seconds. Subsequently you
would reward him for waiting a slightly longer interval of time,
gradually increasing the interval each time you ask him to wait.

Similarly if you want a child to persist at a task even after several failures, you would arrange for him to succeed after one
failure, then after perhaps two failures, gradually but irregularly
increasing the number of failure experiences followed by a success. Most worthwhile endeavors are not accomplished on the
first try. Almost every successful person has learned to persevere
in the face of sometimes monumental difficulties. Those who learn
to persist are lucky to have encountered that combination of successes and failures which has taught them that persistence does
eventually produce success. However, persistence does not necessarily mean repeating the identical behavior again and again.
Success usually comes in varying the behavior, trying different
approaches to solve the problem. Eventually one of the approaches
works and provides the route to success.

LEARNING TO COOK

When Ellen was ten years old, she told her mother she wanted
to learn how to make her favorite dessert, Chocolate Poof, a
complicated dessert receipe involving four separate steps.

Ellen's mother wanted to encourage her in her desire to cook
but feared that starting with Chocolate Poof would produce a
total disaster. Instead they started by making a chocolate layer
cake from a mix. Ellen successfully combined the few ingre-
dients. But as she lifted the first cake pan full of batter into the
oven, she accidentally toppled it, making a sticky mess in the
oven and on the floor. Ellen was quite upset and wanted to give

up cooking right then and there. However, her mother insisted that she help clean up the mess and then asked her to put the other cake pan of batter into the oven. Ellen carefully lifted the cake pan and managed to put it into the oven without incident.

The family ate the one-layer cake with delight. "The garbage disposal ate the other half," explained Ellen.

Several months later Ellen wanted to make tomato soup by herself. Her mother pointed out directions on the can label and said she would be available in the next room. Ellen combined the tomato puree and milk but neglected to stir them well. She complained about the lumpy soup, and her mother advised her how to prevent this problem the next time. The following Saturday she made the soup again, this time without lumps.

Over a period of the next two years Ellen continued to make simple recipes, gradually acquiring more skill. She was not always completely successful, but on the other hand she received some genuine compliments.

It was quite a while before Ellen asked again to try to make Chocolate Poof. This time her mother agreed and gave her directions on how to do it. Ellen did most of the work herself. That evening with great pride she served her favorite dessert to the entire family. Even her younger brother was impressed: "I never thought you'd make a good cook, but maybe there's hope for you after all."

Several factors influenced Ellen's persistence in learning to cook. Her mother was certainly a model for Ellen, but many children observe model cooks and yet never learn to cook themselves.

The key to success most probably was in the sequence of experiences that Ellen's mother provided her. The first task was easy enough so that Ellen could succeed even though her success was accompanied by a partial failure. The accidental failure was probably fortuitous. Ellen learned that if she persisted in the task after spilling half the cake batter, the end result was still satisfying.

The intermittent schedule of reinforcement was partly accidental but partly planned by Ellen's mother. She arranged the tasks in an order of difficulty so that Ellen was constantly having to face new challenges and was usually successful, although meeting with occasional failure and disappointment. If her mother had continued to allow her nothing but easy cooking jobs, Ellen would probably have given up the first time she faced a difficult recipe. If her mother had allowed her to attempt too difficult a task at first, Ellen would have been discouraged and might have given up trying. The gradual increase in difficulty provided just the right combination of new challenges, risks of failure, and the thrills of mastering new skills and producing tasty dishes.

How to Use Intermittent Rewards

NEW BEHAVIOR MUST BE WELL LEARNED FIRST

The value of an intermittent schedule is in helping a child maintain a pattern of behavior after it has once been learned. However, intermittent reinforcement is not as effective as continuous reinforcement in helping a child learn a new behavior originally. Rule of thumb: Reinforce *every* correct or improved response to facilitate initial learning; reinforce intermittently to maintain the behavior.

TOILET TRAINING

When Danny was two years old his mother decided to begin toilet training him. Here is her report of how she proceeded.

I knew I had done a poor job in toilet training Danny's older sister when she was about two years old. I had gotten upset with her whenever she wet her pants. Then she would get upset when I got upset. It was an unhappy experience for both of us, and I was determined not to let this problem occur with Danny.

The first step was getting Danny to have a success experience that I could reward. Whenever enough time had elapsed so that I could predict Danny was about to urinate, I would take him to the toilet. For two days we had no success. Finally on the third day after what seemed to be an interminable time he did urinate in the toilet. I immediately gave him a piece of candy and praised him liberally. From then on the task became rapidly easier. Every time Danny used the toilet successfully I gave him a piece of candy and expressed my genuine delight. When he wet his pants, he received no reward whatsoever. However, I was careful never to get upset or angry at his failures. Within a short period of time Danny seemed to have learned to use the toilet properly, announcing his readiness with the statement, "Toidy, Mommy." Accidents were infrequent and resulted mainly from poor timing.

About this time I remember thinking to myself, "So far, so good. But what if he needs his mother around to reward him for each good performance all his life!" So once I thought he had the habit pretty well established, I gradually cut back on the candy even when he requested it. Instead I continued to praise him highly every time. Gradually over the next few weeks, I found I could reduce the number of times I praised him and I stopped giving him candy altogether.

Danny was toilet trained without either of us getting emotionally upset. His rewards now come from knowing he can use the bathroom like a grownup and from the constant comfort of dry pants.

Danny was learning to discriminate the time and place to urinate. To learn efficiently he needed to be reinforced every time he performed correctly. Once the learning was well established his mother gradually began to interperse the rewards. The rewards that were used to establish the new learning no longer became necessary as Danny learned other benefits of using the bathroom properly.

INTERMITTENT REINFORCEMENT SHOULD BE AN UNEXPECTED SURPRISE, NOT A PROMISE FULFILLED

Some reinforcers cannot be put on an intermittent schedule. For example, the weekly paycheck of a worker represents a monetary reward for services rendered. The employer cannot gradually withdraw this reinforcer. The employer may occasionally pay bonuses for exceptionally meritorious services over and above the stated wages. The bonus could be administered on an intermittent schedule, but the wages which were promised cannot be administered intermittently.

In the same way a child may come to expect certain rewards either because they have explicitly been promised to him or because long experience has led him to believe they will always be forthcoming. Suddenly putting these reinforcers on an intermittent schedule would be perceived as a broken promise. Unfortunate consequences, usually the kind associated with punishment, would result.

NO LONGER MAINTAINING AN ORDERLY ROOM

When Sue was eight years old, her mother and father began reinforcing her for cleaning her room. She quickly learned to complete her duties without being reminded. Her parents praised her continually. As soon as she finished her chores, Sue would ask for reinforcement, "There, Daddy, how's that?" or "Mommy, is that good enough?" Her parents never failed to recognize and praise her work. She took great pride and satisfaction in a clean room. Her father reported what happened then:

We had been reinforcing her after every correct performance for a long time. We began to think it was no longer necessary and so decided to stop reinforcing her so often. But as we stopped praising her for cleaning her room, she stopped keeping it clean. She now finds excuses for not completing her chores. A job that used to take fifteen or twenty minutes now takes an hour. She seemed to lose interest in keeping up her room. She now considers her job a painful task and is somewhat resentful toward us.

What went wrong? With continuous reinforcement Sue cheerfully maintained her room. With the sudden change to intermittent reinforcement she reduced her cleaning effort. On the basis of this brief and incomplete report it is difficult to be certain of what caused the change. Perhaps Sue's parents maintained continuous reinforcement too long after Sue had established the initial habit. Sue grew to depend upon her parents' praise and compliments for a task that benefited her more than anyone else. Possibly the transition from continuous to intermittent reinforcement was too abrupt. A gradual reduction would have been preferable to a sudden shift. Her parents could have continued to reinforce her every time but with diminished words of praise. Perhaps eventually a smile, a wink, a friendly gesture could have replaced the effusive praise.

Sue seemed to feel that her parents had failed to fulfill a commitment to her. To establish a good relationship with Sue and at the same time help reestablish the habit of maintaining her own room, her parents might well have used some alternative reinforcer. They could establish a behavior contract to pay her ten cents a week or whatever amount was mutually agreeable for maintaining her room. The reinforcer under these circumstances would then not be subject to an intermittent schedule but would be paid to her every time she fulfilled her side of the agreement. The agreement would not be a lifetime contract but would only exist for as long as both Sue and her parents felt it was reasonable and fair. It could be renegotiated anytime either of them felt that it should. Eventually her parents would eliminate the reinforcement altogether as Sue assumed more responsibilities and found other financial resources.

Effects of Different Schedules

Psychologists have investigated the effect of different schedules of reinforcement. Most of this research, however, has been done with animals other than human beings. As yet there is no evidence on the precise effect of different schedules for human beings performing a variety of tasks. Nevertheless some useful ideas for scheduling rewards can be inferred from the preliminary research results.

SCHEDULES BASED ON NUMBER OF RESPONSES

A factory worker may be paid on a piecework basis. For example, he may be paid $5.00 for every 300 gimcracks he polishes. The more gimcracks he polishes, the more money he makes. Similarly a child may be paid on a piecework basis for jobs around the house. For example, a boy may be paid $1.00 for mowing the lawn or 75 cents for cleaning out the garage. A girl may be paid $1.00 for every seven times she waters the garden. Such schedules are technically known as fixed ratio schedules because the relationship between the number of responses and the amount of the reward is constant.

Sometimes the number of responses necessary to earn a reward becomes so large that a peculiar thing happens following reinforcement. Instead of behavior increasing immediately after reinforcement, the behavior decreases temporarily. A student may work long, hard hours studying for an examination. He may get an A on the examination but be totally unable and unwilling to study for some days thereafter. A politician may spend long days on the campaign trail hoping to be reinforced by the electorate. Immediately after getting elected he may then take a vacation. After a temporary recovery period both the student and the politician go back to work, but this decreased effort after a difficult task has been rewarded is a natural and frequent occurrence.

Sometimes the reinforcement does not occur after a fixed number of responses but instead occurs after some unpredictable or irregular number of responses, a variable ratio schedule. The slot machine player may win something the first time, or the twentieth time, or the hundredth time. He may hit two jackpots in a row. He has no way of predicting which time, if any, he will receive some pay-off from the machine. This variable ratio schedule usually produces a high, steady rate of response over long periods of time. Anyone who has visited gambling casinos can testify to the steady, rapid rate of response by people playing hour after hour, sometimes playing several slot machines at once, never knowing which time, if ever, they might hit a jackpot.

The following experience illustrates the effect of different schedules of reinforcement on student behavior.

ASSURING THAT STUDENTS PREPARE FOR CLASS

Miss Corpus, the ninth grade Latin teacher, was in the habit of asking her students to translate aloud passages from a Latin reader. Each student was to translate one sentence when his turn came. Students were to study the assignment in advance and be prepared to translate any sentence.

When class started Miss Corpus would start by calling on the person sitting in the first seat in the left-hand row. Next she would call on the person in the second seat in the left-hand row, then the third seat, and so on, moving up the second row, down the third row, up the fourth row, and down the fifth row in a predictable sequence. The students quickly caught on to the system. A student sitting in any given seat could, by counting the number of sentences in the passage and the number of people scheduled to recite before him, determine exactly which sentence he would be called upon to translate. Then while other students were struggling with the preceding translations, he could use his dictionary and make a favorable impression on Miss Corpus by fluently translating the one sentence he prepared even though he would have been at a loss to translate any of the others. As soon as he had finished translating his particular sentence, the student could then relax, knowing that he would not be called upon again until everyone else in the class had had a turn.

Miss Corpus finally got wise to the students' system. Even though many of them sounded fluent when she called upon them in class, their performance on other tests was quite poor. The reason became obvious. The students were not studying in advance outside of class. Most of them would wait until they arrived in class and then would do the bare minimum necessary to make a favorable impression under the fixed ratio schedule Miss Corpus was using.

Changing to a variable ratio schedule, Miss Corpus wrote the name of every student on a separate slip of paper. She mixed the names up thoroughly in a small fish bowl she placed on her desk. Then when she wanted members of the class to translate the reading passage that had been assigned, she would ask for a translation of the first sentence, reach into the fish bowl, pull out a name at random, and ask that person to translate. She would then replace the slip of paper in the fish bowl, stir the names around, pick out another slip of paper, and ask that person to translate the second sentence. Once in a while the same person would be called upon two times in a row. No one could predict when his name would come up. The only way to prepare for class under this system was to have read and translated the entire reading passage in advance. Miss Corpus discovered a surprising increase in her students' test performance under the variable ratio of reinforcement.

The teacher's use of a variable ratio schedule was an improvement over the fixed ratio schedule. However, her teaching methods would be improved still further if she could find a way to keep more of her students actively engaged in learning tasks. Modern language laboratories are a big step in helping every student to get more practice in using the language.

SCHEDULES BASED ON INTERVALS OF TIME

For some kinds of behavior it is more meaningful to give reinforcement after a certain interval of time instead of after a certain number of responses. Most people's salaries are based on units of time, $2.00 per hour, $80.00 per week, $700 a month, or $10,000 a year. As long as he continues working satisfactorily the person is reinforced after a stated number of units of time. These fixed interval schedules are based on a constant relationship between the interval of time (hours, weeks, months, or years) and the number of dollars paid.

In most jobs pay for working an interval of time is more feasible than "piecework" pay. Because so many different responses are usually required, attempting to count the number of useful responses would be wasteful.

Some jobs require continuous alertness and readiness to respond to situations and problems that might arise. Military psychologists, for example, have found that attending to a radar screen image for long hours at a time produces inattentiveness. If an enemy plane were picked up by radar, the radar observer might miss it because he had grown tired looking at the screen. One solution to the problem has been to program "dummy blips" across the screen at irregular intervals of time and to reinforce the radar observer for every blip he identifies. Because the blips appear irregularly, sometimes only a few seconds apart and other times many minutes apart, a variable interval schedule is in use. An identified blip which had not been programmed would of course be a significant event.

Any task or learning skill calling for an attentive response to situations which occur over a period of time may be reinforced on a variable interval schedule.

LEARNING TO BE A SAFE DRIVER

Sixteen-year-old Fritz was learning to drive an automobile. His father was giving him driving lessons, trying his best to note Fritz's improvements and not get angry at his mistakes. As Fritz would drive the car with his father beside him, his father would at irregular intervals say things such as, "You took that corner well," "Now you are a good safe distance behind the car ahead of you," "Great, you've remembered to use the turn signal each time the last three turns."

As Fritz's driving skills increased, his father's favorable comments decreased. Fritz showed signs of developing a real sense of responsibility for driving a car well and safely. He even asked his father what he might do to help reduce the insurance rates.

Most parents find it difficult to teach their son or daughter to drive the family car. The emotional involvements are usually too great. A suggestion sounds like a reprimand. A protest sounds like lack of respect. The family's investment in their car seems too large to risk. For most people it is better to let a professional driver educator do the teaching.

Fritz's father, however, had developed an effective method. He commented only on his son's improvements and successes. At first his comments were frequent, then gradually as he rode with Fritz he allowed progressively longer intervals of time to elapse between favorable comments. With little conscious effort he reinforced Fritz on a variable interval schedule with gradually longer intervals between reinforcements. Appropriately timed suggestions would also have been useful (recall Chapters 4 and 5).

COMBINATION SCHEDULES

Complicated combinations of ratio and interval schedules can be devised. A salesman who is paid at the rate of $500 per month plus $50 for every sale is working under a combined ratio and interval schedule. Few people are aware of combination schedules of reinforcement in the complicated events of life. The following report of a journalism teacher represents one such combination schedule.

LEARNING TO TAKE INITIATIVE

As sponsor for the high school newspaper one of my jobs was to assign tasks to the students working on the paper. I assigned Holly the responsibility of supervising a photographer in taking pictures for the paper.

At first she would take no initiative whatsover. She would ask me for advice on every detail. "Shall I contact the photographer to be sure he will be there?" "Shall I notify the students when and where to appear?" "What size finished photographs would be best?" "What would be a good background for this picture?" "What should the people in the picture be doing to make an interesting shot?"

At first I was tempted to give Holly advice in response to this flood of questions. But soon I saw that answering her questions only prompted more questions. She had to learn to make decisions on her own and accept the responsibility for the result.

I changed my strategy. Every time Holly asked me a question I would say, "What do you think?" And then regardless of her response I would encourage her with "That might be worth trying," or "Why don't you see how it looks?" or "Why don't you try it several ways and see which one looks best to you?" Then after she made a decision, I backed her. When her idea worked out well, I let her know.

To show my interest in her I would sometimes pop into the office and throw her some questions: "Holly, is everything OK?"

or "Did everyone show up?" Sometimes I wouldn't appear in the newspaper office at all but would ask her the next day how things had gone.

Holly's confidence in her judgment grew as she made decisions and found out that the results were good. Even when she made mistakes she discovered that the world did not collapse. She began contacting the photographer without checking with me. She wrote up notification slips to students and merely asked me to sign them. She decided on picture sizes herself. She worked with the photographer as they planned the background and action for each picture. The newspaper experience seemed to change Holly from a shy insecure girl into a self-confident reporter.

This journalism teacher realized that her job was not to produce a school paper so much as to produce competent people. In Holly's case she encouraged what Holly needed—independent thinking. For an impulsive or irresponsible student she would probably have reinforced other behaviors.

Sometimes it is difficult to tell exactly what constitutes a reinforcer. To some extent the lack of attention from the journalism teacher was probably reinforcing to Holly because it demonstrated the journalism teacher's confidence in her ability to make wise decisions. The teacher's confidence in Holly, her insistence that Holly make decisions herself, and her support for the results of those decisions brought about an important change in the girl's willingness to take the initiative. The teacher administered these various reinforcers at irregular intervals and after variable numbers of responses. It would be difficult to plot the precise schedule. Whatever the combination the result was an important positive change in Holly's self-confidence and her ability to take the initiative.

Much Intermittent Reinforcement Is Not Planned

The term *schedule of reinforcement* implies that someone is deliberately planning the schedule. In actual fact such planning rarely occurs. Every person is on a whole series of intricate schedules of reinforcement so complicated that it would be impossible to untangle them. These unplanned schedules sometimes have beneficial effects; sometimes the effects are less desirable.

CARNIVAL   by Dick Turner

"Yeah, that's my Mom calling me . . . but it's only
the second time!"

**Intermittent reinforcement may have either beneficial or un-
desirable effects.**

BENEFICIAL EFFECTS OF UNPLANNED
INTERMITTENT REINFORCEMENT

For most parents it is far more difficult to reinforce a child on a
continuous basis than to reinforce him intermittently. Parents
have problems of their own, and they cannot constantly be attentive to the behavior of each child. Their inattentiveness frequently
occurs when the child is behaving properly. A parent misses many

opportunities to praise his children for proper behavior. Yet these missed opportunities may be beneficial, for in effect the child is being reinforced intermittently. If the behavior is well learned, such intermittent reinforcement will help to maintain it for long periods of time.

Similarly a teacher cannot possibly attend to thirty different individuals working in a classroom at the same time. A student in a classroom may work productively for long periods of time before receiving any kind of recognition or reward from the teacher. This condition is good training for life outside of school, since no one receives constant reward and recognition for every desired response. For the most part all of us have to work for long periods of time without reward or recognition. The inability of the teacher to attend to every pupil has some unplanned benefits.

UNDESIRABLE SIDE EFFECTS OF UNPLANNED INTERMITTENT REINFORCEMENT

A number of undesirable practices are also maintained by unplanned intermittent reinforcement. The prevalence of youthful shoplifting can be explained as a response to an intermittent schedule of reinforcement. If a child steals something from a shop counter without being apprehended, he is reinforced for an undesired social act. Reinforced once, he is likely to try again until eventually he is caught. However, by the time he is caught the child may have been reinforced sufficiently often that being apprehended once does not serve as a sufficient deterrent.

Similarly a child may try a drug out of curiosity, knowing in advance its possible side effects but on that occasion experiencing none of them. This reinforcement may encourage him to try it again and again until he is hooked.

Useless patent medicines enjoy tremendous sales because of an intermittent reinforcement effect. People usually buy a medicine when they are feeling miserable. The recuperative powers of human beings are such that they often will improve no matter what they do. Cures for the common cold are big money-makers because colds always improve no matter what medication the person takes at the worst phase of the cold. The innocent victim willingly ascribes curative powers to whatever "medicine" he took, thus increasing its future sales.

Quack fortune-tellers play on the gullibility of people in somewhat the same way. By making a series of forecasts, some of which are bound to come true eventually, the fortune-teller establishes a reputation for seeing into the future. Forecasts such as "Something good is going to happen to you," or "I see you taking a trip," or "A terrible disaster will happen in this city within the next month" are all virtually certain to happen. The credulous client of a fortune-teller tends to remember the predictions which come true and forgets those that do not. He is intermittently reinforced for consulting the fortune-teller who in turn is intermittently reinforced for making predictions.

Compulsive gambling is another result of intermittent reinforcement. In the long run an ordinary citizen gambling in a casino cannot possibly win because the odds are against him. Occasionally, however, for short periods of time he does win. He may by chance have a long series of wins convincing him that he is on some kind of lucky streak. The dice have no memory, however, and lucky streaks always come to an end, usually on large bets. In an attempt to recoup losses the citizen continues to play, his small gains being erased by larger losses. People can gamble for fun, but when they must gamble to win, it is better to be the professional gambler who arranges the odds in his own favor. The really lucky person at gambling is the one who loses the first time he tries. His gambling behavior may then be extinguished, and he probably will not try again. The variable ratio schedule provided by the gambling casinos keeps professional gamblers wealthy but causes untold suffering among those people unlucky enough to win.

IV

Stopping Inappropriate Behavior

Up to this point we have emphasized ways to help a child learn new forms of behavior. We have seen that children learn both desirable and undesirable behavior in the same way. But if a child has already learned some undesirable behavior, what can an adult do to help him "unlearn" it?

Chapters 8 through 11 present four methods to help stop undesired behavior. For some kinds of behavior one method may be better than another. The four alternative methods from which you may choose are described separately in each chapter but are summarized here.

To stop a child from acting in a particular way, you may

(1)   allow him to continue (or insist that he continue) performing the undesired act until he tires of it (the Satiation Principle, see Chapter 8);

(2)   arrange conditions so that he receives no rewards following the undesired act (the Extinction Principle, see Chapter 9);

(3)   reward an alternative action which is inconsistent with or cannot be performed at the same time as the undesired act (the Incompatible Alternative Principle, see Chapter 10); and/or

(4)   arrange for him to terminate a mild aversive situation immediately by improving his behavior (the Negative Reinforcement Principle, see Chapter 11).

If a child acts in an unacceptable way, remember that somehow he learned to act in that way. If he can learn to act unacceptably, he can also learn to act in an acceptable manner. Your job is to help him learn. These four alternative methods, based on years of psychological experimentation, seem at present to be among the best possible ways of changing undesired behavior. We recommend that you read all four chapters before you choose which method seems best for handling any particular misbehavior.

Letting
Behavior
Run
Its
Course

CHANGING FEELINGS ABOUT A BOY FRIEND

Sixteen-year-old Vicky had been dating Jake, an older boy whom her parents considered "questionable company" for her. Vicky and Jake were getting quite serious about each other, and her mother feared that an early marriage between the two would certainly lead both of them into an unhappy future.

Vicky's parents considered forbidding their daughter to see Jake, but they knew that she would most certainly rebel and sneak out to be with him. She might even run away just to prove her independence. Her infatuation with Jake seemed to blind her to his insensitivity and laziness. Her parents were convinced that if Vicky had an opportunity to see him as he really was, she could come to a more considered judgment. On the other hand they had to admit their own evaluation could also be mistaken.

Instead of forbidding her to see Jake, Vicky's parents included him in virtually every family activity. Her mother invited him over for dinner every night and on week-end excursions with the family. He was around the house constantly, appearing to enjoy the attention and companionship from the entire family. Vicky's mother and father even began to enjoy his straight-forward manner.

Vicky, however, became edgy without a minute to herself. Jake was always around. She began to see him in a different light, commenting on his insensitivity to other people's feelings and his failure to volunteer for any family chores.

After two and a half months Vicky told Jake not to see her any more because she was too young to get tied down. She began dating other boys and now wonders what she ever saw in him.

Vicky's parents took a calculated risk. They relied on her good judgment eventually asserting itself. They figured that by giving her an opportunity to observe Jake over an extended period of time she would find out for herself whether she really felt compatible with him. As it turned out, Vicky discovered that she and Jake were not compatible and so they separated.

The story could well have had a different ending. Her parents could have been mistaken in their original estimate of him. Jake, responding to the warmth of the new family environment, could possibly have changed his behavior. He might have modeled his manners after those of Vicky's family, pitching in with the household chores and becoming a valued part of the family.

However, no matter how the episode might have ended, the strategy of including Jake was clearly superior to forbidding Vicky from seeing him.

Parental injunctions against boy friends or girl friends frequently backfire. Even when they work, a residue of ill-feeling between parent and child remains. It is a mistake for parents to choose friends or marriage partners for their children, but parents can teach their children *how* to choose their friends and marriage partners. By allowing Vicky to become thoroughly familiar with Jake in a family atmosphere, her parents provided an environment where Vicky could learn which traits she valued and which she found incompatible.

Vicky's experience illustrates the first of four possible alternative methods useful in stopping undesirable behavior.

Satiation Principle: To stop a child from acting in a particular way, you may allow him to continue (or insist that he continue) performing the undesired act until he tires of it.

This method is called the Satiation Principle because a child may become satiated with the consequences of continuing his actions as a result of fatigue and boredom. Here are some situations to which the Satiation Principle has been applied:

- Keith neither does his homework nor participates in class.
- Ninth grade algebra is interrupted by horseplay.
- Pepper at age eleven is experimenting with cigarette smoking.
- Two-and-one-half-year-old Randy only wants to eat mashed potatoes.
- Frank runs away from home during his senior year in high school.
- Cissy talks incessantly, whether or not anyone wants to listen.
- Too many clichés in student compositions inspire an English teacher's assignment.

Allowing or Insisting?

Sometimes merely allowing an undesired activity to continue to its natural conclusion is sufficient. However, a child may be inclined to stop of his own accord before he has really tired of it and then to continue again at a later date. When such continuation seems likely, it may be more useful to insist that the activity be continued until fatigue occurs.

ALLOWING THE UNDESIRED BEHAVIOR TO CONTINUE

Following are two examples of ways in which teachers handled undesired activity in a classroom. The first concerns the case of an entire class; the second, an individual in one class.

SETTLING DOWN TO BAND PRACTICE

Rehearsal in the advanced band was not going well. The students were not concentrating on the music but were talking to one another, laughing, and goofing around. The band teacher reports what happened:

The students entered the class noisily, and during rehearsal they failed to settle down despite my repeated efforts to quiet them. Nothing was being accomplished.

I finally stopped and calmly told the class to keep talking and to play around with their instruments; I would return when they were ready to work. Then I left the room and went into my adjoining office, leaving the door open.

Some students tried to have a jam session but it was disorganized and soon they tired of that activity. The talking had begun at a high pitch but gradually it diminished. I guess they were getting tired of an activity that they could do any old time. The only opportunity they had to play their instruments in an organized manner was during class time.

When the noise level began to diminish, I returned to the practice room. As I stepped up on the podium the students quieted down immediately. We then had the best rehearsal session we had ever had. I felt the fifteen minutes of "wasted time" was well spent because it convinced them they did not want to waste any more.

The band teacher's strategy of allowing the talking to continue worked in this instance, partly because the group was an advanced band class already musically talented and eager to produce. Their initial level of excitement, perhaps generated by events unknown to the band teacher, needed time to diminish. After fifteen minutes to settle down the students were ready to get on with the activity they all enjoyed.

The same strategy might not work with a group uninterested in the desired activity. The band teacher counted on the students' mutual interest in practicing together, an activity they could do only during the brief band rehearsal periods. In classes without a common objective the same strategy might have led to pandemonium and chaos.

ENDING A DISRUPTIVE CLASSROOM INFLUENCE

Fourteen-year-old Keith would not do his homework. He would not bring his materials to class, nor would he do anything constructive during the class period. He would talk and disrupt others as often as he could, making comments such as, "What do we need this junk for?" His teacher tells of the following action:

From the beginning Keith made it clear that he was going to do as little as possible in the class. Finally in desperation I said, "All right, Keith, I won't ask you to do any work if you will agree to stay in class and remain quiet. You may sit in the back of the room. You won't have to do anything. Just don't bother anybody else. The rest of us will simply pretend that you are not here."

The first few days after that he made an ostentatious show of his freedom to "loaf." He sprawled out, yawned, and even dozed at times. The rest of the class learned to ignore him.

Then a few days later I noticed he was listening to the class activities. Once or twice during interesting discussions he even tried to participate. The next morning he came in a few minutes before class and handed me his homework assignment for that day.

"Mr. Corman," he said, "I'm getting bored back there. May I take my regular seat again?" I knew what the request implied, so I said, "Sure, go ahead." After this experience Keith's behavior improved considerably. He had relapses, but for the most part his attitude toward class definitely changed. He turned in most of the homework assignments, began to bring his materials to class more regularly, and seldom talked out or disrupted learning activities.

Keith discovered that doing as he pleased was not really what he wanted to do. Sitting in a classroom with nothing to do proved to be less desirable than he had at first thought. However, the only way he could come to this realization was to give it a try. Mr. Corman's desperate move proved to be a successful strategy.

The strategy, however, might have failed. That other members of the class were able to ignore Keith undoubtedly contributed to the success of the treatment. If some class members had been amused, Keith might have continued his interruptions. As the situation turned out, simply giving Keith the latitude to behave as he thought he wanted to behave and to observe the consequences was sufficient to convince him that he would rather participate with the others in class.

The technique of allowing a child to continue performing an undesirable act may be particularly useful with adolescents who resent cueing and other forms of direct control. When possible, the toleration of the undesired activity enables the child to observe the consequence of the act and alleviates the necessity for a patronizing adult to say, "I told you so."

Allowing behavior to run its course is not the same as permissively condoning poor behavior. The Satiation Principle works best when the child discovers for himself that the rewards he received for poor behavior are not nearly as satisfying as the rewards he would get for some alternative behavior. The adult does not condone or reward the poor behavior. He merely allows the child to discover that the anticipated benefits do not live up to expectations.

INSISTING THAT THE UNDESIRED BEHAVIOR CONTINUE

STOPPING HORSEPLAY

While the ninth grade algebra teacher was busy at the blackboard explaining how to solve equations in two unknowns, several members of the class were moving their arms and hands in a peculiar series of motions and paying no attention to the explanation. The teacher reports what happened:

As I turned around from the blackboard, I noticed four or five people in a most unusual state of motion. Their arms were moving in an arc over their heads or were out to their sides moving in an up-and-down motion. As soon as they noticed I was looking at them, they stopped.

"What are you doing?" I asked.

"Nothing," replied one of the students.

"Oh, come on now, you certainly were doing something. Tell us what it was."

Finally one of the braver young ladies explained. "We were just bouncing an imaginary ball."

"What a wonderful idea!" I said. "Let's all do it. Come on. Everybody. Put your arms out to the side and bounce an imaginary ball with each hand. I'll do it with you."

Everyone in class began bouncing an imaginary ball with each hand, laughing and joking as they did it. After a minute the laughing and joking stopped. One of the students put his arms down looking exhausted.

"Oh, no you don't," I insisted. "This is too much fun. Nobody stops. Put your arms back up again and keep on bouncing the ball."

After two more minutes my own arms were getting tired. Others in the class started to drop their arms to their sides, but I insisted that they continue. We all continued until about five minutes had elapsed. Then, exhausted myself, I said, "Okay, that's enough."

No one bounced an imaginary ball in my classroom after that.

By insisting that the students continue bouncing the imaginary ball long after they had first tired of it, the teacher virtually guaranteed that the students would not want to start up that game again very soon.

A whole series of crucial educational questions are ignored by a rather simple procedure such as this. Why were the students engaging in horseplay instead of attending to the mathematical explanation? Was the explanation too difficult for them to understand? Did mathematics seem irrelevant to their everyday living? Or did they in fact need a break from the concentration? Horseplay in the classroom is often a sign that something is wrong with the quality of instruction. Either the course material is not interesting or important to the students, or the methods of teaching make the material unchallenging or too difficult.

The material may be interesting, relevant, and well taught for some members of the class but inappropriate for others. Arranging for these individual differences is one of the teacher's most complicated tasks. A teacher's first question may be, "How can I stop this horseplay?" But the second and more important question is, "What can I do so that the students in my class will not want to engage in horseplay?" An adult must beware of changing children's behavior just to suit his own comfort or convenience without considering whether each child is benefiting.

STOPPING SMOKING

Pepper's mother had discovered that he had been experimenting with cigarettes. On at least two occasions she had found him trying to smoke a cigarette butt that he found in an ashtray. Neighbors had reported to her that they had seen Pepper smoking in the company of other neighborhood boys. Since he was only eleven years old, his mother was eager to have him stop before he acquired the habit.

In her first attempt she used the lecture method to stop him from smoking: She had a serious talk with Pepper, advising him of the dire consequences of smoking. The next time she found evidence of his smoking she punished him by keeping him indoors and not allowing him to go outside after school. The punishment had little effect since one week later she again found him smoking.

"All right, Pepper, you think you would enjoy smoking. I am going to give you an opportunity to smoke right now."

Opening a pack of cigarettes, she gave him some matches and told him to light one. With some protesting he reluctantly and rather sheepishly did as he was told. After taking a few self-conscious puffs he started to put the cigarette out. But his mother told him that would be wasteful. "If smoking is fun, you should be able to continue it." Ten minutes later he had finished his first and his mother encouraged him to light another. Noticing that he was taking the smoke into his mouth but not inhaling it she said, "Smokers who really enjoy smoking breathe the smoke into their lungs. Why don't you try that?" Pepper hesitated, then tried inhaling in an attempt to show her he could, but coughing and gagging he left hurriedly to go to the bathroom. When he came back, she asked him if he wanted to continue. He said, "No more."

Pepper had had his fill. Not only did he stop smoking himself, but he even began to lecture the other neighborhood children against smoking, telling them that it would make them sick.

Pepper's habit of smoking had not progressed far at the time his mother applied this treatment. If he had already been inhaling and if he had become firmly fixed on the habit, his mother's insistence that he smoke cigarettes in rapid succession might not have been an effective way to get him to stop. Her technique involved a calculated risk but one which did prevent Pepper from developing a smoking habit.

The relationship between Pepper and his mother was probably harmed less by her insisting that he experiment than by her lecturing and detective work. The consequences Pepper experienced resulted from too much smoking, not from a hostile or undercover act by his mother, though some would question her judgment (see page 151).

When the Satiation Principle May Be Used

WHEN THE CHILD'S BEHAVIOR IS NOT
SERIOUSLY HARMFUL

Some behaviors are undesirable from an adult's point of view but not particularly harmful.

GROWING HAIR AND GROWING RESENTMENT

I should have had an inkling of what was happening when our son, Buz, fifteen years old at the time, delayed his traditional end-of-the-summer trip to the barber before school opened. It was only the beginning. When he didn't get it trimmed all fall, I was at my wit's end. At Christmas he accused me of constantly nagging and said something jolting about the generation gap in our family. I replied there wouldn't be any if he'd get his hair cut. This sort of argument continued for months and many unhappy hours resulted.

The following June, Buz was getting ready to take a driver education course in summer school. We had to sign permission papers for him to get a learner's permit, and I decided this was the time to act. I knew how badly he wanted to learn to drive.

"Buz, I'll sign those papers if you get your hair cut."

He was furious. But he went to the barber, I signed, and we've been at swords' points ever since. He has not returned to the barber again, and his hair looks positively indecent.

Long hair was not harmful to Buz. Hair styles and clothing styles vary from year to year. Adolescents follow the styles modeled by prestigeful heroes of their generation. Acceptance into the peer group may depend on conforming to current styles. Buz saw his mother's pressure as a threat to his social standing; their relationship suffered as a result.

Some rules are unnecessary. Schools that enforce dress codes tend to create resentment over trivial issues. School administrators and teachers have so much important work to accomplish that it seems unduly wasteful to spend time enforcing rules about slacks, skirt lengths, or hair lengths. If a costume is truly indecent, the police will enforce the appropriate law. If a costume is merely sensational, the attention it attracts will quickly dissipate with time. Attention from the authorities only serves to reinforce sensational behavior. The informal peer group pressure to conform serves as a much more effective dress code than any set of regulations imposed by authorities.

Food preferences are another unnecessary source of conflict.

EATING MORE THAN ONE FOOD

When his mother gave him mashed potatoes for dinner, two-and-a-half-year-old Randy would eat nothing else. When she put other food in his mouth, he would just hold it for a while and then spit it out.

His mother, applying the Satiation Principle, began giving him only mashed potatoes at every meal. After three days of eating nothing else Randy asked for some of the other food that was on the table. Although he would not eat a large variety of other things, Randy did broaden his taste.

Two years later his parents learned that Randy suffered from a severe overbite, making it difficult for him to chew food. His preference for mashed potatoes and other soft foods probably resulted from the difficulty he had in chewing.

Randy's preference for mashed potatoes turned out to be not merely a stubborn whim but in part a result of an undiscovered physical defect. Because some behavior problems may result from physical difficulties, a child should receive proper medical attention and periodic physical and dental checkups.

Allowing a child to stuff himself with mashed potatoes may worry some mothers who are concerned about an unbalanced diet. A parent might use the Successive Approximation and Modeling principles to teach a child to develop a taste for many foods.

ENDING SPITBALL THROWING

Chuck was a high ability member of an eighth grade science class. When there was written work to do, he would finish first. Most of the time he would patiently wait for the others to finish or would take extra time to check over his work. One day, however, he took a different course of action. Here is the teacher's account:

I noticed several spitballs on the floor. I watched out of the corner of my eye to discover their source. Soon I caught Chuck in the act of throwing another spitball. As I gathered up the written work, I quietly informed Chuck that I would like to talk with him after school.

When Chuck reported to me after school, I first pointed out the disadvantages of throwing spitballs during class. "But since you do seem to derive some satisfaction from throwing the spitballs, why not do it now? This is a particularly good time since you can't hit anyone in the eye and can't disturb anyone else." I arranged immediately for his practice session. I asked him to prepare fifty spitballs while I set up a few targets on the walls. Chuck was to aim for the targets and keep count as to how many he hit. After he threw them all, he was to go around and pick them all up, counting them to make sure he had not lost any. When the game began, Chuck was smiling, but he was quite serious by the time the whole procedure was over.

The next day I overheard Chuck's friends ask him what had happened when he stayed after school. His only reply was, "What's it to ya?" He threw no more spitballs in my class.

Chuck's career at spitball throwing came to a sudden stop soon after it began. By satiating him with the activity of spitball throwing, his teacher successfully brought the practice to a halt.

Why did Chuck throw spitballs in the first place? He was one of the brighter members in the class. He finished his work quickly and accurately and usually waited patiently for others to finish. Could other educational activities be arranged for him after he finished his written assignment? Could it not be that the teacher's failure to provide him with enough constructive work brought about his mischief making? The teacher may need to deal with the mischief directly but at the same time he should ask, "What important activities can I devise so that this student will not have time to be mischievous?"

WHEN THE CHILD NEEDS TO LEARN THE CONSEQUENCES
OF HIS ACTIONS

Learning from experience produces a more permanent memory of the lesson. An adult's words of advice about the dire consequences of an impetuous act may fall on deaf ears. Remember that Vicky discovered how she really felt about Jake only after she had had an opportunity to observe him around the home. No one else could have convinced her that Jake had a few unfortunate characteristics to accompany his more desirable ones; she had to discover them for herself.

> *MAKING SCHOOL ATTRACTIVE TO A DROP-OUT*
>
> Frank, at age 17, was an extremely quiet, nonparticipating, surly young man. His only school activity was swimming. He was civil to his swimming coach and other members of the swimming team, but to no one else. When he was a senior, he was elected co-captain of the team.
>
> One day in the middle of the swimming competition season he and a friend ran away from home. They left no explanation and no word as to where they went.
>
> Three weeks later the police found the runaways in a neighboring state working as dishwashers in an all-night diner. The boys' parents, the police, the school principal, and the swimming coach conferred on the problem and reached the decision to leave Frank and his friend alone. The police agreed to keep track of them without making direct contact. Within a week the two boys made their way home. Penniless and exhausted from the long hours of manual labor, they were warmly welcomed back by their parents.
>
> The adventure seemed to give Frank a new outlook on his high school education. He had a great deal of work to make up to qualify for graduation. Never before had he worked so diligently and conscientiously on his school assignments.

We cannot tell from this report exactly what Frank was thinking and feeling about his experience. We can only speculate that his escapade gave him some insights into what life might be like working at odd jobs without a high school education. His parents, cooperating with the authorities, decided not to take any actions to bring Frank back earlier. When they were assured of his physical safety, they elected to let Frank find out for himself what the life of a runaway would be like. He found out. If instead he had found a situation more rewarding than his home and school environment, he might have dropped out of his former existence.

A child may occasionally benefit from learning the consequences of his behavior in a direct confrontation.

REDUCING INCESSANT TALKING

Sixteen-year-old Cissy talked continuously. She talked to almost anybody who was present whether he listened or not. Her teenage companion on an extended bus trip reports the following sequence of events:

At first I listened politely as Cissy rambled on. I tried to insert some ideas of my own, but she only wanted to talk, not listen. Then I tried ignoring her completely. I would turn around and talk to the person in the seat behind me, or I would just stare into space.

Finally I tried a new tactic. When she came to the end of one of her little stories, I said, "Yes, and then what happened?" After she added to her story, I said, "And what happened after that?" Then when she said that was all that had happened, I asked her, "Could you please go through that once more?" She related the story again, although this time in somewhat abbreviated form. As she began to get briefer in her retelling, I encouraged her, "Oh, don't stop. Talk about something else." She started a new story and then interrupted herself, "Do you think I'm talking too much?"

"You figured it out," I said.

"Well, why is it I talk so much and you talk so little?" she asked, genuinely curious and somewhat reticent for the first time. I noticed she finally seemed really interested in listening, and from then on we were able to share ideas instead of giving monologues.

Cissy's listener confronted her with the fact that she was an incessant talker by insisting that she continue her story long after the point had been made and that she repeat the story until she tired of it. Cissy finally became aware of the consequences her behavior had on her companion. The frank confrontation jolted her into listening and sharing ideas. The method is not always successful since it may arouse hurt or anger, cutting off communication entirely.

WHEN THE CHILD NEEDS HELP IN IDENTIFYING ERRORS

Some people are unaware of their mistakes. Deliberately practicing an error sometimes helps. Practicing an error and then practicing the correct response gives the learner control over his behavior. The technique is particularly useful with habitual types of responses. For example, a typist who frequently typed *hte* instead of *the* found that by deliberately practicing the error and then practicing the correct spelling she became aware of the word when it appeared.

A novice drummer had a habit of playing seven strokes instead of five strokes on a particular drum roll. He was asked to practice the seven-stroke roll deliberately in order to help him gain control and distinguish it from the five-beat drum roll.

An English teacher, trying to teach his students to avoid clichés in their writing, generated this relevant assignment, described by one of his students:

ELIMINATING CLICHÉS FROM WRITING

Our instructor felt that we were all using too many clichés in our compositions. She asked us to write a 500-word composition consisting entirely of clichés. It was one of the hardest assignments I ever had to write.

Trying to think of all the trite phrases I knew, I put together a composition consisting entirely of sentences such as, "Driving to the mountains was real swell, but we were all packed into the car like sardines."

After writing that paper I could certainly recognize a cliché when I saw one. It cured me of using them and now I am happy as a clam.

When the Satiation Principle Should Not Be Used

WHEN THE BEHAVIOR MAY BE HARMFUL

When it is clear that a continuation of the behavior will result in someone's being hurt, allowing or insisting that the behavior continue is certainly unacceptable. For example, allowing a bully to continue beating up smaller children might eventually cure the

SEVENTEEN   By Bernard Lansky

"Your little boy was no trouble at all...I just let him do anything he wanted until he wore himself out!"

The Satiation Principle should not be used when the behavior is harmful.

bully of his habit, but a number of innocent children would be hurt. The Satiation Principle is not appropriate under these circumstances.

In some instances it is extremely difficult to judge whether continuing the behavior will be harmful. Pepper's smoking is a case in point. His mother's insisting that Pepper continue smoking cigarettes produced some temporary illness but resulted in his giving up the habit. Smoking also involves some long-range health hazards which must be considered. Someone must decide whether the possible benefit outweighs the possible harm.

WHEN CONTINUING THE BEHAVIOR RESULTS IN ADDITIONAL REINFORCEMENT

Sometimes additional reinforcement is given to a child resulting in a continuation of the undesired act. The child may thus be able to outlast the adult trying to satiate him.

PLAYING WITH MATCHES

The baby-sitter found seven-year-old Jimmy underneath his house playing with matches. She decided to try to satiate him on burning matches by insisting that he continue to light matches, anticipating that he would tire of the activity. A number of Jimmy's friends gathered around the house while he lit the matches. Jimmy would clown and throw the matches about as his friends laughed and joked with him. He would label some of his matches "torpedoes," light them, and slide them toward his audience. He would call others "bombs," tossing them high in the air to watch them fall. The crowd loved the show. After fifteen minutes the baby-sitter gave in, took all the matches away from Jimmy, and made him go into the house.

Later Jimmy bragged to a friend how he had vexed his baby-sitter. A week later his mother caught him playing with matches under the house again.

The baby-sitter made at least three mistakes in dealing with Jimmy. Her use of satiation was not wise under these circumstances since she encouraged the child in the dangerous practice of lighting matches.

The baby-sitter should never have attempted to satiate Jimmy in front of his friends, who gave him additional reinforcement. The technique might have worked if he had been isolated from any audience so that no one could have enjoyed his show.

The baby-sitter made the third mistake when she gave up too soon. Once embarked upon a course of satiation, she needed to stick it out to the end to make it work. Eventually even the playmates would get tired of the show and wander off. Jimmy could not continue indefinitely. Stopping the activity after fifteen minutes and at the peak of the show only convinced Jimmy that there was a great deal of reinforcement value in playing with matches.

WHEN THE REPEATED BEHAVIOR DIFFERS FROM THE UNDESIRED BEHAVIOR

One old-fashioned discipline method is to have a child repetitiously write about his misbehavior. For example, the child might have to write 100 times "I will not whisper in school." A better means of satiation is to ask the child to come in after school and whisper for an hour. Asking him to come in and write "I will not whisper in school" will only make him tired of writing. If the Satiation Principle is to work, the adult must insist that the child repeat the identical behavior that he wishes to stop.

The Satiation Principle is the first of four alternative ways of helping a child stop an undesirable practice. In Chapter 9 a second method is described.

9

Eliminating
Rewards

ELIMINATING AN INSULTING NICKNAME

Dear Ann Landers: I'm writing about the wife who didn't like it when an old schoolmate greeted her husband with, "If it isn't Dirty Neck Swanson." I don't blame her for not appreciating the nickname dredged up from grammar school.

You advised Mr. Swanson to tell his old friend with the big mouth to "knock it off." You said: "When dealing with insensitive clods the direct approach is the only way."

I disagree. Cloddish types are heartily encouraged when they discover their needling has struck a raw nerve. Here's my story:

When I was 17, I was a shade under 5 feet 5 inches. A few friends began to call me "Shorty." Dad was afraid I'd develop a complex so he gave me this advice: "Son," he said, "you will never be stuck with a nickname you don't answer to."

And he was right. From then on, when I heard "Shorty," I looked straight ahead and played deaf. Anyone who wanted my attention had to try another name.

If it worked for me I'm sure it will work for others, so please pass it on.—E. B. C.

Dear E. B. C.: Your Dad was a wise man. I wish I had thought of it. I'll use his advice the next time I'm asked.

By refusing to give any attention to those who called him "Shorty," E. B. C. stopped his "friends" from using that nickname. The insulting nickname was intended to rile him. Any protest on his part would reinforce those who were attempting to get him angry. Even when nicknames are used affectionately, they may still offend. When the intent is friendly, a direct approach might well be more effective: "You know, Les, I'm trying to forget that I'm not the tallest guy in class, so why don't you call me 'Ed' from now on."

Attention is reinforcing for most people. Like the actor who said, "I don't care what you print about me as long as you spell my name correctly," some people want to be noticed whether the notice is favorable or unfavorable. For them any action which gains the attention of others will tend to be repeated; any action which fails to gain the attention of others will be eliminated. One of the more effective ways of stopping an undesirable action is to pay absolutely no attention to it.

The Extinction Principle: To stop a child from acting in a particular way, you may arrange conditions so that he receives no rewards following the undesired act. The Extinction Principle represents the second alternative way of helping a child stop an

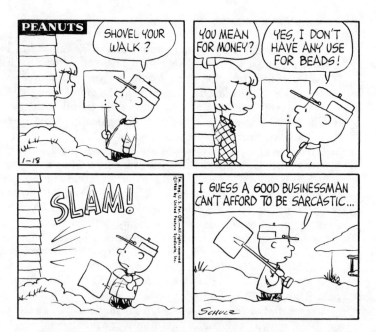

Behavior not followed by reinforcement tends to be extinguished.

undesirable type of action. It is the opposite extreme of the Satiation Principle described in Chapter 8.

A child may stop a behavior when he is tired of the behavior and its "rewards" (Satiation Principle) or when he never gets rewards for the behavior (Extinction Principle). One principle may be better than the other depending on the situation.

Do not alternate between principles. Choose one and apply it consistently. If you always reward an undesired behavior one day and never reward it the next, you will be intermittently rewarding the behavior you do not want. As we saw in Chapter 7, inconsistent rewards strengthen an established behavior.

Let us examine some situations where the Extinction Principle has been used.

- When Benjy has a temper tantrum, he throws himself down and bangs his head on the floor.
- Glen loves to "play ape" during tutoring sessions.
- Ginger interrupts whoever is talking when she thinks of something she wants to say in class.

- Teddy has acquired a salty vocabulary.
- Lenny fights with his younger sister.

When Omitting Rewards Is Likely to Work

WHEN THE BEHAVIOR ITSELF IS RELATIVELY HARMLESS

Some undesirable behaviors are annoying but not particularly harmful to the child or anyone else. Eliminating the reinforcement the child gets after the undesired behavior is one effective way of bringing that behavior to an end.

TERMINATING TEMPER TANTRUMS

Whenever he did not get his own way or did not receive the attention he wanted, Benjy would throw himself down, yell, scream, and hit his head on the floor.

Benjy was the first child in the family, and the arrival of his baby sister seemed to upset him terribly. The only way he could get his parents' attention now seemed to be to make a terrible racket and cause them to fear for his safety. When Benjy knocked his head on the floor for the first time, possibly accidentally, his mother quickly turned from the baby sister and picked him up and held him. Frequently when Benjy threw a temper tantrum his mother would yield to his desires, sometimes taking him out in the yard to play with him.

Benjy's parents felt his temper tantrums were growing worse and wondered if perhaps their actions were creating the tantrums. Therefore they decided to institute a new policy.

Whenever Benjy went into his temper tantrum act, his parents agreed that neither one would pay the slightest bit of attention to him. During the next several head-banging sessions he would ask his parents for a favor and if they denied it, he would bump his head some more. It was difficult for his parents to watch these episodes, so they simply walked out of the room. No longer did they grant favors after a tantrum.

Within a remarkably short time Benjy stopped the worst of his head-banging tactics. The action no longer paid off and, besides, it was painful to him.

As long as Benjy's parents knew that he would not seriously injure himself by hitting his head on the floor, the omission of reinforcement was a valuable technique. If he had been in danger of hurting himself seriously, they should have taken an alternative course of action. But if a child finds that he gets his own way after some self-destructive act (hitting his head, holding his breath), he will continue to use the only method that works for him.

Benjy's parents should help him learn some other ways of getting their attention. When a new baby arrives in the household, it may be wise to give the older child special jobs helping to care for the new baby so he won't feel left out. The newborn child knows only one way to get attention—yelling and crying. But as he grows older, the child needs to learn more acceptable ways of attaining it. The arrival of a second child is a convenient time to begin teaching the oldest child to assume some new responsibilities. He can learn to get attention by helping rather than by annoying.

WHEN YOU CAN CONTROL ALL SOURCES OF REINFORCEMENT

All reinforcement, not just part of it, must cease if the Extinction Principle is to work. Even though one adult no longer reinforces the behavior, other people in the environment may deliberately or unintentionally reinforce the same undesired behavior. Sometimes the parent or teacher may find it impossible to ignore the problem.

The Adult May Find It Difficult to Omit Reinforcement

Many people find it hard to ignore behavior they do not like. Just as a "poker face" is difficult for some card players, so is a "straight face" difficult for many concerned adults. In one family the children developed considerable proficiency in belching at the dinner table because their grandmother always spoke the name of the guilty belcher immediately after the belch in a tone of utter disgust and contempt. The other children mimicked their grandmother's tone of voice, calling out the name of the guilty party and thus providing a great deal of recognition for those proficient in belching. The grandmother could not bring herself to ignore a behavior she found undesirable.

The following report from a private tutor illustrates how his momentary uncontrolled reaction maintained an undesired behavior for some time.

"Try ignoring him."

The Extinction Principle stops another person's undesirable behavior only when you can control all his sources of reinforcement.

ENDING MONKEYSHINES

I was tutoring two brothers, ages seven and nine. One day when I was trying to get the children to do their assignments, Glen, the seven year old, started walking like an ape. Kent, his older brother, said, "You look like an ape!" Glen's quick reply was, "You're my brother, you're my brother!" At the moment this struck me very funny and I laughed uproariously.

For days thereafter whenever things became quiet or dull, Glen would play ape. Even though I never again laughed at his antics, it took several weeks for his ape attacks to subside.

As long as he could control his own behavior and ignore Glen's antics, the tutor was able to bring the apeplay under control. His own uncontrolled laughter at one time gave Glen the reinforcement to continue for several weeks.

Anyone who has tried to omit reinforcement completely knows how difficult it can be. However, either intentional or spontaneous reactions can reinforce behavior.

Reinforcement from Other Sources Must Also Be Controlled

STOPPING CLASSROOM INTERRUPTIONS

Ginger would not wait her turn to share ideas in the third grade classroom but would interrupt whoever was talking whenever she thought of something to say. The teacher discussed with the class the rules for sharing ideas,and the class agreed on a "courtesy rule" of raising hands and waiting turns before sharing ideas during class discussion. Even though she had taken part in establishing the new courtesy rule, in the next class discussion Ginger again broke the rule.

The class then agreed that they simply would not listen to anyone who broke the courtesy rule. When Ginger interrupted, the teacher and the class would try not to look at her or give any indication that they heard but would continue to devote their attention to the person who had permission to speak. After being ignored three times in a row, Ginger stopped interrupting, raised her hand, and waited her turn to speak.

The teacher wisely involved the whole class in establishing the courtesy rule. The teacher alone could not ignore the interruptions; instead the entire class had to agree upon the rule and enforce it by simply ignoring those who violated it.

ELIMINATING OBSCENE LANGUAGE

Four-year-old Teddy had begun to insert terms such as "Oh, shit" into his vocabulary around the house. He was picking up the vocabulary from some of the older neighborhood boys. The first time she heard Teddy use this language, his mother was inwardly startled but she checked her immediate reaction both to laugh and scold. Instead she pretended not to have heard anything that Teddy said. She waited until Teddy said something else without using his newfound vocabulary and then responded to that. When her husband came home that evening, she informed him of the latest development and both parents agreed to pay no attention to anything Teddy said if it involved the use of words they considered undesirable.

Since the words produced no attention for him whatsoever and since he had no models using these words at home, within two weeks Teddy stopped using his obscene vocabulary around the house.

We do not know from this brief example whether Teddy used more salty language outside the home. Children learn to use the language that gets them what they want. Teddy could quite possibly have learned one language for use at home and, if he were reinforced by his peers for it, another language for use on the street.

Important Cautions

OMITTING REINFORCERS DIFFERS GREATLY FROM TAKING AWAY REINFORCERS

Not giving candy to a child has a far different effect than giving candy to a child and then taking it away again. Although the end result may be the same—that is, the child ends up without any candy—the psychological effect is quite different. Taking away a reinforcer which has already been received is a form of punishment and has definite effects on the child. These effects (see Chapters 11 and 12) are so risky that punishment cannot be recommended as a regular and dependable procedure for stopping undesirable behavior.

Taking away a reward or privilege which has already been given constitutes punishment; *withholding* a reward or privilege not yet given is not punishment. For example: "Since you didn't work yet, I'm taking away what you earned last week" is punishment. But "Since you didn't work yet, you don't get paid yet" is withholding a reinforcer (not punishment). The distinction is an important one because of the different effects on a child's behavior.

A Broken Promise Is Punishment (Reinforcement Taken Away)

QUELLING QUARRELS

"Lenny, I have a surprise for you. This afternoon I'm going to take you with me when I go shopping and we'll get a chocolate ice cream cone."

At lunch time Lenny began quarreling with his younger sister and spilled his soup all over the floor. His mother became angry and said, "Just for that, I'm not going to take you to get an ice cream cone this afternoon after all." Lenny broke into great sobs and screamed, "You promised, you promised. I didn't mean to. I didn't know you'd do that!"

Alternative episode

"Lenny, if you are able to play with your sister today without quarreling or fighting with her, we'll have a surprise this afternoon. I'll take you to the shopping center and buy you a chocolate ice cream cone. But only if you and your sister get along peacefully until then."

That noon Lenny quarreled with his sister and spilled his soup. His mother said, "Lenny, did you notice that you were quarreling with your sister?"

"Yes."

"Okay, I just wanted to make sure that you noticed." Lenny says, "Does that mean that I don't get any chocolate ice cream cone this afternoon?"

"What did I say earlier this morning?"

"Okay, I know what it means but I don't like it."

In the first episode the mother promised an ice cream cone with no conditions attached. Then when she became angry at Lenny's misbehavior, she broke her promise to him by in effect taking away the ice cream cone she had promised. Even though it had not actually been placed in his hands, the ice cream cone had definitely been promised. The mother's withdrawal of the ice cream cone was a punishment. Lenny screamed and protested at this broken promise. The relationship between mother and child suffered as a result.

In the second episode the promise of the ice cream cone was contingent upon the absence of quarreling between Lenny and his sister. When he did quarrel with his sister, his mother called the fact to his attention. She actually would not necessarily have had to remind him that there would be no ice cream cone that afternoon except that he decided to ask about it. Lenny certainly was not happy about what happened, but the result was clearly due to his own behavior, and he knew that no special reward would be forthcoming if he engaged in quarreling behavior. Having no justifiable complaint, his respect for his mother's integrity remained unimpaired even though he did not enjoy the outcome.

Adults need not feel guilty about enforcing the rules for fear that their children will dislike them. Children respect consistency. If Lenny's mother had surprised him with an ice cream cone anyway, she would have taught him that quarreling is rewarded and that her word is not to be trusted.

Unspoken Promises Are Sometimes Inferred from Past Behavior

ANNOYING OTHER SWIMMERS

In swimming class Bert would splash water in the faces of other children, particularly younger girls. Despite repeated scolding, explanations, and warnings he continued to splash water and disturb the other swimmers when he thought the instructor wasn't looking.

Every day at the end of the regular swimming class the students had a free fifteen-minute period. One day when Bert continued his splashing of younger children, his instructor told him that he could not stay in the pool for the free swim. Bert became very upset.

When his instructor mentioned that the free swim period was a special reward for those who behaved themselves, Bert complained that everyone else was being allowed to swim and he should be too. He said that he had been allowed to swim during the free period every other day he had splashed, and he didn't see why today was any exception. The instructor stuck to his decision.

Bert went home and complained to his mother about how unfairly he had been treated. She in turn phoned to hear the whole story. The instructor concluded, "I think his mother finally understood the situation from our point of view, but I don't think Bert ever did."

An alternative procedure could have made a difference in the way Bert reacted to virtually identical circumstances. The swimming instructor might have said, "Bert, we have decided that you have received enough warnings. The free swimming period after instruction is a special privilege. Beginning tomorrow if you splash water in the faces of any of the other children, I want you to know that you will not receive that special privilege. Do you understand that?" If Bert clearly understands the contingencies in advance and still goes ahead and splashes the smaller children, then he has no justifiable complaint.

The instructor might argue that the free swim period had always been a special privilege. However because the privilege had been granted to everyone regardless of their behavior and because Bert had received it despite his many previous splashings, an implicit promise did exist. Taking away a privilege that has long been established through custom will be perceived as punishment. It seems the better part of wisdom to make clear in advance any changes in the contingencies of reinforcement so that a child knows beforehand what consequences his behavior will bring.

GOOD BEHAVIORS MAY BE EXTINGUISHED UNINTENTIONALLY

DISCOURAGING PARTICIPATION BY IGNORING INITIAL CONTRIBUTIONS

Helen was shy in her high school classes. She would come into her American government class quietly and unobtrusively. Although she always handed her written work in on time she never participated in class discussions.

Helen had been on a committee to investigate the organizational structure of the city hall. Her committee had interviewed the mayor, the police chief, and the city manager. When the five committee members gave a report, Helen read hers also. It was the first time she had spoken in class. The class members asked questions of the other four committee members who then became involved in an animated discussion. Neither the teacher nor any other class member made any effort to include Helen in the discussion. Helen did not volunteer. She continued to sit quietly, making herself as unnoticed as possible. If anything, she seemed less comfortable than before.

If the teacher were concerned with helping Helen increase her participation in class activities, the actions described here certainly could not have helped. Helen's efforts to participate met with no reinforcement whatsoever. Undoubtedly the teacher did not intend to extinguish Helen's efforts to participate, but good intentions are irrelevant. No reinforcement was given as Helen made what for her must have been a strong initial effort to participate. Desirable behavior as well as undesirable behavior can be extinguished by the failure to reinforce it.

YOU CAN WITHHOLD REWARDS AND STILL BE UNDERSTANDING

Children sometimes complain that adults don't understand them. Too often the complaint is well justified. We may fail to listen and understand problems from the child's point of view. However, an adult can understand a child and let him know that he is understood without necessarily doing what the child wants. Understanding a child's problem does not necessarily require acquiescence to his requests.

When Leta was eight years old, her family moved ten miles away to a new community. Leta was unhappy with the move since she had to leave her friends and familiar surroundings. She would mope around the house, bemoan her loneliness, engage in crying tantrums, and ask her mother to drive her back to see old friends.

Her mother was understanding. She would say to Leta, "I know exactly how you must feel. You feel lonely without your good friends. You miss all the good times you had playing in our old neighborhood."

The mother was so sympathetic to her daughter's point of view that she spent much of her free time transporting Leta back to the old neighborhood.

We do not know exactly what the mother's goals might have been. Certainly she was reinforcing Leta's whining and crying. Perhaps she too resented having to move to a new community and deliberately (or unknowingly) reinforced Leta's behavior to pressure her husband. Whatever her motivations, the effect on Leta was clear: By whining, crying, and complaining about her loneliness, not only could she elicit sympathy and understanding from her mother, but she could wrangle a trip back to her old neighborhood as well.

It is important to distinguish a sympathetic understanding from the actions that would remedy the problem. The mother did a good job of letting Leta know that she did understand. But what action would be most helpful? Returning to the old environment took time that Leta could have used to make new friends. How could she learn to get acquainted in the new neighborhood? After initially expressing her understanding of Leta's feelings, her mother might have begun to talk with her about what could be done. Helping her locate playmates in the new neighborhood and encouraging her to invite new classmates to her home would probably benefit Leta more in the long run.

Leta will have to move many other times during her lifetime if she is like most people in our society today. Her first move is a good opportunity to learn the skills needed in getting reestablished.

An unhappy person makes himself unhappy by something he is doing. To overcome these unhappy feelings he must do something different—something incompatible with feeling unhappy. Leta needed to make some new friends so she would not be lonely in her new neighborhood. Chapter 10 presents other examples of how a person can be reinforced for engaging in behavior incompatible with unhappy feelings.

10

Rewarding
Alternative
Behavior

LEARNING TO CARE FOR PLANTS

My five-year-old daughter, Shelley, seemed to have no appreciation for the effort and pride I put into my garden. She would
wander across my flowers and vegetables, trampling them and
digging them up, probably thinking she was imitating me. My
scoldings produced tears but no lessening of her desire to "help"
me.

Finally inspiration struck. "Shelley, would you like to have a
garden all your own?" I arranged a tiny plot of land that would
belong only to her. I gave her some seeds that would grow at
different rates during the summer and showed her how to plant
them. I put some beans in a little glass dish between pieces of
damp paper towel so that she could see how the roots formed
as they anchored the plants in the soil.

One day I noticed how pleased Shelley was when she showed
some tiny carrots to her neighborhood friends. As she began to
take pride in the work she was doing in her garden she became
careful not to trample or destroy her plants and so learned not
to destroy mine either.

Neither of the two methods for stopping undesirable behavior in
Chapters 8 and 9 would be appropriate here. Shelley's mother
would not want her to trample the garden until the child tired of it
(the Satiation Principle). Shelley could not be prevented from
receiving intrinsic rewards and satisfactions from walking and
digging in the garden as her mother did (the Extinction Principle).
Her mother came on the most valuable way of helping a child stop
an undesirable behavior—arranging for the child to engage in an
alternative type of behavior which she could reward.

To some mothers the extra planning and work would have
seemed too burdensome. Shelley's mother saw the work not only
as a way to save the flowers but as a way to help Shelley learn to
share her love for gardening.

The experience of Shelley's mother illustrates the third and most
important way of helping a child stop some undesirable type of
behavior.

**The Incompatible Alternative Principle: To stop a child from
acting in a particular way, you may reward an alternative action
that is inconsistent with or cannot be performed at the same time
as the undesired act.**

Here are some illustrative situations adaptable to the Incompatible Alternative Principle:

Encourage incompatible alternative behavior.

- Walt likes to spit sunflower seeds and throw banana peels around at school.
- Alex spends his evenings loitering with friends on the street corner.
- Three-year-old Becky thinks washing the car is great fun, much to the consternation of the neighbor who is trying to get the job completed.
- Allison loves putting her sticky hands on the windows to see the imprint on the glass.
- Yvonne, sent to the office for disciplinary reasons, distracts the principal's secretary from her work.
- Ray prefers watching television to helping his father with the ranch repair jobs.

Finding Suitable Alternative Behavior

The most appropriate kind of alternative behavior is that which is diametrically opposite to the undesired behavior. Sometimes, however, it is not possible to devise a behavior diametrically opposed, but only one that cannot be performed at the same time. The alternative behavior may at a minimum be only a distraction. In any event the problem is to devise some alternative behavior that can be rewarded and is incompatible with the undesired behavior. Let us review some examples of each type.

ALTERNATIVE BEHAVIOR WHICH IS OPPOSITE TO THE UNDESIRED ACTIVITY

One method of helping a child find satisfaction in a behavior opposite to that previously performed is to give him a new responsibility that will be rewarding. The new job may be to prevent the kind of problem behavior that the child previously exhibited himself.

LITTERING VERSUS HEADING THE ANTI-LITTER CAMPAIGN

Walt seemed to have little respect for the junior high school property. He had the habit of eating sunflower seeds and spitting the shells out in the corridor, in the classrooms and on the playground. During the lunch hour he threw banana peels, waxed paper, and food around the lunchroom. A teacher reported what happened next.

In a school staff meeting someone suggested the idea of having an anti-litter committee. I suggested putting Walt on the committee. The students elected the chairman and guess who it was —Walt! It was like putting a wolf in charge of the sheep. The principal made a bit of a ceremony out of appointing the committee, asking the members to come to the front of the auditorium during a school assembly at which time Walt was announced as the chairman.

When he was asked for his advice about the kinds of things he thought his committee could do to help make the school a cleaner place, Walt had more ideas than anyone else. Perhaps it takes a thief to catch a thief. The committee launched a poster campaign designed to remind litterbugs to use the garbage cans and waste baskets. They posted monitors in the lunchroom to remind children about the proper disposal of their lunch remnants.

Walt received a great deal of recognition for his success. The school took on a new appearance, littered now mainly by anti-litter posters. Miraculously, although no one said anything directly to Walt about it, we no longer found any sunflower seed shells on the floor.

Perhaps it was dangerous to give responsibility for the anti-litter campaign to the person most responsible for producing litter. The principal could have structured the situation so that it appeared that Walt was being chastised for his littering. Instead he gave a responsibility to Walt and arranged for him to have recognition. To be successful in this new responsibility Walt had to engage in behavior diametrically opposite to the behavior he previously exhibited.

If one can identify and describe precisely what kind of behavior is undesirable, then the opposite behavior can also be described. The very first indications of the new, more desirable behavior should be rewarded when they occur. For example, we may reinforce cooperative play instead of fights, neatness instead of sloppiness, accurate statements instead of lies or exaggerations. The key to success is in making the desirable behavior yield more positive consequences than the undesirable behavior.

ALTERNATIVE BEHAVIOR WHICH CANNOT BE PERFORMED AT THE SAME TIME AS THE UNDESIRED ACTIVITY

The adult may not always be sufficiently in control of the situation to reinforce a behavior in diametrical contradiction to the undesired behavior. However, it might be possible to reinforce activities taking up the time that otherwise would be involved in undesired activities. One such example is provided by a community recreation worker.

ENDING POTENTIALLY SERIOUS VANDALISM

Fifteen-year-old Alex hung around with two or three friends who frequently got into minor trouble. He and his buddies would loiter on street corners, harass and annoy passersby, and occasionally engage in minor mischief such as breaking street lights.

I was in charge of a neighborhood youth center, so I invited Alex and his buddies to come over some evening to play basketball. I had to invite them six times before they finally showed up, but I made certain they got involved in a good basketball game their first night. After that they came around almost every evening. Alex's parents learned of this new activity and encouraged him by buying him a pair of basketball shoes. I think we got to Alex before he became involved in any really serious misdemeanors.

Playing basketball was not in direct opposition to breaking street lights, but both activities were impossible to do at the same time.

ALTERNATIVE BEHAVIOR WHICH DISTRACTS FROM UNDESIRED ACTIVITY

Distractions may work better with small children who cannot appreciate logical consequences.

SWIMMING IN SHALLOW WATER ONLY

Four-year-old Bruce was unafraid of the water, in fact so unafraid that he would wander out toward the deep end of the pool even though he was unable to swim well enough to protect himself. I knew I could frighten him into staying on the shallow side of the rope, but I did not want to make him afraid of the deep water. I simply wanted him to stay in the shallow water until he was a better swimmer.

Whenever we went swimming I would arrange for one of his brothers or sisters to play one of his favorite water games, "Dunk the Doughnut" or "Ring Around," in the shallow end of the pool. The games improved his swimming ability and kept him diverted from the deep end of the pool. We were able to teach him to swim without instilling a fear of deep water.

Another successful diversionary tactic is illustrated by a neighbor who was trying to wash his car while a three-year-old girl tried to "help."

DISTRACTING A FRIENDLY PEST

Every time I tried to wash my Volkswagen, little Becky would hang around, be in the way, and get splashed. I tried to reason with her and then, exasperated, I tried force—that was a mistake. She began to wail. I didn't want her parents to think I was mistreating her, but I didn't want her under the hose either.

Finally, I said, "Becky, how would you like to pretend you're driving my car in the rain?" She loved playing inside the car (keys were removed), especially when I would squirt water at the window. She was out of my way, happy inside the car, and I had a clean car without having to wash a little girl.

In the short run this method may have been unbeatable. The possible danger is that Becky might at some future time find keys in the car and really try driving. Becky would have to be taught when it was, and when it was not, permissible to get inside the car alone (see Chapter 5).

Practicing Alternative Behavior in Advance

As children grow older they will inevitably have to face increasingly complicated problem situations. We cannot anticipate what all of these problems will be, but we can prepare for some.

REFUSING DRUGS

Katie's parents knew from the local newspaper that the junior high school in their community had a problem with marijuana. Although thirteen-year-old Katie was not yet involved, they wanted to help her anticipate what might happen. According to her father the conversation went something like this:

"I see by the paper, Katie, that five students at the junior high school were picked up by the police for possession of marijuana."

"I don't know why kids use that stuff."

"You sound as if you're not interested in trying it out."

"They've told us at school about some of the dangers of using it, and we've seen a movie about drugs. I don't think I'd ever want to try it."

"But Katie, someday your friends will put pressure on you to try it, and you may not be able to refuse."

"Well, what would you do if your friends tried to get you to do it, Dad?"

"I'd just say 'No thank you'."

"I wonder if I could do that."

"Well let's try it and see. Let's pretend that we're at a party. I'm one of your good friends. A bunch of kids at the party are all smoking marijuana. You be yourself. Pretend I come up to you and say, 'Katie, why don't you try one of these joints?' What would you say?"

"No thank you."

'Don't be such a super-straight, Katie. Come on, join in the crowd. Everybody's doing it. It really won't hurt you a bit. It will make you feel good.'

"Thanks for the offer, but I really don't care to."

'Just one puff, Katie. You'll really love it. Look around. All the kids are doing it. Everybody thinks it's all right. Don't be so uptight.'

"Thanks all the same, but I'm really quite happy as I am."

'Katie, give me just one good reason why you won't at least try it. Don't you believe in experimenting? Don't you think it would be fun to try something new and different? You don't want to be one of those hung-up straights do you?'

"I believe everybody should do his own thing. Some people get high on marijuana. I get high on fresh air."

"Katie, that was a beautiful answer so let's stop play-acting. You really stood up to all that pressure without even getting angry at them."

"It wasn't so hard, Dad."

One such role-playing episode is, of course, no total solution to Katie's future exposure to the complex drug scene. Nevertheless it does illustrate a useful technique for helping a child anticipate a problem and practice some alternative behavior. Sometimes parent and child can exchange places in the role-playing. The child can then observe how the parent would have handled the same situation. The child can then try his own part and experiment with alternative responses until he finds some that seem useful.

Providing Rewards for Alternative Behavior

NEW BEHAVIOR MAY HAVE ITS OWN REWARDS

HELPING TO KEEP WINDOWS CLEAN

Six-year-old Allison had the habit of putting her sticky hands on the window as she looked out of her house. She also pressed her face and nose against the glass, leaving spots and smudges.

Allison's mother asked her if she would like the job of washing windows. With the aid of modern spray-can window cleaners Allison relished her new responsibility. She would spray the window cleaner, rub vigorously, and beam with pleasure at the polished result. After that day she was critical of anyone who attempted to touch her clean glass.

No extra reward was necessary to encourage Allison to substitute window washing for window dirtying. The reward was in performing the new activity—pushing the button on the spray can—and in seeing the results—clean windows.

Being trusted with a responsibility is in itself highly reinforcing to a child who up until then has seldom been trusted.

REDUCING HOSTILITY TOWARD SCHOOL

When there is a disciplinary problem in the classroom of one of the summer session high school classes, the troublemaking student is sent down to the office of the principal. Often the principal is not there so the student must wait. With nothing to do many of these students cause more trouble. The principal's secretary described one event:

When Yvonne came in I noticed her hostility immediately. Instead of waiting quietly she would stop other students walking down the hall, make a lot of noise, and distract me from my work. That day I was extremely pressed with extra jobs, so I asked Yvonne if she would be willing to help me with a rush job that had to get out. She jumped at the chance to do the stapling job, and right away I could see a change in her attitude. She worked diligently at stapling and asked me if she could help with something else when she finished.

As we began talking, I learned about the source of her difficulty. She felt that her parents were forcing her to go to summer school to take a class in which she had no interest.

The principal conferred with Yvonne and her parents, and eventually they all agreed that she would work part-time in the high school office as a student helper and still receive some partial summer school credit. I found her a responsible, pleasant person to work with, and we had no repetition of the troublemaking either in or outside of class.

A combination of factors led to Yvonne's hostile attitude: She had no desire to attend summer school, she was taking a class in which she had no interest, and probably the teacher in that class was doing little to arouse her interest. A normal reaction to these aversive conditions is resistance. Yvonne fought back by causing trouble in the classroom and then in the principal's office. The school secretary, more out of her own necessity than out of concern for Yvonne, asked her to assume some small responsibilities in the office.

Yvonne may have been rewarded by this evidence that someone thought she could be useful, or she may have enjoyed working at a job where she could clearly see the results. In any event she

"We want something real nice to give our daughter for not rebelling."

Reward some specific alternative action, not merely the absence of the undesired behavior.

found positive rewards in an alternative activity and probably learned more than she would have in class.

EXTERNAL REWARDS MAY BE ADDED

Some alternative behavior does not provide a sufficient amount of reinforcement in itself. Added reinforcement may be necessary.

INCREASING WILLINGNESS TO DO CHORES

At the age of twelve Ray could hardly be moved from the television set. He procrastinated about doing his chores because he would rather watch almost any television program. One Saturday afternoon his mother finally persuaded Ray to go out to help his father repair some fences on the ranch. His father was a man of few words and said nothing directly to Ray about his work.

That evening a family friend dropped by and Ray's father mentioned the work his son had done in the afternoon: "Ray worked like a real man." The boy overheard the remark.

After that Ray began to be more cooperative in doing his chores. His father remained as taciturn as ever, but the two of them seemed to work together as a team.

Responsibility was nothing new to Ray. He had responsibility for many chores but apparently got little satisfaction out of performing them. When Ray overheard his father's praise, it held much significance for him. Sometimes such indirect recognition is more powerful than direct praise.

Cautions

THE SUBSTITUTED BEHAVIOR MUST NOT BE A REWARD FOR THE UNDESIRED ACTIVITY

REWARDING AGGRESSION UNINTENTIONALLY

Kurt was the most aggressive boy in nursery school. He would knock down other children's block towers, take away their toys, throw water around the room, prevent other children from going about their business, and generally make a nuisance of himself.

The policy at his nursery school was never to reprimand a child for bad behavior. The main technique was to distract the troublesome child. Whenever Kurt engaged in an aggressive act, a teacher would try to divert his attention. Frequently Kurt would end up sitting on a teacher's lap having a story read to him. He seemed to get more love and attention when he was hostile than when he was not. However this "love" was insincere since the teachers came to dislike Kurt.

Kurt's behavior progressed from bad to worse. He began kicking and spitting at other children and at the teachers, knocking children off their tricycles and hitting them. Finally he was asked to leave the school.

The difficulty here is that the teachers distracted Kurt immediately *after* his inappropriate behavior. These distractions proved to be highly reinforcing. In effect they reinforced Kurt for his hostile and aggressive behaviors, increasing such behavior to the point where he had to be removed from the school.

Kurt's hostile behavior might have lessened or stopped entirely if the teachers had rewarded him for engaging in some behavior incompatible with aggressive responses: playing cooperatively with another child, sharing one of his toys with another child, helping another child to build a block tower, helping to clean up the playroom, or playing quietly by himself. If the teachers had given Kurt special attention, read to him, let him sit on their lap after successive approximations to behaviors like these, the outcome might have been quite different. The teachers might then have found that they did sincerely love him.

Whether a child might see an alternative activity as a reward for the original behavior is difficult to gauge in advance. The adult may have to wait until he can observe the child's reaction to the substituted behavior. The test is in the frequency of the undesired behavior. If the frequency increases, the alternative rewarded it. If the frequency decreases, the substitution was successful.

THE SUBSTITUTED BEHAVIOR SHOULD NOT PRODUCE UNPLEASANT CONSEQUENCES

LEARNING THAT HONESTY IS NOT THE BEST POLICY

Spike was frequently lectured on the importance of telling the truth. However, he was often caught in lies.

One day Spike accidentally swung his arms about carelessly, knocking over his mother's glass vase. It crashed to bits on the floor. When his mother questioned him, he denied all knowledge of the event. Finally, when questioned again several days later, he admitted that he had knocked the vase over. His angry mother said that he could not play outside after school for the rest of the month. She told him, "You should never have lied to me. For two days you have been telling me that you didn't do it. This will teach you a lesson."

After that Spike seldom admitted the truth when it could possibly do him any harm.

People learn to tell the truth or to tell lies depending upon the consequences that arise after either kind of action. Those who are rewarded for telling the truth will tell the truth; those who are rewarded for telling lies will tell lies. Spike avoided aversive consequences as long as he lied about his responsibility for the broken vase. However, as soon as he told the truth, he was severely punished. His lying was rewarded; his honesty was punished. Under these circumstances he will almost certainly learn to be a liar.

His mother might have responded, "Spike, I am pleased that you were able to tell me how that vase came to be broken. I'm sure you didn't mean to break it. Maybe you could go with me to help pick out a new one. Would you be willing to help pay part of the cost of a new vase by working around the house to earn some money?" Spike's honest report would be rewarded, but he would not be absolved of responsibility for doing something about replacing the damage he caused even though the damage was accidental.

The traits of honesty and dishonesty are learned through a series of concrete events that are usually soon forgotten. But the results of these events may shape a career.

11

Ending
an Aversive
Situation
When Behavior
Improves

ENDING SURLINESS

Some days my eight-year-old daughter Kim would "get up on the wrong side of the bed." She would be touchy or downright grouchy. Nothing I could do for her was ever quite right. On such days she could find fault with an angel's halo.

For a long time I tried to be unusually understanding and cooperative with her. I went out of my way to humor her and tried to comply with her demands, assuming that she was not feeling on top of things and needed extra sympathy. But the nicer I was, the worse she got.

When I finally realized that I had actually been reinforcing her grouchiness by my extra attentions to her, I knew I had to change my own behavior. Unfortunately I had been reinforcing her in this way for years, and I knew it was not going to be easy to change either my behavior or hers.

One day she came storming into the living room demanding in a disparaging voice, "You have to sew this button on my dress. You never take care of my clothes. How do you expect me to wear this dress when a button is off?"

At first I was tempted to run to get my needle and thread. However, I realized I would simply be rewarding her demanding behavior. So I tried to extinguish it by refusing to respond.

But Kim escalated the battle by yelling and hurling insults at me for neglecting her clothes. "You're a terrible mother. If you loved me, you would take care of me. You must hate me or you would sew on this button."

I knew now that the time for confrontation had arrived. In a voice more controlled than I really felt, I said, "Kim, I would like you to ask me politely to sew on that button. When you ask me in a calm, polite voice, I will do it." However, my studied reasonableness only sent her into a more violent tantrum.

Finally I said, "Kim, the way you are behaving annoys me very much. I want you to go to your room and stay there until you can come out and ask me in a polite way to sew on your button. You may come out of your room as soon as you can be sweet. Now go."

Kim stomped into her room, slammed the door, and howled and cried for fifteen minutes. It seemed even longer than that to me. Then she came out and in a sarcastic tone said, "Won't you please sew on my button like you're supposed to?"

"When you can come out and ask me in a polite and sweet way, I will do it. What you just said was sarcastic. Go back and try again. Wait until you feel that you can be sweet and then come out and ask me." She burst into tears and returned to her room. The crying simmered down after about ten minutes and then all was quiet for an hour. Kim opened the door and quietly

approached me. "Mom, could you please sew on this button?"
"Certainly," I said, dropping everything else I was doing.
"What color thread do you think we should use?"
"I think light green would match the best," said Kim.

Kim's mother was quick to reward her polite request. Kim needed to learn that a polite request got prompt attention whereas a sarcastic request got nothing. However, her temperamental behavior had been reinforced for so long that more drastic action was needed when the situation became too much for her mother to tolerate.

Kim was sent to her room but was permitted to leave as soon as she felt she could behave better. She was not sent to her room for an hour or for fifteen minutes or for any other fixed period of time. As soon as she felt she could ask politely, Kim could terminate her own aversive situation. When she came out of her room the first time, however, she did not ask politely but continued in an offensive tone of voice. Her mother could not accept this behavior and therefore asked her to return to her room again.

Finally Kim was able to come out of her room and ask politely. Under these circumstances Kim was in control of her own behavior, for as soon as she asked politely, she terminated her own isolation.

Kim's behavior provides a good illustration for the fourth method of stopping inappropriate behavior, stated as the **Negative Reinforcement Principle: To stop a child from acting in a particular way, you may arrange for him to terminate a mild aversive situation immediately by improving his behavior.**

Note that the child terminates the aversive situation by improving his own behavior. The noxious conditions exist only as long as the child's behavior is unacceptable. Don't confuse this negative reinforcement with the use of punishment.

THE BORN LOSER   By ART SANSOM

Negative reinforcement is ending an aversive situation.

Why Punishment Is Not Recommended

It is possible to punish a child in two different ways: You can do something aversive or painful to him—spank him, slap his hand, insult him, or belittle him with sarcastic remarks. Or you can take away something he considers rewarding—his toys, his television privileges, or his freedom to move about (such as by confining him in his room).

Neither type of punishment is necessary or desirable except in rare instances. Yet most adults use punishment more frequently than they would wish, perhaps because they know no alternatives o. because they cannot control their own hostilities (see the self-control suggestions, pages 233–34).

NEGATIVE REINFORCEMENT IS BETTER THAN PUNISHMENT

Let us take another look at the case of Kim and her mother. Suppose at the height of Kim's fussiness her mother had said, "I can't stand it when you talk that way. As a punishment you must go to your room and stay there for one hour."

Four things are wrong with such a punishment:

1. When the hour is up, Kim can come out even though her behavior has not improved. She will have served her sentence and "paid her debt to society," but she may well continue to be just as grouchy as she was before she went in.

2. Although she knows that her mother did not like something she did, Kim may not know exactly what behavior she is expected to change. This punishment tells the child that something is wrong but does not necessarily help her understand what it is.

3. The child may well decide to be sweet in much less time than one hour. It is wasteful and inefficient to require an hour for a job that may take only a few minutes.

4. If she gains control of herself quickly but is required to spend a full hour in her room, she may revert to her grouchy state. If she is released from her room at the end of one hour while she is still grouchy, then her mother will unintentionally be reinforcing her for grouchiness. The behavior occurring just prior to release from an aversive condition tends to be strengthened.

But didn't Kim's mother use punishment? How does the Negative Reinforcement Principle differ from the use of punishment? At the moment her mother sent Kim into her room depriving her of her freedom she was using punishment, but the punishment was to *end* when Kim's behavior improved—that is the crucial point. The Negative Reinforcement Principle has three advantages over punishment:

1. The child must know what behavior is expected of him and must demonstrate this behavior for the punishment to end. The child must therefore behave properly at least once after which something relatively good happens to him (his aversive situation ends).

2. The child remains in control of his behavior. He is free to terminate the aversive situation whenever he chooses to behave properly. He is not powerless as he is when punishment continues regardless of his behavior.

3. Negative reinforcement is more efficient. As soon as the child's behavior improves, punishment ends.

If the Negative Reinforcement Principle is not appropriate, there are still three other principles for stopping undesirable behavior. At least one of them is more likely to work than punishment. Remember the Satiation, Extinction, and Incompatible Alternative Principles.

PUNISHMENT WORKS UNPREDICTABLY

If negative reinforcement has so many advantages over punishment, why does anyone ever use punishment? Punishment does work—sometimes—for a while. If it never worked at all, no one would ever use it. When Kim is sent to her room, Kim's mother is relieved of her daughter's whining. At that moment the mother is reinforced for having separated herself from an aversive child. A technique producing a feeling of relief once will ordinarily be used again. The use of punishment is often rewarding to the punisher even though it does not necessarily produce the long-term benefits desired.

Sometimes punishment does by chance produce long-term desirable effects. Unfortunately we cannot always predict when the desirable effects will occur. But let us imagine that Kim's mother requires her to spend exactly one hour in her room as punishment for being fussy. As luck might have it, at the end of that hour Kim may very well be happily playing with her toys. When her mother comes to release her, Kim comes out cheerfully and speaks politely to her mother. Her mother will then feel that the punishment has been successful and will tend to use it in the future. By chance the punishment happens to end when the child is behaving in a desirable manner.

But why leave the timing of when punishment ends to chance? You can control when punishment ends. By arranging the proper conditions you can make certain the punishment stops when the child's behavior starts to improve. His behavior need not be perfect, but it does need to be an improvement over the undesirable behavior you are trying to change.

PUNISHMENT CAN BE DANGEROUS

Not only does punishment tend to work less reliably than negative reinforcement, but punishment also has some serious dangers:

1. Attempted punishment may actually serve as reinforcement. A teacher who punishes a child by making him sit in front next to her desk or by writing his name on the blackboard calls attention to the child. Other children notice him. Such attention may actually be reinforcing, thereby increasing rather than reducing his undesired behavior.

2. Punishment may produce intense fears and anxieties which may last a lifetime (see Chapter 12).

3. When a child receives frequent punishment and sees no course of action that will enable him to escape that punishment, a foundation is laid for later neurotic behavior.

4. Children tend to resist punishment by fighting back, by actively escaping, or by withdrawing into passive apathy. Vandalism, truancy, and uncooperativeness are the names frequently given such forms of resistance when they occur in school. They are the direct result of the punishment adults mete out to children.

5. The child tends to avoid the punisher whenever he can. A child who has constantly been punished by his parents does not want to be near them any more than he has to be. Parents with grown children sometimes wonder why their children seldom come to visit them. In families where punishment is frequently used, the children, when they grow up, may feel uncomfortable near their parents. Children can develop severe feelings of guilt if they have been taught that they should love their parents but in fact do not. When you love someone, you want to be near him. But you do not want to be near someone who punishes you. You cannot want to be

near a person and simultaneously not want to be near that person without undergoing some kind of inner conflict. Parents and teachers who want their children to love them should maximize the opportunities to use positive reinforcement and minimize the use of punishment.

ON RARE OCCASIONS PUNISHMENT MAY BE NECESSARY

The natural occurrences of life administer so many punishments to most people that it is seldom desirable for us to design additional punishment. These few occasions may include situations such as the following:

1. A mild punishment may be necessary to teach a child what no means. A young child learns the meaning of the word no or no-no by having the words spoken at the same instant that something unpleasant happens to him, for example, a loud, gruff voice or a slap on the hand. Establishing this connection is discussed further in Chapter 12.

2. In emergencies a punishment may be the only way to save a person from greater danger. A tetanus shot is punishing but is considered worthwhile to save a child from greater danger. Dental work may be punishing but is less painful in the long run than bad teeth or gums. Knocking a child to the ground is punishment, but if it removes him from the path of a line-drive baseball or a rifle bullet, then the punishment is the lesser of two evils.

3. Punishment may be the only way to get a child to try some alternative behavior which can then be reinforced. An undesirable pattern of behavior may be so well established that the child would never try any alternative without some shakeup in his regular routine.

Many persons testify to the beneficial effects that some adverse conditions have had. People who have been fired found better jobs. People whose marriages broke up found more compatible mates. A failing grade shocked a child into realizing that he had to do something differently. A serious heart attack made a habitual smoker stop smoking. The occasional instances where adversity is met with even greater constructive effort tends to be news and occasionally makes the daily papers. However, even the people who profit from adversity do not necessarily recommend it. At least they do not seek more of it for themselves. People can conquer unplanned adversity. In rare instances planned aversive consequences may also shock people into an awareness that their behavior needs to change. But the punishment should if possible be accompanied by the opportunity to try alternative behaviors which are likely to be reinforced. Otherwise the punishment cannot have its desired effect.

Negative reinforcement has different effects than punishment. Let us look at some problems where the Negative Reinforcement Principle has been applied.

- Annoyed by a nose bleed apparently caused accidentally by a member of the opposing basketball team, Terry lashes out to get even.

- Miss Clark yells at her class to be quiet, but they ignore her and continue irrelevant, noisy activity.

- Diane does sloppy math work so that she has more time to play.

- By continually blurting out answers before anyone else has a chance, Stan interferes with the learning of other students in his class.

- Ella's parents want assurance that if she is unable to return home from dates by 1:00 A.M., they will know immediately without having to wait up for her.

What Is an Appropriate Aversive Condition?

THE AVERSIVE CONDITION SHOULD BE EASY FOR A
CHILD TO TERMINATE WHEN HIS BEHAVIOR IMPROVES

CHANGING UNSPORTSMANLIKE CONDUCT

As high school basketball coach, I felt good sportsmanship was a major part of my responsibility. Here is what happened at one of our tournament games:

Terry was our starting center and one of the best players on our team. The game was progressing normally until he got a nosebleed from an accidental bump. Embarrassed and angry, he started to retaliate by throwing his elbows around unnecessarily and injuring some of the other players.

Even though the team needed Terry I pulled him out of the lineup. I told him, "You'll sit on the bench until you tell me that you can play in a sportsmanlike manner." He was mad—at me as much as at our opponents. I thought he might sit out the whole game. But after a long five minutes he said, "I'll play fair now, coach." He played the rest of the game without a foul.

For Terry, having to sit on the bench was an aversive situation that was easy for the coach to control. It required no effort, except some worry about losing the game, and it was easy to terminate when Terry promised to "play fair."

These are some other situations where the aversive conditions were easy to terminate when the child's behavior improved.

- Mr. Christal and his son Peter made an agreement that Peter could use the family car to drive to school as long as he kept it clean inside and out. When Mr. Christal discovered the car was dirty, he denied Peter permission to use it until the car was clean.

- When Duke became rowdy, pushing and shoving several other boys at the Teen Club, the director asked him to leave, telling him he could return whenever he was ready to be orderly in the building.

- Jill, dawdling unnecessarily when getting ready for bed, was told that she could not turn on the television to watch her usual evening program until she put on her pajamas and completed all other bedtime preparations.

The Precise Instant of Termination Can Be Important

REGAINING CLASSROOM CONTROL

Miss Clark felt the first day of school had been a success. In fact her third period class had gone so well that she finished everything she had planned a little early and allowed the class to talk until the lunch bell rang. On the second day of school the third period class members again started talking among themselves before the bell rang even though she had not given them permission. By the end of September the last fifteen or twenty minutes of class were out of Miss Clark's control. Although she yelled at the class to be quiet, they would settle down only momentarily, then resume giggling, "horselaughing," or calling to someone across the room. By the end of October she had absolutely no control over the class from beginning to end. Any student wishing to work would have found it impossible.

Miss Clark consulted the school principal, Mr. Campbell. After learning what had happened, Mr. Campbell said, "Miss Clark, tomorrow when the third period class begins, I wish you would announce that you expect them to do their assigned work, that they are not to talk to each other, and that no one is to leave for lunch until the room is quiet. I imagine they will ignore your announcement as usual. But just before the lunch bell rings I want you to place yourself in front of the door and repeat the announcement. I will be just outside the door in case you need me."

The next day Miss Clark made the announcement, and as expected the students continued their uproar. One minute before the bell rang Miss Clark moved into position blocking the exit, "No one goes to lunch until it is absolutely quiet in this room." The bell rang. Students surged toward the door. Miss Clark stood her ground. The students shouted at her that they wanted to go to lunch. Miss Clark repeated, "No one goes to lunch until this room is absolutely quiet and everyone is in his own seat." The students milled around for a few moments, but some sat down. Finally all were sitting but there was still an undertone of muttering. Miss Clark repeated, "No one goes to lunch until this room is absolutely quiet." Finally there was silence. One whole second of complete silence. Miss Clark said, "Class dismissed," and stepped quickly aside.

Miss Clark had regained control. The students knew it, Mr. Campbell knew it, and most important of all Miss Clark knew it. Months later several students told her how glad they were that she had shown them she meant business. "Otherwise we would have wasted the whole year."

In this case having to remain in class during the lunch hour was the aversive situation. It had to end promptly as soon as the class had met the required behavior of maintaining silence, however briefly. Miss Clark was able to choose the precise second that the aversive stimulus would end. If she had dismissed the class while their muttering was still audible, she would have confirmed the students' view that she did not mean what she said. If she had waited just a few seconds too long, the talking might have started up again and she would have had a new confrontation. She had to follow through consistently with what she requested of her students if she were to maintain control.

Such extreme measures should seldom be required. If a teacher can keep each child busy and successful with relevant learning activities, discipline problems are rare. But once a teacher loses control of the whole class, no relevant learning activities can even be started. Somehow the teacher has to regain sufficient control so that students will have an atmosphere conducive to work. Students prefer it this way.

The Best Aversive Situations Require Little Energy From the Adult

Conventional punishments require too much work. For example, spanking requires a great deal of energy just to hold a squirming child in position. Few adults can keep spanking for more than fifteen or twenty seconds. Furthermore whatever behavior the child is engaging in when the punishment ends is the behavior that is being rewarded. Since the child is usually crying when the spank-

SIDE GLANCES   By Gill Fox

© 1966 by NEA, Inc. T.M. Reg. U.S. Pat. Off.

"My problem is largely of a financial nature. I have to cry harder and harder for what I want!"

Establishing an aversive condition should require little energy.

ing ends, the adult is rewarding the crying behavior. A "cry-baby" is a child who has learned that he gets what he wants by crying. He learns to cry because either he is positively rewarded for crying or his punishment ends when he is crying.

Physical punishment is undesirable for many reasons. Not only does it not work predictably, but it requires so much energy from the punisher that inevitably he must end the punishment when he tires, not when the child's behavior improves. Thus he may be rewarding the very behavior he does not want.

Lectures are usually aversive to a child, but they too require energy. The lecture ends when the lecturer tires, but the child may not necessarily be better behaved at that instant. As a cue to better behavior verbal instructions have maximum impact just prior to the expected action, not after (recall the Cueing Principle in Chapter 4).

BLUFFING IS RISKY

The adult should avoid implausible threats. Even though the adult may be able to deceive a child a few times, eventually the child may call his bluff. The following example illustrates a dangerous and not recommended use of negative reinforcement, recalled fifteen years later by the child on whom it was used.

DANGEROUSLY BLUFFING A CRY BABY

One time when I was four years old I was carrying on a loud crying marathon. I don't remember what I was unhappy about. My mother asked me to stop crying, but I decided I wasn't going to stop.

She went into the bedroom and put on her fur coat, which she only wore on special occasions. She told me that she wouldn't live in the same house with a cry baby. She opened the front door and walked out.

At first I didn't believe her, but she didn't even look back. I was sure she meant it then. I stopped crying and ran out after her. I promised her that I would stop crying and pleaded with her to come back. She returned to the house, hung up her coat, and everything was fine again. I was scared to think that I might have caused her to leave home. I felt I was going to be abandoned, and I felt guilty that it would have been my fault.

Threatening to abandon a child is not a mildly aversive situation —it is cruel and inhuman treatment. Even though it may have accomplished a temporary tactical victory in this instance, it left a residue of fear, insecurity, and guilt remembered too well fifteen years later.

The mother was acting out an impossible threat, one which an older child would quickly recognize as a bluff. What would the mother have done if the child had not conformed to her wishes? She was abandoning her child and leaving her house. Suppose the child had said, "Good. Go away and stay away." Eventually the mother would have had to return. The child could have called the mother's bluff.

The Negative Reinforcement Principle is the least desirable of the four alternative methods of stopping undesirable behavior. Before using it an adult should be able to answer "yes" to this question: If the child *accepts* the aversive situation that I have set up, would I be willing to live with the consequences? In the preceding example the adult would probably not want to move out of her home to maintain an aversive condition.

THE AVERSIVE SITUATION SHOULD FIT THE THE BEHAVIOR TO BE CHANGED

The Negative Reinforcement Principle will work even though the aversive situation is not logically related to the undesired behavior. However, justice seems to have a more compelling logic if there is some relationship between the two.

TAKING TIME TO BE ACCURATE

In order to encourage her children to learn their addition and subtraction facts well, Miss Lee planned the math period just before recess and announced that any child could go to recess as soon as he finished his math problems.

Diane quickly caught on to the system. She would write down any answer—right or wrong—so she could be the first one out to recess. Diane pulled this trick three days in a row before Miss Lee caught up with her.

Miss Lee then asked Diane to come in after school and do the arithmetic problems until they were all correct. No fixed interval of time was set. Diane was told she could go home as soon as the problems were done correctly.

After that day Diane took additional time to do the problems correctly before recess.

Recess should not be used as a reward for speedy accomplishment of academic work. All children need to have a break and some exercise, not just those who fortuitously have the ability to finish quickly. Diane wanted extra time to play but did sloppy work to get it. The teacher established an aversive condition which in effect subtracted from Diane's play time until she did satisfactory work. The aversive situation was logically related to the offense. However, the entire situation could have been avoided if Miss Lee had insisted upon accurate work originally.

Here are some other short examples where the aversive situation was designed to fit the behavior to be changed:

- Although no medical problem was apparent, seven-year-old Brian had not learned consistent bladder control. In an effort to help him control the problem Brian was given the job of washing his soiled clothing.

- Bunny frequently forgot to put her bicycle in the garage at night even though one bike had already been stolen from the yard. She was told that any day after she had forgotten to put away her bike, she would have to walk to school instead of biking.

- We live in a neighborhood where we have to keep the house locked at all times. I gave our eight-year-old son Quent a key to come in whenever he wanted. Unfortunately he would childishly tramp through the dirt outside and, forgetting to wipe his feet at the door, would track dirt into the house. So I temporarily took away his key privilege. I told him to ring the doorbell at which time I would ask him whether he had wiped his feet. After he remembered to wipe his feet several times in succession I returned his key to him with the reminder that it was a privilege dependent upon adultlike behavior.

AVERSIVENESS IS IN THE EYE OF THE BEHOLDER

A situation considered aversive by an adult may be rewarding to the child.

REWARDING SELFISHNESS UNWITTINGLY

Even for a six-year-old Pam was possessive with her toys. She would quarrel with friends who came to play and try to prevent them from using her things.

When I noticed the children arguing over the toys, I would take the contested toy away and put it up on the closet shelf telling Pam, "As soon as you feel you can share this with the other children I will take it down." However, so long as her friends were in the house Pam would never ask to get the toy down. She seemed to gain some satisfaction from having the toy put out of reach of her friends. I began to suspect that she deliberately started quarrels to have toys taken out of circulation.

Removing a toy was not an aversive situation for Pam. On the contrary it was a reward for her quarreling. She was able to prevent her friends from using her toys even though temporarily they were out of her own reach.

Pam's mother would probably have found the Incompatible Alternatives Principle more successful. Since she wanted Pam to learn to share her toys, she could have arranged some reward for Pam if she shared them and played cooperatively with her friends for a specified period of time.

An identical event can be either rewarding or aversive depending upon how it is presented. Recall (page 110) how blackboard washing was a reward in one elementary class but a punishment in another.

GETTING HOMEWORK IN ON TIME

When I was teaching United States history, many of my high school students would fail to get their weekly assignments in on time. They always had innumerable excuses as to why the work was not done.

I told them that I would keep a record of their weekly work. Only those who got their work in on time would be allowed to take the scheduled examinations.

At first the students thought it was great that they could get out of taking tests by not doing their weekly assignments. They soon realized, however, that their grade for the year would depend upon the test results. Taking the test became a privilege. It was a rare occasion when the weekly assignments were not in on time.

A previously aversive situation (test taking) became a reward partly because the teacher said it was a privilege and partly because it enabled the students to earn a satisfactory grade.

Teachers sometimes forget what they are trying to accomplish with their teaching. The purpose of education is not to get weekly assignments in on time. A good education should not only help children learn but should also help them *love* to learn. Punishment and negative reinforcement are both aversive techniques which detract from ultimate educational objectives. It is hard to love an activity in which participation is motivated by fear of punishment.

There is an alternative way of structuring the classroom situation to meet these ends: The teacher can help each child set his own standards of performance for what he would learn and reward every child for making progress toward his particular goals. A test is merely a way to find out what the child has learned so he can be rewarded for it and a way to diagnose what difficulties the child may have so he knows what he has yet to learn. A weekly assignment then takes its proper place as one possible method for learning rather than as an objective which deserves to be rewarded itself.

OTHER SITUATIONS MAY BECOME AVERSIVE BY ASSOCIATION

LEARNING TO DISLIKE THE PLAYPEN

Lucy was only sixteen months old but she could make as much noise as an amplified rock band. Before dinner she would look at the box of crackers which was on a high shelf and scream for them. Trying to be a dutiful mother I attempted to ignore her, but every look at the crackers only renewed the strength of her yelling. She could go on for long periods of time until I wanted to scream myself. (OK, I admit that I had been rewarding her crying by occasionally giving her a cracker.)

To keep from listening to her I would pick Lucy up, take her into the other room, and put her in her playpen. I would then close the door and leave her there to scream by herself. As I became consistent in never rewarding her with crackers when she cried and always putting her in her playpen when she started crying, Lucy stopped her habit of crying for crackers.

Unfortunately she also came to hate her playpen. When I put her in it at other times, she would raise a terrible fuss. She used to play peacefully there with her toy duck, but no longer. Maybe she had just outgrown it. But I suspect that my putting her so often in the playpen when she was unhappy made it an unpleasant place to be.

The intended aversive situation was supposed to be simply the isolation from her mother. However, when isolated in her playpen, Lucy associated it with punishment. She was approaching the age in which confinement in a playpen would soon become aversive under any circumstances, but the process was undoubtedly hastened by the associated events.

The aversive situation may easily become generalized and spoil a desirable activity. For example, some teachers assign homework as punishment for classroom misbehavior. Such a procedure can almost be guaranteed to make youngsters hate homework. Homework should be given to help the child learn something he needs to know; it should be as interesting and as pleasant an experience as possible. Assigning homework as punishment defeats a major objective of education, helping the individual learn to love the process of learning.

How Should the Aversive Situation Be Presented?

GIVE A WARNING CUE IN ADVANCE

Sometimes a simple warning is sufficient so that the aversive situation is not needed.

RESTRAINING UNTIMELY COMMENTS

Stan, one of our better high school students, was a source of irritation to me and to his classmates because of his impatient disregard for even the most basic parliamentary rules. He would blurt out answers and make running comments during the whole class hour without ever raising his hand for permission to speak. Although he was doing well in the class, his behavior obviously interfered with the learning of others.

I tried ignoring his comments, but since his answers were almost always correct, I could not ask the same question of another class member after Stan had obviously given away the answer. Bawling him out did not do any good either. Finally I asked him to stay for a minute after class so that we could talk. I explained to him that he had been disrupting the class and that something had to be done about it.

"After this I'm going to ask you to come in after school and write down every answer that you blurt out without permission during class. I'll warn you just the first time. That one slip puts you on probation for the rest of the day. If you speak out of turn again after that, I'm going to ask you to come in after school to write out the answers."

This one conversation caused an abrupt change in Stan's behavior so that he ceased to be a problem. I congratulated him on his improvement and told him that it was obvious he didn't need help to restrain himself any more. "I believe good manners are a habit with you now," I said, "so you can forget about coming in after school." Stan said that he had never realized how frequently he had been blurting out answers. He said that he was just trying to show how much he knew.

With Stan a warning was sufficient, but it does not always work so well. Even when a warning does not work by itself, it provides an element of fairness to whatever follows. Stan would never be able to complain, "But I didn't know I was disturbing anyone. It isn't fair to punish me without warning." If the teacher had called Stan in after school, the boy would have had to admit that he had been given fair warning. The warning called Stan's attention to his blurting-out behavior and demonstrated to him that the teacher recognized his knowledge. Stan no longer needed to show-off.

Other ways of handling such a problem are available. One way is to use the Extinction Principle as was done in a similar context with Ginger (page 160). A preferred way in Stan's situation would be to use the Incompatible Alternatives Principle. Stan did good work and wanted to show his teacher how much he knew. The teacher might well be able to give him special work in the class which might stimulate him further, allowing him to demonstrate his competence in more socially acceptable ways. For example, several students might be small group discussion leaders on a list of questions. Stan could not simultaneously ask the questions and blurt out the answers. As a group leader he might begin to appreciate the value of well-timed contributions. It is usually not enough to disapprove of one type of behavior without helping the individual learn other modes which he can substitute to his ultimate benefit.

DESCRIBE THE AVERSIVE SITUATION POSITIVELY

A child's undesirable behavior may make you angry. However, if you see misbehavior simply as the result of inadequate learning, then you may be able to phrase your correction in a way that will create a little better feeling.

Instead of:

"Dammit, you little punk, get in here and stay here until you can remember not to throw those blasted rocks."

Try:

"Please plan on staying in the house until you tell me you can go outside without throwing rocks."

Instead of:

"Absolutely under no condition will I allow you to let a boyfriend come for supper if you don't warn me first. You show me no consideration at all and never have."

Try:

"I'm sorry but from now on I'm going to have to turn you down when you bring a boyfriend home for supper without phoning first to see if it's convenient."

Instead of:

"You won't eat your carrots so I'm not going to give you any dessert even though everyone else gets some."

Try:

"If you feel you are able to finish your first helpings of food, you may have some dessert."

Instead of:

"You're a terrible class today. You'll stay in your seats until dark if you don't stop moving around the room."

Try:

"When you show me you are all ready to continue by getting into your seats, we will proceed."

REMEMBER TO FOLLOW THROUGH

Any warning must be followed through if the behavior does not change. Parents and teachers sometimes make empty threats. Children quickly learn whose warnings they can safely ignore.

Students test the limits of a new teacher. Each fall students spar with teachers they have not had before and test each substitute teacher, teacher's aide or student teacher because the students want to see whether this person really means what he says. A teacher's actions must be consistent with his words.

ESTABLISHING CLASSROOM DISCIPLINE

In my first year as a new teacher I began by telling the class that they were old enough to handle themselves in the room without strict rules about what they were permitted or not permitted to do. I wanted them to like me so much that not only did I permit some students to take advantage of me but I allowed others to practically ignore me. I simply lost control over the class and the students lost respect for me. At one point when things were bad two boys kicked my wastebasket all the way down a flight of stairs and into another part of the building.

During the summer after the first year, I read up on discipline and interviewed experienced teachers to get help. When school began the second year, I had formulated some ideas that involved keeping the class orderly so more learning could take place: "Windows are not to be opened or closed without teacher permission," "Raise your hand first if you wish to sharpen your pencil," "Students are to be courteous and quiet when a teacher or student is speaking to them as a group."

Having laid down the rules that I felt were essential for classroom order and without being punitive, I made certain the students knew I meant business, and then I watched to be sure they carried out my rules. I made few threats, but those I used were ones I could follow through on, and after a warning I always did. Whereas the previous year I had a steady run of students heading for the principal's office, this year I almost always did my own disciplining instead. Although I had difficulty at first, partly because my reputation from the previous year had followed me, I stuck to my guns, and after about a month I began to notice that all my efforts at following through with the rules I had set up were having some effect.

Then around Thanksgiving time I began to relax some of the rules gradually but deliberately. I started out something like this: "Since the class has become so orderly, I would like to suggest that whenever anyone has a pencil to sharpen, he simply comes up quietly and sharpens it without waiting for my approval first. So long as he can do it without disturbing the others I'll know he can take the responsibility himself."

A week or so later I told the students that, since they were not disruptive sharpening pencils, they could begin handling the shades, and later on the windows themselves, in what was really a reward for showing courtesy toward others and accepting responsibility.

From Easter time on we had a classroom in which students freely came and went to recess as they completed their work and in which small group discussions on projects were taking place simultaneously in different parts of the room. If someone spoke loud enough to disturb another group, he was reminded by the group, not me. Teaching became a pleasure, and I felt the students had grown a great deal by learning to conduct themselves in a more mature way. All of us had the pleasure of learning in a more relaxed and pleasant atmosphere.

Sometimes the adult may find it inconvenient to follow through in person.

COMING HOME ON SCHEDULE

Ella's parents had a rule that she must be home by one o'clock in the morning from any party or date on a weekend night. An alarm clock was placed in the hall and set for 1:15. If Ella returned home by 1:00 or even shortly thereafter, she would be able to push in the alarm plunger and prevent the alarm from sounding. Only if Ella were late would she be put in the embarrassing position of waking up the rest of the family.

An automated aversive situation made it unnecessary for Ella's parents to wait up for her. If she came home on time, they could sleep undisturbed; if she did not, they were automatically awakened. Not all aversive situations can be instituted so easily and automatically. However, the adult should enforce all rules consistently if he wants his children to value his word. Furthermore he should periodically reexamine the rules to see that they are still wise for maturing youngsters.

INSIST ON ACTION, NOT PROMISES

A child can easily say, "I'm sorry" or "I won't do it again." Apologies may be desirable but they are not sufficient.

APOLOGIZING INSTEAD OF ACTING DIFFERENTLY

In our neighborhood Mrs. Evans always insisted that her children apologize whenever they did anything wrong: "Tell Don you're sorry you stepped on his foot," "Tell Aarie you won't ride his bike again without his permission," "Say you didn't mean to hit him." Once she made one of her children write a note of apology and deliver it in person to another child he had offended.

Even as a child I remember thinking about the strange paradox that even though her children were the most profuse apologizers among us, they were also the ones that nobody trusted. In retrospect I realize that her intentions were good but that she erred in an important respect: she assumed that an apology automatically meant a change of behavior. She followed through on apologies, but she did not follow through on what the apology meant. As a result her children became astute at apology making but seldom changed their behavior.

Mrs. Evans might have helped her children to have less to apologize for. She should have rewarded the change in behavior, not merely the apology. "You promised Aarie you wouldn't use his bike without asking first. I don't want you using the neighbors' possessions without their permission, so we are going to delay our trip to the amusement park for one week. If you can remember not to borrow without permission during this week, we will then go to the park and you can take a friend along." Such a statement is not punishment for a fixed period of time because the child gets the trip only if he refrains from "borrowing." A punishing statement would be, "Just for that you can't go to the amusement park for a week," implying that after a week the child can go no matter what he has done during that week. A one-week probationary period may be needed to test whether the child lives up to his promise. If he has not changed his behavior, then the adult can extend or reestablish the aversive situation, for example, postpone the trip for still another week contingent on good behavior. If you must use the Negative Reinforcement Principle, then be sure to use it consistently.

Which of the Four Principles on Stopping Inappropriate Behavior Should You Use?

To decide which of the four principles you should use, ask yourself these questions:

1. *Is the undesirable behavior all that bad? Does it really matter whether it continues?* If it does not matter very much, then the Satiation Principle is probably most appropriate. The

child will eventually tire of the reinforcers from the undesired activity.

2. *Can I arrange conditions so that the child is not rewarded for the undesired behavior?* If you can control the rewards, be sure to arrange conditions so that the child is not rewarded following the undesired act. The Extinction Principle is valuable primarily when you have major control of rewards. When you do not, one of the other three principles would be more feasible.

3. *What would I really like the children to be doing instead?* If you can describe what the child is doing that you do not like, then you should be able to describe some behavior that is just the opposite. By far the most useful and effective principle is the Incompatible Alternatives Principle. Try to devise a way to reward behavior incompatible with the undesired behavior. The child will learn more if you do.

4. *Have the other three principles failed to work?* If so, you may need to try the Negative Reinforcement Principle. The aversive situation ends when behavior improves. But the aversive situation must nonetheless be instituted, so negative reinforcement still suffers from some of the same disadvantages as punishment.

In general, the best possible way to help a child stop behaving inappropriately is to find some incompatible alternative behavior to reward instead.

Modifying
Emotional
Responses

12

Learning
to Avoid
Danger

CONVERTING A RECKLESS DRIVER

My older brother taught me to drive. He enjoyed working with motors and had assembled a race car that he kept in top condition. He taught me a great deal about the mechanics of cars but not much about the rules of driving.

During a six-month period I was cited four times for speeding and was threatened with having my driver's license revoked. The judge sentenced me to attend a driver education course. I was not happy about being forced to go to class. Learning the rules was dull; I felt I was beyond all that.

What began to make an impression, though, were the color films we were shown. The films showed on-the-scene pictures taken at accidents with the causes of accidents described. The pictures were repulsive, showing people splattered with blood, lying in contorted positions. One picture showed two girls who had been smashed against a wall. I don't think I'll ever forget that scene. Another film showed what would happen to the driver and passengers on impact if a car hit something at various speeds. Then the teacher read a local account of several serious accidents in our community, naming the intersections where the accidents had occurred and stating the citations of the offenders. It all came much closer to home.

Shortly after that I drove by an accident in which someone had been killed, and I remember thinking to myself, "That could happen to me." I learned that accidents don't just happen to other people; they could happen to me because of my own actions.

With the traffic violation record I started out with at age sixteen, it's hard to believe that I have not had a single citation since that course and I'm now twenty. Every time I see an accident I still find myself saying, "That could be you, Stew, old boy."

A person tends to avoid situations in which he has been harmed. But it is not necessary to harm a child physically in order to teach him that danger may be associated with that situation. We have just seen how authentic color movies of accident victims served as an effective representation of a danger. The method was to present simultaneously the situation to be avoided (speeding and unlawful driving) with pictures of aversive conditions (accident victims).

Stew's report serves to illustrate the **Avoidance Principle: To teach a child to avoid a certain type of situation, simultaneously present to the child the situation to be avoided (or some representation of it) and some aversive condition (or its representation).**

Stew could have learned to avoid speeding in a more costly manner. If he had been painfully injured while actually speeding,

Stew might have learned more vividly to fear speeding cars. Fortunately he was able to learn by representations of the aversive condition and the speeding situation: The color pictures of shattered bodies represented the aversive condition; the instructor's verbal descriptions with films represented the speeding situation. Representations do not work with everyone as well as they did with Stew. They work best with more mature individuals.

A more vivid fear-producing experience could cause Stew to fear all cars. People who have actually been injured in automobile accidents are frequently afraid to get into a car again. The driver education course had to pinpoint the dangers of speeding and unlawful driving without allowing the class to generalize that all use of automobiles is necessarily harmful.

Simultaneous timing is important to establish the association. For example, suppose a toddler has just run out into the street. To teach him the danger associated with being in the street, the child's parent might give the child one sharp spank as he picks the child up out of the street. This spanking would teach the child to associate the middle of the street with danger, but a spanking after he is safely back on the curb is poor timing. The child should associate the street with danger; the curb, with safety.

The world contains many things that children must learn to avoid: matches, stoves, hot irons, poisons, busy streets, deep water, weak branches, rusty nails, electric outlets, rattlesnakes, strange men, growling dogs, and even delicate valuables. A young child can usually be protected by simply separating him from these things. Poisons and matches can be put on a high shelf, electric outlets can be covered, rusty nails can be removed, hot objects can be kept out of reach. But as he grows older, the child will inevitably become exposed to dangers from which he cannot be protected. He needs to learn what kinds of objects and what kinds of situations he should avoid. He must learn to respond sensibly and realistically without becoming frantic or anxiety ridden.

- Wendy at fourteen months does not know that she should leave delicate objects alone.
- Mickey does not know what "hot" means.
- A young boy considers carrying stick matches a status symbol.
- Packy has never learned some of the basic spelling rules and performs accordingly.
- Bonnie notices her mother has a terrible fear of yellow jackets.

How Do You Teach a Child to Avoid Harm?

SIMULTANEOUSLY PRESENTING THE HARMFUL OBJECT
AND THE AVERSIVE CONDITION

The simplest and most direct method of helping a child learn to avoid a harmful object is to present some kind of noxious stimulation just as he approaches the harmful situation. Few people grab a thistle twice. Yet what can you do when the object is not harmful to the child but the child is harmful to the object?

LEAVING BREAKABLE OBJECTS ALONE

Wendy was only fourteen months old when my wife and I took her to visit my Uncle Alex. Alex had a hobby of constructing delicately-webbed sailing ships which were on display in many accessible places throughout the house. I knew we were headed for trouble since Wendy had just learned to walk and would have loved to get her hands on some of those sailing ships.

By chance I noticed that Uncle Alex also had one of those old-fashioned bulb-type automobile horns which goes "oogah" when you squeeze it. That gave me an idea: When Wendy approached the nearest model sailing ship and started to reach for the main mast, I sounded the horn. It made a loud, harsh noise that startled her. She withdrew from the ship. A little later she approached another ship, and again I repeated the process. All told it took four more "oogahs" until Wendy stopped approaching the model sailing ships with that destructive gleam in her eye.

A loud noise is aversive to most people. By presenting the aversive noise just as Wendy was reaching for the fragile objects, her father taught her that the object was something she should avoid. At that stage of her life Wendy had not yet learned what "no" meant. Her parents could have taken the opportunity to teach her the meaning of "no" simply by saying the word "no" just before sounding the horn each time.

TEACHING WORDS THAT REPRESENT THE AVERSIVE
SITUATIONS

Fortunately an actual aversive situation is not necessary every time you want to warn a child. Children can learn words that signal danger, but the word must occur at approximately the same time as the aversive condition.

AVOIDING HOT OBJECTS

Mickey was sitting on my lap at the breakfast table when he suddenly grabbed for my coffee cup. I warned "hot" just as he got one finger into the hot coffee. He jerked his hand away and started crying.

The next day I deliberately had him touch a piece of hot toast that I had just removed from the toaster while at the same time I was repeating the words "hot, hot, hot." Mickey just barely touched the toast, jerked his hand away and for the first time said "hot" himself.

In the same way a child learns the meaning of "hurt" by hearing the word when he has skinned his knee, bumped his head, or pinched his finger.

Other kinds of representations for dangers are familiar: A picture of a skull and crossbones represents poison; red flags or red flares on the highway signal a dangerous traffic situation ahead; a fog horn warns ships. Pictures of aversive situations can influence us as they did Stew at the beginning of this chapter. We learn many kinds of sounds, pictures, whistles, signs, and words as representations of dangerous situations.

REASONING WITH A CHILD

Once a child learns the language, you can reason with him about the possible consequences of various actions. When you reason with a child you use language to describe, or get him to describe, the possible consequences of alternative actions. Let us look at some examples of reasoning.

- "The reason you do not accept rides from strangers is that you do not know why they want to give you a ride. Some people actually hurt little children. They may pretend to be good by offering you candy to get you into their car. A stranger probably would not offer you something nice unless he wanted something from you in return."

- "Why do you suppose I don't want you kids to throw this dried mud at each other?"
  "I don't know."
  "Feel how hard it is, almost as hard as a rock."
  "You're afraid that I might hurt myself or somebody else."
  "Right. Now let's think of something to do that's just as much fun but not so dangerous."

Because the child can describe the possible consequences, he can decide for himself to avoid the dangerous situation. His decision is not based on blind obedience. It is an informed decision because he anticipates some possible harm to himself or others. The difference between blind obedience and reasoned action is in the ability to anticipate possible consequences. Although it is quite easy to teach a child to obey blindly, it is not usually in the best interests of the child, his parents, or society. Through reasoning with him we can inform the child that his actions have consequences which he might not anticipate. Of course, if we pose dire consequences which are untrue or extremely unlikely, the child may come to distrust our warnings. A responsible person can describe the probable consequences of alternative actions and act accordingly.

LEARNING BY EXAMPLE

Children learn fears by example too. Dangers avoided by parents are likely to be avoided by their children. Fears expressed by parents are likely to be shared by their children.

IGNORING SHORTCUTS

The playground and school were on the other side of a heavily traveled street. The shortest way to get there was to cross in the middle of the block; but from the beginning my mother or father would walk with me, and we always walked the extra half block to reach the pedestrian crossing. They explained that the traffic was dangerous. When I began walking to school alone, I cannot remember a single time using the shortcut even though I knew it was more direct.

Since parents are powerful models particularly for younger children, the patterns established in early childhood usually form lasting habits. The same parental modeling may not be nearly so effective if it is begun during the teen-age years when youngsters begin to adopt models from outside their family.

Children may learn to cope adequately with dangers, or they may learn irrational ways of responding to danger, from the examples provided by others.

GROWING AFRAID OF YELLOW JACKETS

One summer day a yellow jacket flew through the open door of our home. I am petrified of these bees. Since my husband was not at home I shrieked and rushed out to a neighbor's house with my little girl Bonnie at my heels. The neighbor's son came over to our house and killed it.

That evening as I described the incident to my husband I mentioned that Bonnie was as scared as I was. "Isn't it funny," I said, "that females always seem to be much more afraid of insects than males are?"

"Hmmm," he muttered from behind his newspaper, "Maybe it is just that you are such a wonderful example for your daughter."

Cautions

STRONG AVERSIVE CONDITIONS MAY CREATE IRRATIONAL FEARS

A mild aversive condition is usually sufficient to teach a child to avoid a harmful situation. If the aversive condition is too intense, too strong, or too powerful, fears may persist long after the actual danger has passed.

- "One summer when I was young our family spent several weeks at a Minnesota lake. I can remember being severely spanked for going near the lake shore by myself. My mother screamed at me that I could drown. Her apprehension was so great that it sticks with me even now. I avoid large bodies of water and have actually made up excuses to keep from joining people at swimming parties."

- "Everyone at our house used to eat corn on the cob. When I was four years old I asked to have some too. My mother told me that I could not eat it because I might choke to death on it. Having choked on other things, I was so scared of corn on the cob that I never wanted to try it and have not tried it to this day."

A healthy respect for the water can be taught without hysterical screams about the dangers of drowning. Corn on the cob can be withheld from a child until he is old enough to eat it without making him worry that he may choke to death on it. The aversive conditions in each case were more intense than they needed to be and engendered fears that lasted far longer than intended. Reasoning and frightening are not the same.

How intense should an aversive condition be? The borderline between a mild and an intense aversive condition is hard to draw and will vary with the individual child. The dangers of an intense aversive condition, however, are great enough that one would be wise to start with the mildest aversive condition.

What makes an aversive condition intense? Is it the severity of the anticipated punishment, for example, death by choking? Or is it the manner in which the threat is uttered, for example, screaming it at the child? Even though they cannot assess the actual danger, children are easily frightened when they sense that adults are frightened. Probably the manner of expression contributes more than most adults realize to the intensity of a warning.

FEARS MAY GENERALIZE TO RELATED SITUATIONS

- Wayne was frightened by a dog, barking and jumping upon him. Since then he has shown fear of all furry animals and even began crying when he saw a lady wearing a fur coat.

- As a child, Ginny was locked in a closet as punishment. Even now she is uncomfortable entering elevators and small, closed rooms.

- Max did not learn as fast as the other children in school. He received low grades and derogatory remarks from the teacher. Now he hates books, school, and learning.

Children generalize their fears easily. Intense aversive conditions make it difficult for a child to distinguish the cues of real danger from the irrelevant cues. A school child needs help in identifying exactly what he should do next to improve his performance. Punishment for doing a poor job only teaches a child to fear or dislike the punisher and things associated with the punisher.

SOME AVERSIVE CONDITIONS MAY PRODUCE FEELINGS OF GUILT OR WORTHLESSNESS

SPELLING POORLY

When he was seven, Packy missed several weeks of school because of illness and had to spend considerable time making up the major part of what he had missed. For a while he was taken out of class to work with a specialist for extra help with reading. Unfortunately this extra help was during his spelling period, and he continued to make low marks in spelling even though his reading improved. In the later elementary grades he received many papers with encircled misspelled words.

In seventh grade English he was again confronted with his spelling problem when he was asked to correct and return stories he had written. One paper handed back said in red pencil, "You are a poor speller. Work on it." No other help was offered.

By the time he reached eighth grade he thought of himself as a "poor speller." An analysis then of Packy's spelling errors

Some competitive events produce many losers with feelings of worthlessness.

showed he had never mastered the rules about when to drop the e in making *ing* endings and when to drop the y in forming plurals, among other things. The analysis further showed he also frequently misspelled words he really knew. When this was pointed out, his response was simply, "Well, gee, I'm just a lousy speller, that's all."

Parents and teachers should be careful about the labels they attach to children. There is an important distinction between a bad act and a bad child. An adult might say, "That was a bad thing to do," but it is dangerous to say, "You are a bad child." Children may easily come to believe the labels that are attached to them.

A girl whose mother thoughtlessly told her, "You are my ugly duckling," grew up with an intense feeling of worthlessness even though she developed into a beautiful woman. The names by which children are jokingly called sometimes find their marks and stick, with long-range, harmful consequences.

Good labels stick too. An adult might correct a child by saying, "You usually use such good judgment, but this one thing you did might cause some trouble. Let me show you why." The child can be labeled as good, but the act can be labeled as harmful and the reasons explained. In this way the child is more likely to grow up feeling good about himself and will be better able to analyze which actions produce desirable or undesirable consequences.

Fears Develop Accidentally Too

Many fears develop as the result of accidental contingencies. Both helpful and debilitating fears can be created by accident.

HELPFUL FEARS

FEARING MATCHES

When I was about nine or ten years old, I used to carry wooden stick matches around in my pockets. It was a sort of status symbol. My mother discovered them one wash day and gave me a stern lecture, but I continued the practice anyway. One day one of my best friends was playing near a large revolving grindstone. He apparently nudged against it just long enough to ignite about twenty or thirty wooden matches in his front pocket. His clothes were badly burned, and he was admitted to the hospital for treatment of leg burns. When I visited him, he showed me a handful of charred matches and a badly burned and blistered leg.

Then, just two days later, another boy who was fooling with matches caught his shirt on fire. His right arm was burned. Since his uncle owned the town's only newspaper, he got his picture and story in the local paper.

After that time, not only did I not carry matches any more, I warned my neighborhood friends. I still avoid matches to this day. I do not smoke or even carry safety matches.

A drastic way to avoid smoking! The accidental burnings of two other boys made an indelible impression on this youngster. Not all accidents have positive side effects.

DEBILITATING FEARS

- Boo hates the game of Bridge. In college she was teased about her mistakes. Her companions deliberately would deal her peculiar hands and laugh at her confusion. She now refuses to play the game at all.
- Rachel has an uncontrollable fear of moths ever since several got caught in her hair when she was standing under an outside light one summer night.
- Scott was playfully dunked one time when he was just learning to swim and swallowed too much water. Ever since he has found it almost impossible to put his head under the water.
- Telling ghost stories around a campfire gave nine-year-old Steve intense fears about shadows in his room at night.
- When she was a child, Julie was taught that sex was bad and has never adjusted to sexual relations in marriage.
- Warren was taught that God was watching him all the time and writing down each bad thing he did. When he grew old enough to discard this view of religion, Warren rejected all religious beliefs.

Fears accidentally or deliberately engendered in children have long-range consequences. Since it is possible to teach children how to respond appropriately without deliberately inculcating fears, the deliberate use of intense aversive conditions should be avoided whenever possible. However fears are sometimes accidentally produced by conditions outside of one's control. Under such circumstances there are ways of reducing these fears and anxieties as explained in Chapter 13.

13

Overcoming
Fears
and Anxieties

OVERCOMING FEAR OF THE DARK

I'm not sure how our small daughter, Barbie, first became afraid of the dark. I know that sometimes she had terrible nightmares. She would yell and scream if we did not leave a light on in her room or leave her door open to a lighted hallway.

We tried a lot of things to help her get over this fear. Sometimes I would play a "hide the toy" game with her in a poorly lighted room so that she would be having fun while she was "in the dark."

When she was four years old, we went for a vacation to the beach. In the evening we would look for shells and explore the tidepools as night fell. We would watch the sunset with her so that she could associate the approaching darkness with beauty rather than with strange, frightening apparitions.

That winter during a heavy storm the lights went out while Barbie was sitting in the living room playing a game with her father. I immediately said, "Oh, how exciting! Let's get some candles and we'll pretend we're pioneers." When the lights came back on again Barbie seemed a little disappointed.

By the time she was eight, Barbie actually seemed to like the dark. She would play hide-and-seek outside after dinner in the dark. Sometimes she would "camp out" in the back yard with her friends. Her nightmares and her fears of the dark had completely disappeared.

Barbie's mother could have made two serious mistakes: She could have forced the child to remain alone in the dark, or she could have left lights on so that Barbie never had to experience the dark. Force would only have intensified Barbie's fears. Continual light could not be provided forever.

Instead of making either mistake, her mother gradually exposed Barbie to increasing amounts of darkness while she was feeling secure or having fun. Sitting with her in the dark would give her the assurance that a loved one was near. Each activity helped Barbie to discover that she could be having fun or feeling secure when it was dark.

Barbie's experience illustrates the **Fear Reduction Principle: To help a child overcome his fear of a particular situation, gradually increase his exposure to the feared situation while he is otherwise comfortable, relaxed, secure, or rewarded.**

Fear must be faced, but it can be faced gradually in small steps while the child is engaged in pleasant activities. The stronger the fear, the more gradually it must be presented and the longer it will take to overcome it. Here are some additional ways which have been used to help children overcome fear of the dark:

1. Provide a night light, gradually moving it farther away from the child and eventually into another area.

2. Leave a flashlight available by the child's bed.

3. Stick bright, florescent colored stars on the ceiling.

4. Play relaxing games in the dark.

5. Eat in the dark.

6. Have a friend who is not afraid of the dark sleep over night in the same room.

Childhood may contain many fears. Here are a few childhood situations we will look at more closely in the pages that follow:

- Jennie has heard so much about other children's trips to the dentist that she is unrealistically fearful about her first experience.

- After falling down a flight of stairs three-year-old Nicky is terrified of them.

- Dick is unwilling to go into the swimming pool.

- Jody's father is a fearful stranger to her when he returns after two years overseas.

- Corky, competing with a fluent older brother, begins to stutter.

- A science class is squeamish about laboratory specimens.

Pair Comfort with Fear

A person cannot be anxious and relaxed at the same time. The incompatibility of anxiety and relaxation is often used by professional counselors to reduce anxieties of their clients. Parents and teachers can also use incompatible activities to help a child overcome his fears or anxieties.

RELIEVING ANXIETY ABOUT THE DENTIST

Jennie was the youngest of four children and had often heard her older brothers and sister compain about their visits to the dentist. When I told Jennie that she had to visit the dentist for

"You've got to learn to relax."

A person cannot be anxious and relaxed at the same time.

a check-up before she entered kindergarten, she burst into tears and begged, "Please, don't make me go to the dentist!"

I inquired of my friends about dentists who were especially understanding with children and finally found one who was willing to work on a way to overcome Jennie's fear.

On the first visit Jennie only had to stay in the waiting room, an attractive place with some child-size furniture, an inviting array of colorful books and some well-chosen toys. She entertained herself with the toys while I talked a few moments with the dentist. I introduced Jennie to the dentist who gave her a plastic ring as she left.

On the second visit the dentist lifted her up into the dental chair and let her look at the tiny dental mirror. He rinsed out her mouth with a syringe filled with a peppermint-flavored mouthwash and gave her a coloring book.

On the third visit she climbed into the chair herself and allowed the dentist to clean her teeth, remarking afterwards, "That's fun, it tickles!"

Later when some actual dental work had to be done on her teeth, Jennie showed little apprehension.

Finding a dentist who will cooperate in a program like this might not always be easy. Sometimes a dental hygienist can be found who will serve the same purpose and at less expense. A series of painless, pleasant visits to the dentist's office will help a child who has learned to fear the dentist to relax. If the dentist anticipates that he will inflict some pain to accomplish the necessary work, he should warn the child in advance that "This will hurt." The child's fear in the long run will lessen if he can count on the dentist's telling him the truth.

REDUCING APPREHENSION ABOUT STAIRS

When my son Nicky was about three years old, he fell down about twenty steep stairs in our apartment building. After this incident he was terrified of the stairs; he resisted using them and would stand at the top shrieking with fear.

I realized that I was going to have to help him overcome this fear. At first I would make extra trips and carry him up and down the stairs myself. Then I would hold his hand and chit-chat with him while going toward the stairs and walking down with him, but I could tell by the way he tightened his grip on my hand that he was still tense. Later for a few days we sang nursery rhymes as we went down the stairs.

What finally did it was a "Slinky" toy, one of those cater-pillar-like coiled springs which can be placed on the top step and once started proceeds step-by-step to the bottom. I would send Slinky down the stairs first, and we would follow right after it. I then suggested to Nicky that he go down first, and I would send Slinky down to him so he could catch it before it hit the bottom. Nicky thought this was fun. After that time he seemed to have forgotten that he was ever afraid of the stairs.

Note the kind of conditions that help a child become comfortable, relaxed, secure, or rewarded: associating with someone the child loves or respects; engaging in familiar activities such as talking, singing, or playing games; investigating some novel, interesting, or pleasant situation, such as a new toy or a pleasant mouthwash.

A pediatrician who has a skillful knack with children is able to carry on a constant line of chatter while at the same time his hands are busy administering shots, drawing blood samples, or testing reflexes. Another wears a straw hat and false mustache. Still another arrives with his stethoscope and other instruments in a bright beach pail. Simply keeping the child's attention focused on distracting ideas or activities helps to reduce the tension that would be generated if the child's full attention were devoted to the situation he fears.

Gradually Expose the Child to the Feared Situation

Exposure to the feared situation must progress in slow, gradual steps. The child must accomplish each step successfully with little or no apprehension before going on to the next step.

LESSENING FEAR OF THE WATER

Dick was eight years old but still afraid to go near the water. I lived in the same apartment building and learned from his parents how fearful he was. They had bought him a little battery-powered swimming fish, hoping that it might encourage him to play near the water. The toy fish did get Dick closer to the water. He enjoyed walking around the side of the pool controlling the fish with the remote control unit. One day, however, the wire connecting the fish to the battery broke and the fish sank to the bottom of the pool. Dick started to cry. I dove into the pool, brought the fish to the surface, and told him, "Your fish was having a good time swimming down to the bottom." He then threw the fish into the pool again just to see it "swim to the bottom."

Dick and I soon became good friends. One day he sat down beside me at the edge of the pool. I started splashing water with my feet. I bet Dick that he couldn't make as big a splash. At first he hesitated but then took the dare. I made sure that he always made bigger splashes.

After several days of splashing at the edge of the pool, I suggested sitting on the first step—it was only about twelve inches deep—for our game. Again he hesitated but eventually agreed. We continued to splash and to play with the disconnected fish. One day on my way up from the bottom with the fish I blew big bubbles just before coming to the surface. Dick laughed. I said, "You may be able to beat me at splashing, but you can't beat me at blowing bubbles." After three days Dick could blow bubbles as big as mine.

Next I suggested that he hang on to one end of a kick board and see how much fun his fish had swimming in the pool. He practiced kicking in the shallow end of the pool while he held on to the board. We also continued blowing bubbles.

Dick's family moved out of the apartment building before I had actually taught him to swim, but there was no doubt that his fear of water was greatly reduced.

Working through gradual steps takes patience. An impatient adult might want to throw a fearful child into the water, but such a traumatic episode might cause fears that would last a lifetime. The success of any technique is based on its results. The safest approach is gradual exposure to increasing amounts of the feared situation under pleasant conditions.

Fear of the water is common. Here are some other gradual approximations that have been tried:

- Walking beside the water with a friend.
- Watching others play in the water.
- Eating lunches on the beach, gradually moving close to the water.
- Building sand castles on the beach.
- Accompanying a friend who has no fear of the water.
- Entering the water at first only when the surface is calm.
- Splashing, then taking turns ducking.
- Playing alligator (head out, arms walking along bottom of shallow water).
- Playing motorboat (blowing bubbles at the surface while moving along).
- Riding piggyback in the water.
- Reaching for discs at the bottom of a shallow pool.

The child must feel comfortable accomplishing each step before advancing to the next. If the steps have not been arranged in an increasing order of difficulty, rearrangement may be necessary. Big steps may need to be broken into smaller ones.

OVERCOMING FRIGHT ABOUT A NEW PERSON

When I returned home after two years overseas my two-and-a-half-year-old daughter Jody had completely forgotten me. I remember rushing over to greet my wife, then grabbing Jody and lifting her high above my head. You can imagine my dismay when Jody started crying hysterically. Too late I realized she was accustomed only to other children and their mothers. She was extremely frightened of me.

That evening my wife and I talked over what we could do. Beginning the next night when Jody went to bed my wife talked with her, wound up her musical teddy bear, and told her a short story. For a few evenings I went into the room with them but kept my distance. After Jody became used to my presence, I wound up the teddy bear for several nights. Then we gradually progressed so that I would sit at the end of her bed and tell her stories.

One day I picked up her favorite book and pretended to be reading it. Jody came up and asked me to read it to her. This was a golden day for me—the first time she had reached out to her Dad.

Jody's father's first natural and impulsive greeting was frightening to his daughter. Fortunately after that he did not force himself on her but proceeded gradually to fit himself into Jody's usual routine under conditions that would keep her feeling relaxed and secure.

Identify the Exact Source of Fear

The child may not know or may not be able to explain exactly what troubles him. He may, therefore, try to avoid a whole situation when only a small part of that situation frightens him.

- A child who seems afraid to get up at night by himself may actually fear the deep hole of the toilet in the bathroom or the mysterious shadows cast on the window shades by moonlight.
- Fear of a physician may actually be fear of an injection or fear of a cold instrument in the ear.
- Fear of a vacuum cleaner may only be fear of the noise it makes.
- Fear of school may in fact be fear of one particular teacher, a grouchy bus driver, a mean schoolmate, an inability to understand what the teacher wants, a recess game, or a lonely walk home.

Make an effort to identify exactly what the real trouble is. With older children patient and sympathetic listening may help them describe exactly what troubles them. With younger children careful observation will help to identify exactly when and where they begin to express their fear. Different fear-reduction activities are needed if the child is only afraid of a certain recess game instead of the entire school.

Once the adult has identified the exact source of the fear, the general treatment process is identical. If the child is to overcome the fear, the adult must gradually expose him to greater degrees of the feared situation at the same time keeping him comfortable, relaxed, secure, or rewarded.

If the fear is based on the child's current misconception, the adult's merely identifying the source of the fear correctly may be sufficient.

IDENTIFYING THE SOURCE OF A BEDTIME FEAR

Val was afraid to go to bed at night. His mother finally discovered that he believed ghosts were making weird noises and trying to frighten him. She agreed to come into his room and listen to the "ghost noises." Sure enough, she did hear some soft rustling and crackling sounds. She traced the sounds to the leaves of a tree which in a gentle wind would brush back and forth along the sides of the house outside Val's window. The next day Val's father duplicated the sounds by deliberately moving the branches of the tree against the side of the house. When the boy saw exactly how the noise was made, he completely lost his fear of going to bed.

Is insight into the source of fear sufficient to overcome it? Traditional psychoanalytic theory has held that recalling the early traumatic situations which originally created their fears gives people an insight which is sufficient for them to overcome their current fears and anxieties. No evidence has yet been produced to support this point of view. On the contrary, many people are quite able to describe the circumstances which produced their original fears and yet continue to be irrationally fearful. Recalling the past originating events is seldom sufficient to reduce current fears. However, if current fears are being produced by misinterpreted current events, as was the case with Val, then correctly identifying the source of the fear might be sufficient to eliminate it.

A fear can be overcome without tracing its origin. A person

afraid of insects, for example, need not discover how that fear originated, but it would be important to analyze the current fears so as to discover the exact type of insect or the circumstances under which the fear is now greatest. A counselor, psychologist, or psychiatrist trained in the process of systematic desensitization would be able to diagnose and treat complicated fears and anxieties.

How to Prevent Fears

Children can be helped to anticipate potentially fearful situations and prepare for them. All traumatic situations cannot be anticipated, but some, such as thunderstorms or hospital trips, can be handled in a way to prevent unnecessary fears from arising.

PREVENTING ANXIETY OVER THUNDERSTORMS

Mr. Edwards was determined that his daughter Sally would not develop the tremendous fear of thunderstorms he had as a child. When Sally was about two years old and the first violent thunderstorm of the season approached, Mr. Edwards bundled her up in a warm sweater and took her out on the screened-in porch to watch.

When the distant lightning flashed, Mr. Edwards waited a few seconds and then made a rumbling sound like the anticipated thunder, saying, "Listen for the boom-boom." When they heard the actual thunder, Mr. Edwards laughed and Sally laughed with him.

Sally sat snuggled on her father's lap as the thunderstorm came closer. She imitated the "boom-boom" sound when she saw the lightning flashes and then laughed with glee as nature appeared to echo her.

After that time Sally seemed to delight in thunder and lightning storms.

Mr. Edwards' prevention project was successful because of the manner in which he exposed Sally to the thunder and lightning. He made sure she was comfortable (the warm sweater), he tried to make her feel secure (snuggled on his lap), and he anticipated the loud noises until Sally was able to anticipate them herself. Sally learned to associate thunderstorms with joy rather than with fear.

PREVENTING WORRY ABOUT HOSPITAL TREATMENT

Children who come to the hospital for intensive lung therapy are sometimes afraid of the Bennett machine which provides this therapy.

When I was in nurses' training, I observed how a 22-month-old girl was gradually introduced to the different parts of the machine just before her nap time while she was warm, had just been fed, and was being held. The parts of the machine were brought closer to the child and were put together ready for use. The child was cuddled and played with throughout this time. Finally the machine was turned on at low pressure, enabling the child to get used to the noise. Then she was put down for her nap, after which time the actual treatment was conducted. Under these circumstances the girl developed no fear of the machine.

The usually fearful machine was slowly assembled while the child was happy, playful, cuddled, warm, and full. Fears were prevented by gradually introducing the machine to a comforted child.

DISPELLING FEAR OF BIOLOGICAL SPECIMENS

As a science teacher I have observed many children extraordinarily squeamish at the sight of dead laboratory animals and preserved specimens. I wanted to help the youngsters in my class develop a more matter-of-fact scientific attitude toward the wonders of nature.

When I brought an animal heart to class, there was "ooing" and "ahing," groans and moans. I told the children that no one had to look at or touch anything he didn't want to but that I didn't want any silliness or nonsense about these objects: "We are going to act like scientists."

I was relaxed and objective myself in describing the parts and their function. Those children who were interested gathered around me while others went off to read or work on some other project. No one was forced or even urged to come near. However, the group discussions were lively and fun for those who chose to participate.

More children began to join the group as time went on. At first some would listen to the discussion but avoid looking at the animal parts. I brought these children into the discussion without commenting on their reluctance.

The specimens were left on display so that the children might examine them. Some would pick up the parts and try to imagine how they worked.

After about a month almost all the children acted matter-of-factly about these specimens. The "silliness" and "nonsense" disappeared. In fact when another class was brought into the room and groaned like my class did a month earlier, I was amused to note the disgust of my new scientists at the behavior of the visitors.

Here we see how a teacher arranged an environment to prevent or dispel an aversion to biological specimens by modeling the behavior herself, by arranging a rewarding discussion for the children who developed the necessary objectivity, and by not calling attention through ridicule or sarcastic remarks to those children who remained reluctant to approach.

REDUCING STUTTERING

For a four-year-old our son Corky continually surprised my wife and me. He did well keeping up with his three older brothers.

One night at dinner, however, it suddenly occurred to me that Corky was having to try too hard. Encouraging the boys to discuss the day's events at the evening meal always required some refereeing as to who should talk, but that night Corky repeated words and sounds so frequently that one brother laughingly started to imitate him. I realized that Corky had been stuttering more lately and that something must be done.

"OK, kids," I said, "Let's all stop a moment. You will each get your turn. But from now on let's make sure each one also gets uninterrupted time. When someone talks, let's all give him our attention quietly. No butting in. No laughing."

I made certain the rule was observed at the table. And I also talked to the older boys privately about the importance of listening to Corky and not teasing him. Corky's speech improved almost immediately.

Stuttering can become a serious problem requiring the attention of a speech therapist. Corky's case is not at all unusual since it occurs more frequently among boys than girls and often among younger children competing with older siblings. Since it tends to occur in stressful interpersonal situations, stuttering is a problem that adults can help to prevent. Stuttering is an indication that the child is experiencing tension when he tries to communicate. The following suggestions may be useful:

- When the child tries to communicate, allow him to talk uninterruptedly without correcting him or anticipating what he is going to say.
- Make certain the child is not mimicked or ridiculed.
- Do not show concern or anxiety about the stuttering. Such attention is apt to reinforce the disfluency.
- Since speech is easily modeled from those around, be sure the child has models of adults who speak well. Recall, for example, Larry McMonihan (page 48) who said, "M'nim 'Ar' M'Mahun'."

Changing
Your
Behavior

14

Summary, Questions and Answers

Summary of the Thirteen Principles

To strengthen new behavior

1.   *Positive Reinforcement Principle:* To improve or increase a child's performance of a certain activity, arrange for an immediate reward after each correct performance.

To develop new behavior

2.   *Successive Approximations Principle:* To teach a child to act in a manner in which he has seldom or never before behaved, reward successive steps to the final behavior.

3.   *Modeling Principle:* To teach a child a new way of behaving, allow him to observe a prestigeful person performing the desired behavior.

4.   *Cueing Principle:* To teach a child to remember to act at a specific time, arrange for him to receive a cue for the correct performance just before the action is expected rather than after he has performed incorrectly.

5.   *Discrimination Principle:* To teach a child to act in a particular way under one set of circumstances but not another, help him to identify the cues that differentiate the circumstances and reward him only when his action is appropriate to the cue.

To maintain new behavior

6.   *Substitution Principle:* To reinforce a child with a previously ineffective reward, present it just before (or as soon as possible to) the time you present the more effective reward.

7.   *Intermittent Reinforcement Principle:* To encourage a child to continue performing an established behavior with few or no rewards, gradually and intermittently decrease the frequency with which the correct behavior is rewarded.

To stop inappropriate behavior you may choose from four alternative principles

8.   *Satiation Principle:* To stop a child from acting in a particular way, you may allow him to continue (or insist that he continue) performing the undesired act until he tires of it.

9.   *Extinction Principle:* To stop a child from acting in a particular way, you may arrange conditions so that he receives no rewards following the undesired act.

10.   *Incompatible Alternative Principle:* To stop a child from acting in a particular way, you may reward an alternative action that is inconsistent with or cannot be performed at the same time as the undesired act.

11.   *Negative Reinforcement Principle:* To stop a child from act-

ing in a particular way, you may arrange for him to terminate a mild aversive situation immediately by improving his behavior.

To modify emotional behavior

12. *Avoidance Principle:* To teach a child to avoid a certain type of situation, simultaneously present to the child the situation to be avoided (or some representation of it) and some aversive condition (or its representation).

13. *Fear Reduction Principle:* To help a child overcome his fear of a particular situation, gradually increase his exposure to the feared situation while he is otherwise comfortable, re-laxed, secure, or rewarded.

Questions and Answers

Individuals who work with children, especially teachers and parents, frequently raise a number of questions about applications, theory, and ethics involving the thirteen principles. Here are our answers to the most frequent and important of these questions.

APPLICATION QUESTIONS

1. *How can a person be taught self-control?*

A person who lacks self-control is unable to act as he wishes. Self-control can be taught.

One problem in maintaining self-control is "avoiding tempta-tion." People trying to lose weight seem unable to control their eating behavior. They find that when food is available they simply cannot stop from consuming it. Teaching them self-control is teaching them to arrange their environment so that temptation is removed. They can be taught to keep tempting food in out-of-the-way places, such as keeping candy out of the living room. Smokers can be taught ways of making access to cigarettes difficult. One man taped his cigarettes to his thigh so that whenever he wanted a cigarette he had to take down his pants. Another smoker put cigarettes in the freezer and put the freezer key under his child's mattress. It soon became just too much work to go upstairs, wake up the child, remove the key, go down to the freezer to take out a cigarette. A basketball coach who would run out on the court whenever he disagreed with a referee's decision, costing his team many technical fouls, eventually found the solution: he fastened himself to the bench with an automobile seatbelt.

The other problem in maintaining self-control is sticking to a difficult task which may not have many immediate reinforcing consequences. Difficult jobs need to be broken down into small parts and rewards arranged frequently for accomplishing each small part. A person can promise himself a cup of coffee as soon as he finishes a predetermined part of the job. Two people can help each other: "I'll reward you if you finish your job by Tuesday if you reward me when I finish my job by Monday."

A self-controlled person arranges for his own rewards when he engages in behavior he desires. He also removes temptations that he would not be able to resist if they were present. A person who controls his own environment controls his own behavior.

2. How can a person possibly learn to be altruistic following the behavioral approach you recommend?

"Altruistic behavior" involves the sharing of time, effort, or possessions with people who are unlikely to repay the giver. How are people taught to engage in altruistic behavior? They watch respected people who engage in this kind of behavior so that they begin to model these individuals. They are praised when they give "unselfishly" of themselves and win the respect and honor of their fellows for their "altruism." In short they receive many kinds of rewards for being "selfless." The man who gives a million dollars to a college usually has his name put on a building. Perpetuating his name may be worth a million dollars to a wealthy donor.

Some people are taught that anonymous giving is the most desirable. They are told of people who give anonymously, and they read Bible verses extolling the virtues of the left hand's not knowing what the right hand doeth. A person who adopts this ideal can then give anonymously and reward himself with the knowledge that he is indeed living up to his ideal. Such self-reward is sufficient for some people.

Fund-raising organizations have found ingenious ways to reward people who give large gifts but do not explicitly want to be identified with the number of dollars they give. Honorary titles are sometimes given, "Friend of the College" to those who give more than $100 and "Patron of the College" for those who give more than $1,000. Altruistic behavior is amply rewarded.

3. *Can I use several principles at the same time, or must I choose one principle and use it exclusively before trying the next?*

Use as many principles as you can at one time. The principles are listed and described singly in order to make it easy to understand each one. But in actual practice you often are able to use more than one at a time. For example, in toilet training not only would you reward successive approximations, as explained in Chapter 2, but you might also provide cues, perhaps allow an older brother or sister to model the desired behavior if you have no aesthetic or modesty objections, help the child identify the appropriate times and conditions for elimination, develop some relevant rewards (allowing him to flush the toilet), gradually withdraw rewards as the behavior becomes self-reinforcing, avoid giving special attention when he soils his clothes, and make sure that you do not establish fears and anxieties by punishing his failures. The Satiation and Extinction Principles, of course, could not be used at the same time.

4. *Are there times when certain principles should not be used?*

The test for using any principle is whether it works. If use of the principle produces the desired outcome without undesirable side effects, you will be rewarded. If it does not work as you desire, and you feel you have applied it correctly, you should stop using that principle. As you gain more experience in applying principles, you will gradually learn which principles work best with which kinds of situations. Observe the consequences. Trust your common sense and good judgment.

5. *What if nothing I try works?*

Here are several questions you can ask yourself in an effort to diagnose the difficulty.

A.   Am I trying to teach the child something he is not yet ready to learn? It is impossible to teach a child to read or to tie his shoe before he has developed the necessary verbal and physical skills and it would be unwise to try.

B.   Is the reward sufficiently powerful and given immediately?

C.   Could the final behavior I desire be broken down into a number of intermediate steps each of which might be accomplished in turn? The child may need help in learning prerequisite skills. Reward accomplishment of these intermediate steps toward the more complex task.

D. Are there some preliminary experiences that I can provide which might motivate a child to try new activities? A child initially afraid of playing "Charades" was given a one-word television program to enact ("Lassie") and instructed that she could act like a dog. When her team quickly and successfully identified her act, her fear of the game disappeared and she begged to play again. An early success encourages further efforts.

E. Am I giving each principle a sufficient amount of time and a sufficient number of trials to test it adequately? Some people change principles too soon. Most of the principles depend upon consistent application over a period of time if they are to have much chance of succeeding. Think about which principle or combination of principles you wish to apply and then do so consistently. To illustrate, if you try rewarding an incompatible behavior one day but not the next, the child merely learns that you are inconsistent. If you try extinguishing a response for a few hours and then allow it to be rewarded later, the child is rewarded on an intermittent schedule. His undesirable behavior will persist since he finds he can get his way by outlasting you. If you do not think you can consistently carry through a principle for some logical period of time, then perhaps you should not start its use. On the other hand you may be relying on the same principle for too long when another principle might in fact work better.

F. When should I change principles? If you have tried one or more principles over a period of time without success, then perhaps those you have chosen are not appropriate or you do not have sufficient control of the environment to make them useful. You may then wish to experiment with a different combination of principles which will enable you to exercise greater control.

G. Would it be useful for me to discuss my child's problem with a professional counselor, psychologist, or psychiatrist trained in behavior therapy or behavioral counseling? Most people have difficulty diagnosing behavior problems in which they are personally involved. Sometimes the help of an objective well-trained professional will enable you to identify the difficulty more precisely and discover how to overcome it. It is helpful to have another person give you support and encouragement as you help a youngster accomplish a difficult behavior change.

6. *Wouldn't it be much easier and just as effective to let the child grow up naturally?*

If the "natural" environment provides consistent rewards for good behavior, then the child will learn to engage in good behavior. If the "natural" environment rewards lying and stealing, then the child will learn to lie and steal. If you really care how your child turns out, you will want some "say" about what behavior is rewarded regardless of whether it occurs naturally or is deliberately planned.

7. *What if one parent reinforces behavior that the other parent does not?*

Parents should discuss their goals for childrearing and try to reach some agreement. If they cannot agree, the child will learn to behave one way for one parent and another way for the other. Children quickly detect inconsistencies in parental policy and play one parent against the other for their own advantage.

8. *What if one of the two parents does not agree that this behavioral method of raising children is good?*

Behavior has consequences whether or not a parent "agrees." Any parent who sometimes notices his child but pays little attention at other times is reinforcing some behavior and extinguishing other behavior whether or not he realizes it. A parent may be unaware of the behavior he is rewarding and may even consider it advisable to be unaware, but the differential attention affects the child's behavior regardless of parental intent or agreement with the method.

9. *Isn't the behavioral method useful only for people who have substantial control of the environment like parents and teachers but practically useless for occasional-contact people like recreation workers, social workers, and policemen?*

The adult who controls the environment of a child for longer periods of time does have a greater chance of influencing his behavior. For instance a parent cannot influence an older child as much as a younger child because the older child spends more time in the presence of other people who may reinforce quite different behaviors. However, even people with brief contacts can produce positive results using these principles.

10. *In the family can anyone besides the child's parents apply these principles?*

Yes. A babysitter, a sibling, or a grandparent can apply these principles just as well as any parent. Not all may agree, however, on what behavior is to be encouraged.

11. *Do these principles apply to slow learners, fast learners, "ghetto" youngsters, emotionally disturbed youngsters, the physically handicapped, and delinquents as well as the so-called typical child?*

Yes. These principles apply to all youngsters, but specific reinforcers and goals may vary.

12. *If it is true that the major formative years are from birth to six, how useful can these principles be for school-age children?*

The early years are extremely important, but learning continues throughout life. The principles apply throughout a lifetime.

13. *Isn't it necessary to know the reasons for a child's behavior before trying to change it? For example, if a baby cries because he is hungry, he should be fed and not ignored because you wrongly think he simply wants attention.*

An infant begins life by applying the Negative Reinforcement Principle. When he is hungry, he sets up a loud, persistent howl which is aversive to most adults. The parent then casts about for some socially acceptable method of quieting him. If the parent gives the hungry baby a warm bottle of milk, the child is rewarded, stops his crying, and thus negatively reinforces the parent with some temporary peace and quiet.

However, suppose that when the warm bottle of milk is put into the baby's mouth he rejects it and continues crying. The adult must then cast about for another possible source of discomfort. Perhaps the child's diapers are wet. Perhaps the child has stomach gas. One can change diapers to see if that works. One can "burp" the baby to see if that helps. The "reason" the child is crying is "explained" by the reinforcing circumstances which stop the crying.

It is important to know the reason for a child's behavior as long as we understand this to mean that we must discover the present combination of circumstances which might change an undesirable pattern of behavior to a more desirable one. However, many people who talk about understanding reasons for a child's behavior are referring to events long past, over which we no longer have any control. Although it is true that these events of the past have consequences in a child's present behavior, merely understanding the past is not sufficient to help a child improve now.

14. *My parents believed, "Spare the rod, spoil the child." Although I basically agree with the thirteen principles, I sometimes without thinking revert to handling children the way I was treated as a child. What can I do?*

Be pleased that you recognize your error. Congratulate yourself the next time you react more appropriately.

15. *You make this whole process seem too logical and rational. Sometimes I'm in a bad mood and my kids make me so angry that I can't help myself. I lash out and give them a swat. Even if it's not the best for them, it makes me feel better at the moment. How can I learn to control myself?*

Fortunately children are resilient enough to be able to take a certain amount of punishment without much harm. Let's not worry about what you have done in the past. You wisely ask what you can do to control yourself in the future. Here are a few ideas other people have found useful. You would have to judge, of course, when they would be appropriate to your situation.

A.   Remove yourself. Quietly, without creating a scene, go somewhere else. Maybe you can find peace and quiet if you lock yourself in the bathroom for a few minutes.

B.   Point out matter-of-factly that you are not in a good mood. Let your children know that you are edgy and irritable. "I'm in a bad mood right now. Better leave me alone for a while." They may respond with uncanny humaneness.

C.   Engage in some alternative activities which will dissipate your anger and hostility. Try walking, running, bicycling, playing the piano, pounding a punching bag. Activities which involve some strenuous exercise are usually best.

D.   Anticipate problem situations and bring them up at a time when you and your children are better able to deal with them. If you must announce an unpopular decision, for example, you usually need not give the decision immediately. Tell them that you will let them know in the morning (when everyone is fresh and rested). Perhaps at that time not only will you be able to deal with their hostility and arguments more effectively, but they too may be more amenable to what you have to say.

E.   Confront the real problem that put you in a bad mood. Children are sometimes victims of situations beyond their control. If you are angry at your mother-in-law for giving you unsolicited advice, it would be far more fair and courageous to tell your mother-in-law you would "rather do it yourself" than displace your anger on innocent children.

F.   Enlist support for a self-control project. Ask help from a friend, your spouse, or a colleague. Tell him you are having a problem blowing up at children when you are in a bad mood. The help might consist of his listening to you blow off steam, sharing ideas about possible actions, joining in some alternative activities if he is available, giving you courage to face up to the actual source of your discontent, or arranging to reward you when you make progress in controlling your temper.

16. *On those occasions when I simply haven't controlled my temper with the kids, I find later on I feel guilty for what I've done, so I try to make it up to them to ease my conscience. I might fix them big treats or give in to unreasonable requests, no matter how they're behaving. Sometimes I think the kids deliberately bug me so they'll get something extra later. Is this likely?*

You want to see your children treated fairly, so it is only natural that you would feel guilty when you are provoked into some unjustified action. However, you do see that the unjust punishments and undeserved rewards may teach your kids how to provoke you. If you slip, make it up to them when they deserve it—not when your conscience is bothered.

THEORETICAL QUESTIONS

1. *Isn't it necessary for a person to be aware of the underlying reasons for his own behavior to change it?*

No. People frequently change their behavior without being aware of the "reason." Furthermore, people can give elaborate verbal explanations for the origins of their inappropriate behavior and still continue to engage in it. The elaborate explanation of "causes" may serve as justification of the behavior and excuses them from any effort to improve. The idea that "insight" is necessary for change is a Freudian notion which has misled psychiatrists and psychologists for years. Some kinds of insights may be useful but are not essential for change.

2. *If people engage in behaviors that are rewarding to them, how do you explain some people's engaging in behavior harmful to themselves, for example a lonely person who refuses to go out and meet people?*

Some people do get into a vicious cycle. A lonely person may want friends, but he is so afraid of being rejected that it is less painful to avoid people than to approach them and risk rejection. He thereby fails to learn the skills of meeting new acquaintances. Other people fail to respond positively to his inadequate approach behavior, so he withdraws still further. He continues to engage in a pattern of withdrawal because in the short run withdrawal is less unpleasant than the alternative, although in the long run withdrawal is destructive of what the person wants.

Neurotic vicious circles make the lives of many people miserable. In such cases behavioral counseling or behavior therapy may be used to intervene and start a person experimenting with a new pattern of behavior in a nonthreatening environment. Small initial successes can be used to encourage greater risk taking. The same basic principles explain both the negative cycle of despair and the positive cycle of accomplishment.

3. *Shouldn't children be given the freedom to develop on their own, allowing their natural impulses to unfold?*

If we want them to learn what? Children are being rewarded for some behavior and not being rewarded for other behavior whether or not adults intend such a result. If rewarding consequences do not follow the good behavior of children, the good responses will be extinguished. That children should be allowed to do whatever they want whenever they want has a deceptive appeal. As adults we cannot withdraw from the child's environment and automatically expect that he is then "free." If we lessen our influence, other forces increase theirs. The child is being shaped and influenced by the natural consequences of his actions and by the other people with whom he comes in contact. If these other influences are positive, then the child will turn out well. If they happen to be negative or inconsistent, difficulties will arise. As an example, a clique of "established" children in either a school or a neighborhood will often tend to exclude a new youngster unless a sensitive adult helps them learn how to include the newcomer. It is naive to believe that children's "natural impulses" are going to provide the most desirable environment for helping every youngster develop optimally. Why leave to chance the development of a child's character?

4. *How can a child feel happy, secure, and loved by adults who enforce their rules and insist that he abide by them?*

If an adult "enforces" his rules with punishment, then as we pointed out in Chapters 11 and 12, he decreases his child's feelings of happiness, security, and love. However, if he enforces his rules by positively rewarding improvements and by providing a good example, then he increases the child's feelings of happiness, security and love. The consistency with which the adult rewards good behavior contributes to the child's feeling of security. The child knows where he stands, he knows what he needs to do to earn his rewards, and he is confident that nothing he can do will cause the adult to reject him.

The goal of keeping a child happy will keep him from being a happy child.

5. *Isn't it harmful to a child's happiness to frustrate him by not letting him do as he wishes?*

No. The goal of keeping a child happy will keep him from being a happy child.

"Dear Abby" puts it this way: "So many mothers make the same mistake. They think the most important thing in raising children is to make them happy. It's not. If you raise your children to be dependable, industrious, honest and considerate of others, they will make themselves happy."

6. *If I can afford to buy something my child has asked for and I can't think of any reason it would harm him, I feel I have to get it for him. Do I?*

What are you teaching your child? You are placing the burden of proof on yourself to come up with some reason to deny his request. You seem to think he can have whatever he wants if you cannot think of contrary reasons. Why not instead put the burden of responsibility on him to justify his request. Why not ask him, "What can you do to earn this thing you want?" If you think he already deserves it, tell him what he has done that merits this reward. Do you want your child to learn that his demand or request is sufficient to get whatever he wants unless you can come up with contrary reasons? Or would you rather have him learn that he can get what he wants if he engages in some worthy actions?

7. *Which philosophy of childrearing do you subscribe to: permissive, authoritarian, stimulus–response, or reward and punishment?*

None of these philosophies. We believe that parents and teachers should design learning environments that will enable children to develop into independent, self-respecting, creative, and productive citizens. Neither a permissive philosophy allowing the child to do whatever he pleases nor an authoritarian philosophy advocating absolute obedience will produce that kind of citizen. An adult can be firm and consistent without being authoritarian. A child should experience success by gradually learning more difficult skills for solving the problems of life. As he grows older, the child should be consulted about the kinds of things he wants to learn; he can provide information about the effectiveness of our educational methods. If we are successful, a child gradually learns to take control of his own behavior.

Our method cannot be labeled "stimulus–response" either. Human beings do not respond automatically and predictably to any given stimulus. They may learn to use a stimulus as a signal for what action may be beneficial or harmful. But each person can still choose whether to act and does so on the basis of anticipated consequences.

Neither is our method a "reward and punishment" method. We use rewards but minimize punishment. Punishment has too many undesirable consequences, as we explained in Chapters 11 and 12.

Any label for a method is a short-cut summary that is likely to create misunderstandings and misconceptions. We refer to our method as "behavioral" because the term reminds us that specific observable behaviors result from the environment we help create.

But do not judge a system of childrearing by its label; judge it by its consequences.

ETHICAL QUESTIONS

1.   *If you reward a child with material objects such as tokens, gifts, candy, or money, won't he then value only material things and not learn to value the intrinsic merits of learning?*

If he is not now engaging in any worthwhile learning activities, the child is not going to discover their intrinsic merits. Somehow he must get started. Contrived rewards such as tokens, candy, or money are simply a way to get him engaged in a new activity which may produce its own intrinsic rewards once the child experiences them. Unfortunately they are sometimes continued when they are no longer necessary or desirable. As the child discovers that the activity produces its own rewards (the joy of reading, the excitement of hitting a baseball, the thrill of personally creating a new work of art), the importance of the contrived rewards is greatly reduced.

The best way to get a child to appreciate the intrinsic values of, say, playing the piano is for him to associate pleasant things with piano playing. A child is more likely to enjoy music if he is rewarded for an improved performance than if he is punished for not practicing. (See Chapter 6 for further discussion of changing rewards.)

2.   *Doesn't rewarding a child really tend to coddle and weaken him rather than toughen him for "real life"?*

It depends entirely upon what kind of behavior you reward. You can reward a child for weak, dependent behaviors, or you can reward him for coping successfully with a progressively tougher set of real life problems. The way in which rewards are scheduled (see Chapter 7) influences the extent to which the child will continue to persist in the face of adversity. Certainly it would be a mistake for a child to grow up believing that every good action of his will immediately be rewarded. "Real life" is not like that. But if he has experiences in which a sequence of good actions eventually gets rewarded, he has a somewhat more constructive pattern of behavior to tide him through periods of frustration. An ability to cope successfully with the problems of adulthood may best be learned by coping successfully with the problems of childhood.

3. *Why should I reinforce a child for something he should be doing anyway?*

If he is not doing what he "should" be doing, how then are you going to get him started? Obviously if the child is already doing what he should and is finding natural satisfactions in "performing his duty," no further rewards are necessary. If not, rewards may be helpful. It seems strange that an adult expects a child to work under conditions that the adult himself would not tolerate. If you are employed, you most likely do what you should be doing on the job. But if your employer stopped paying you, would you continue performing the parts of the job you didn't enjoy, or for that matter any part of the job? Why then should we expect a child to perform without reinforcement simply because we think he should?

4. *Isn't it unethical to pay a child for doing work around the house where he eats and sleeps and is a part of the family? Shouldn't children work simply because they are part of a family unit and share in the family's well-being?*

Children should learn that there is a connection between the work they do and the benefits they share. One good way to make sure this connection is learned is to find specific chores for which they would like to be responsible in exchange for specific money or privileges that they are entitled to receive in return. A way to develop family unity is to make a whole family's reward contingent on the contributions of everybody in the family. ("We'll all go to the lake as soon as everybody finishes his job.")

5. *Aren't these methods really subtle forms of manipulation and indoctrination designed to control people's thinking and make little Hitlers? Don't they conflict with true morality?*

No. There is nothing subtle or hidden in the application of these behavioral principles. The entire procedure is open and may be known to everyone who participates in it, including the learner. The principles themselves are morally neutral. However, they could be used for evil purposes, good purposes, or anything in between. They could be used to develop little Hitlers, or they could be used to develop good citizens. They could be used to develop dependent, subservient slaves, or they could be used to develop independent, creative, productive citizens. The result depends upon the kind of behavior rewarded and the kind of models made available to young people. The thirteen principles in this book are simply a description of *how* people learn, not *what* people learn. If we live in a society which uses knowledge for the betterment of human welfare, we can guard against the abuse of these principles. However, knowledge can certainly be misused. The widest possible dissemination of these principles of human behavior is the best defense against their misuse in the hands of a few.

6. *Wouldn't you have to call these principles a form of coaxing or bribery?*

No. But if this important question bothers you, see page 25 for a more detailed discussion.

7. *Isn't there danger in a system which at first glance appears to be reinforcing but actually is aversive to those who do not perform correctly?*

Ideally everyone could be receiving rewards as he learns to improve his performance. Everyone should have success experiences as well as occasional failure experiences. Unfortunately in most school situations a few people receive almost all the success experiences while many others are consistently punished and almost never rewarded. The difficulty is that the typical educational system does not reward people for improving over their previous performance. Instead it pits them against each other, constantly rewarding the better performances and constantly punishing the poorer ones. Children from disadvantaged backgrounds start slowly, seldom catch up, and are humiliated by low grades and teacher disapproval. They are seldom rewarded for the progress they do make. It is no wonder that they often become drop-outs, truants, or vandals. The present system is aversive to those who do not perform correctly. An ideal grading system based on the principles in this book would arrange for every child to be rewarded as he makes progress over what he did previously.

8. *What happens to spontaneous love and affection? Real emotions seem to be withheld until the right moment. Isn't this cold and detached?*

Nothing that has been said in this book should inhibit you from expressing your spontaneously felt love for a child. For his well-being a child should be assured of love and know he is valued by the adults in his life. Your love should never be contingent upon the child's behavior. You can still love him even if he is at the moment misbehaving. But to extinguish inappropriate behavior you may nevertheless withhold certain rewards simply because you do care for the child. You do not have to prove your love for him by rewarding actions which are inappropriate or undesirable. True love for a child is in helping him to learn to cope successfully with the problems of life, secure in the knowledge that he is loved and respected by those close to him.

9. *Aren't these principles really a crutch so that adults applying them can avoid understanding what the child's real problem is?*

To be understood is rewarding. A sensitive adult tries to learn how children see things and tries to understand their problems from their point of view. Children feel better about their problems when they know that someone else understands. However, for many problems merely understanding the child's perception of the problem is not enough. To assist the child the adult must take action. These principles are to help adults construct useful actions based on their full understanding of the child's difficulty.

10. *Don't children learn the reinforcement methods and use them on their parents and teachers?*

Yes. We find that our children reward us when we do things that they like. "Thank you for taking us out to dinner." "I sure like the chocolate cake that you baked." "Thanks for explaining

"*THAT'S* A GOOD GIRL!"

Children learn to reinforce adults, too.

how to do this homework assignment." We fully realize that our children are attempting to influence our behavior in the same way we are influencing theirs. They are telling us what we do that pleases them just as we tell them what they do that pleases us. It feels good both ways.

11. *Isn't the child's self-esteem the most powerful factor in his behavior?*

Maybe. If so, how do you develop a child's self-esteem? You make sure that he is learning to master the tasks in his environment, that he is praised and rewarded for his accomplishments and assured that he is loved and respected by those around him. The end result of these behaviors is the development of a feeling in a child which we label "self-esteem."

The evidence is quite clear that the pattern of reinforcement provided by teachers and parents can produce or destroy self-esteem. An adult who punishes unsatisfactory behavior but ignores good behavior tends to develop a child with a fear of failure. An adult who rewards satisfactory behavior but ignores unsatisfactory behavior helps a child develop a positive attitude toward achievement.

In his newspaper column Charles McCabe reported his feelings on being unworthy. "I don't know about you, man, but I was brought up to feel unworthy. Maybe worthless . . . At home I would do this, that or the other thing, or be thought to be doing this, that or the other thing (which was equally bad) and my mother would make her usual statement. It was generally toneless and without emphasis, because it had been repeated so often, and because it had the ring of revealed wisdom: 'You'll end up in Sing-Sing.' . . . And away from home I would go to church and listen to the lordly platitudes and smell the incense and join the congregation in singing one of the favorite hymns of the time: 'Oh Lord I am not worthy . . .'

"And I wasn't kidding about that. I wasn't worth a nickel and I knew it. How I would ever fit into that great grown-up world where people wrote books and built homes and repaired plumbing and sailed boats and planted trees I could never figure out. I had daily assurance that I was a misfit which certainly did not fit me for not being one. . . .

"I know that I am anything but unique in having this kind of training. Millions of Americans, in many kinds of religious denominations, had the same kind of upbringing. They were told they were conceived in original sin, and were never allowed to forget it . . . If there is any point to life at all, it is that it should be embraced joyously. And the task of education, at home and abroad, should be to persuade the child of his eminent fitness for joyous embracement. . . . The slogans might be: 'You will end up in the White House, my boy.' or, 'You will end up on the board of overseers at Harvard.' . . . We are, to an unfortunate degree, what we are told we are. If we are assured, unremittingly, that we are budding felons, then felony will have irrational lure for us.

"Life is to be lived. The essential ingredient for this great adventure is confidence that it can be lived, and well. The job of instilling that confidence in a child is perhaps a parent's most important function. If it is not performed, the parents are guilty of cheating the child out of his most important heritage: the relishing of his years."

12. *Wouldn't the application of these behavioral principles tend to represent the very kind of cultural values that have caused so many young people to "drop out" of society?*

Quite the contrary. Young people tend to be repelled by a society that "puts them down" for trivial differences in dress and hair style, that punishes them when they are unable to master irrelevant academic exercises at a prescribed pace, and that fails to find ways to involve them in socially constructive and rewarding activities. Every family and every school has the power to arrange an environment for its young people which can reinforce them for meaningful contributions to the group, for learning socially useful skills, for improving their talents, and for joyful creativity. Families and schools which consistently apply the principles in this book toward socially relevant ends will capture the enthusiasm and cooperation of young people. A harmonious society is one in which all members feel reinforced in their contacts with one another.

Annotated
Bibliography

BANDURA, A. *Principles of Behavior Modification.* New York: Holt, Rinehart and Winston, 1969.
A thorough technical summary of the research evidence on which the principles of behavior modification are based.

FRANKS, C. M., ed. *Behavior Therapy: Appraisal and Status.* New York: McGraw-Hill, 1969.
A collection of articles by experts in the field on problems of applying behavior change principles.

HOLLAND, J. G., and SKINNER, B. F. *The Analysis of Behavior.* New York: McGraw-Hill, 1961.
A programed self-instructional manual which teaches the vocabulary and fundamental principles of behavior change.

KRUMBOLTZ, J. D., and THORESEN, C. E., eds. *Behavioral Counseling: Cases and Techniques.* New York: Holt, Rinehart and Winston, 1969.
A collection of 43 detailed descriptions of applications of behavioral principles for counselors and school psychologists.

MISCHEL, W. *Personality and Assessment.* New York: John Wiley and Sons, 1968.
A technical discussion of the problems of measuring behavior change for psychologists.

PATTERSON, G. R., and GULLION, M. E. *Living with Children.* Champaign, Illinois: Research Press, 1968.
A brief programed book to teach parents the basic principles of behavior change.

SKINNER, B. F. *Science and Human Behavior.* New York: Macmillan, 1953.
A basic source book by the man whose fundamental experimental work first enabled psychologists to make substantial progress in the control of behavior.

SKINNER, B. F. *Verbal Behavior.* New York: Appleton-Century-Crofts, 1957.
The application of behavioral principles to the understanding of verbal behavior.

STAATS, A. W. *Learning, Language and Cognition.* New York: Holt, Rinehart and Winston, 1968.
An attempt to extend behavioral principles to the learning of language, reading, and cognitive understanding.

STAATS, A. W., and STAATS, C. K. *Complex Human Behavior.* New York: Holt, Rinehart and Winston, 1964.
A summary of basic principles of behavior and their application in language, personality, social development, childhood education, educational psychology, and the treatment of behavior problems.

THARP, R. G., and WETZEL, R. J. *Behavior Modification in the Natural Environment.* New York: Academic Press, 1969.
The application of an experimental behavioral program for the modification of delinquent behavior.

ULLMANN, L. P., and KRASNER, L. *A Psychological Approach to Abnormal Behavior.* Englewood Cliffs, New Jersey: Prentice-Hall, 1969.
The application of behavioral principles to the origin and treatment of abnormal behavior.

Behavior *(cont.)*
mostly learned, xvii
desirable and undesirable, xvii
exceptions, xvii–xviii
outgrowing, xviii
precise descriptions of, need for,
xvi–xvii
stopping inappropriate, 135–202,
232–33
strengthening existing, 1–28, 232
understanding not sufficient, xviii
Behavioral approach, 243–44
annotated bibliography on, 251–53
Bicycling. *See also* Physical skills
motivation to learn, 52
putting away bike, 193
Biology
dispelling fear of specimens, 226–27
enthusiasm for, 62
Biting fingernails, 78
Blackboard, cleaning, as reward and
punishment, 110
Bladder control. *See also* Toilet
training
taking responsibility for, 193
Blind obedience, 95, 208–9. *See also*
Hitler
Bluffing dangerously, parent, 191–92
Books
avoiding, 211
learning to like, 14–16
Boredom in school, 6, 54–56, 141–42,
142–43, 147, 148–49, 196–97, 250
Bouncing imaginary ball, until
satiation, 142–43
Boyfriend
changing opinion about, 138–39
inviting for dinner without
permission, 198
parental injunctions against, 139
Boy Scout skills, 3
Brainwashing, 61, 244
Breakable objects, avoiding, 207
Breath control in singing, 68
Bribery, not same as reinforcement,
25–26, 246
Brother. *See* Siblings
Bulletin board for recognition, 20–21,
46, 112

Calling for help, appropriate
conditions for, 95–96
Camp counselor, 98–99
Candy. *See also* Reinforcer
giving and taking away, 161
offered by stranger, 208

Candy *(cont.)*
removed to resist temptation, 233
Carelessness, cueing to overcome,
66, 76–78
Cars. *See* Driver education, Driving
Changing your behavior, 229–50
Charm course, as aid to height
problem, 53
Charts. *See* Checklists, Graphs
Checklists as cues
for family cooperation, 81–82
to overcome thumbsucking, 82–83
self-cueing, 81–82, 82–83, 84
Chess, enjoyment of and persistence
at, 117–18
Child-centered approach, 243
Child rearing, philosophy of, 243
Choral singing, 12–13, 68. *See also*
Music
Chores, 17–18, 24–25, 37, 46, 66, 79–80,
81–82, 101–2, 111, 113, 114–15,
121–23, 124–26, 174–75, 177,
188, 193
Classroom activities. *See also*
Classroom control, Grading,
Homework, School, Teachers
cueing by teacher, examples of,
78–79
discouraging shy child through, 164
displays of class work, 46
encouraging responsibility in,
130–31
importance of success in, 21–22
increasing participation in, 141
insuring thorough preparation for,
127–28
library skills, improving, 31
making assignments accurate for,
192–93
reason for truancy from, 185
test taking, 194–95
Classroom control
aggression, unintentionally
rewarded, 177–78
anger at class, 198
boredom and, 141–42, 142–43, 147,
196–97
class "courtesy rule," enforcing, 160
establishing, 199–200
disruptive influence, ending,
141–42
horseplay, terminating, 142–43
promptness, 9
punishment as positive reinforcement, 23–24, 185
punishment and truancy, 185
regaining, 188–89